AUTOMOTIVE SUPERCHARGING & TURBOCHARGING MANUAL

A Technical Guide

John D. Humphries

Foulis

Haynes
®

J. D. Humphries

A FOULIS Motoring Book

First published 1992

Published by:
Haynes Publishing Group
Sparkford, Nr Yeovil, Somerset
BA22 7JJ, England

British Library Cataloguing in Publication Data
Humphries, John
  Automotive Supercharging and Turbocharging
  I. Title
  621.43
  ISBN 0-85429-880-0

Printed in England by J. H. Haynes & Co. Ltd.

Table of Contents

Acknowledgements

The author wishes to express his grateful thanks to Geoff Kershaw of Turbo Technics who gave up his precious time to find and fix all the technical bugs in the original draft text. Also many thanks to Ralph Swinhoe and his colleagues at Garrett Automotive who gave the author the confidence to take on the project of writing this book. The assistance of Jesse Cross and the Society of Motor Manufacturers was much appreciated. They opened up their network of contacts amongst the press officers of numerous companies.

This book has been built on the foundations laid by previous authors dealing with the subject, and any readers who want to expand their knowledge should study these earlier works. The author acknowledges his indebtedness to these books written by McInnes[26], Allard[39] and Watson[42].

The assistance of all the automobile manufacturers who are listed in Appendix A is gratefully acknowledged. They not only took the time to sort out the data for the tables in the Appendix, but also supplied other useful information and illustrations used elsewhere in the book.

In addition the following organisations provided information and illustrations without which this book could not have been written, and their help is gratefully acknowledged:

ABB Turbo Systems, Alfa Romeo (GB) Limited, BMW (GB) Limited, Robert Bosch Limited, Citroën UK Limited, DPR Forced Induction Systems Limited, Eaton Limited, ERP Limited, Fleming Thermodynamics Limited, Iveco-Ford Limited, Aktiengesellschaft Kühnle, Kopp & Kausch, Lotus Cars Limited, Napier Turbochargers Limited, National Motor Museum, Adam Opel AG, Porsche Cars Great Britain Limited, Power Engineering, Saab Great Britain Limited, Sabre Engines Ltd, Superchargers UK, Torque Developments Limited, University of Manchester Institute of Science and Technology (UMIST) Department of Mechanical Engineering, VAG (UK) Limited, Volvo Concessionaires Limited, Weber Concessionaires Limited.

Foreword

The turbocharging principle has been known and practiced since the early part of the twentieth century. However, despite both the accumulated experience and the boost given to development by the Second World War, it took until 1978 for the turbocharger to be applied to cars on a volume basis. This was made possible by the increasing need to improve fuel economy and reduce emissions. These needs gave impetus to the manufacturers of both cars and turbochargers simultaneously to develop the 'turbo car'. Prior to 1978 only a few enthusiasts – probably followers of Indianapolis racing – had heard very much about 'turbo'. In that year Saab added the word to the popular dictionary, followed shortly afterwards by Mercedes in Germany and Buick in the USA. The remainder is history.

I first became involved with turbocharging during the late nineteen sixties, and count myself fortunate to have been at the centre of the turbocharging business during the middle and late seventies as the scene unfolded. To be involved in such an important stage of development of the car engine was indeed exciting, perhaps ever more so in retrospect than it felt at the time. Because of my involvement, initially with the early development and first volume production applications, and latterly in the specialist performance field, I find myself in an almost unique position to comment on the developments, technical and otherwise, that have taken place throughout the turbocharging industry.

It can be said that the optimisation of any system involving more than seven variables is an art and not a science. In this respect, the design and application of any turbocharging system is more an art form than a scientific discipline. It is, however, vital to apply scientific engineering principles in order to create a successful turbocharging system, and John Humphries' explanations will help many people towards a greater understanding of these principles.

Several books have been written on the subject of turbocharging over the past decade or so for the professional engineer or engineering student, but these are heavy going indeed for the technically interested layman (and for some professionals too!). There has long been a need for a book on the subject which is both interesting and readable, and at the same time technically accurate and explicit. *Automotive Supercharging & Turbocharging* fills a very real need, spanning both early and contemporary history of the subject, with excellent clarity of technical explanation.

The final chapter has yet to be written on the subject of turbocharging, and I believe it will be many years before this happens. Numerous ideas have been advanced to improve both the turbocharger as we know it, and its application to the reciprocating engine. The supercharging system of a decade hence may well be different to what we see today, but there can be no doubt that forced induction will play an increasing role in the car engine of the future.

Geoffrey Kershaw
Managing Director
Turbo Technics Limited

Introduction

The basic idea of supercharging, providing some form of forced induction system, is nearly as old as the internal combustion engine itself. In 1896 Rudolf Diesel introduced his supercharger design, only 18 years after the first successful Otto engine. The idea of using exhaust gas energy to provide the supercharging was not far behind, and in 1905, the Swiss engineer Büchi was granted the first patent for a practical turbocharger.

Despite this early appearance, supercharging remained for a long time something of relevance only to motor-racing fanatics, aero engine designers and a few other specialist users. In recent decades the application of the

The traditional image of supercharging. A drag racing car with a Roots type supercharger mounted on top of the engine.

turbocharger to heavy trucks has gradually increased until, suddenly, in the 1980s turbocharged automobiles appeared everywhere.

Now 'turbo' has become a generally used adjective associated with anything fast or powerful with its own image completely separate from the automotive industry. When this book was being written, a brief check revealed a 'turbo' candy bar, an insulating house-brick, a men's aftershave cosmetic, and a logo on a pair of pyjamas! This does not include the more obvious connections such as a domestic fan heater and a vacuum cleaner, and automotive shock absorbers and cam-shafts.

This fashionable use of the word clearly has followed from the general appearance of turbocharged automobiles on the road, which has brought the public into contact with the concept of supercharging. The purpose of this book is to help the interested, but non-specialist reader to understand what supercharging is all about, and in particular the workings of turbochargers. The focus of the book is on passenger automobiles and light commercial vehicles, but much of the material is equally relevant to larger truck engines, marine craft up to about 20 metres, and light aircraft.

According to the dictionary, a supercharger is a 'device for increasing the pressure in an internal combustion engine', and this generic, technical sense is the way in which it is used in this book. However, in many automotive discussions the word is used loosely to mean a traditional, mechanically driven compressor as distinct from an exhaust driven turbine/centrifugal compressor combination. Where it is necessary in this book to distinguish between the two different basic types of supercharger, the shortened terms 'turbocharger' and 'mechanical supercharger' are used.

Why supercharging?

What then are the key factors which make supercharging important? By increasing the density of the air drawn in, supercharging an internal combustion engine allows more fuel to be burned. This, in turn means a greater power output from a given size of engine, or conversely allows a smaller and lighter engine to be used for the same power requirement. There can also be some engine efficiency improvements which can reduce fuel consumption. These benefits naturally focused early attention on the maximum power requirement applications such as racing-cars, and military use in aircraft. The idea of apparently getting something for nothing by using the engine exhaust gas energy to drive a supercharger made the turbocharger concept very attractive. However, the limitations in theoretical knowledge and materials technology made the practical development of turbochargers a slow process. The need to improve the power/weight ratio and the maximum power from the large diesel engines used for main propulsion in ships, and for electrical power generation, provided the driving force for the early developments. The introduction of aircraft jet

engines forced improvements in the production of the special materials which can operate at very high temperatures, and the ready availability of these materials gave a new impetus to turbocharger manufacture in the early 1950s.

The turbocharged diesel engine was introduced for trucks in 1957 and its usage has grown until it now dominates the heavy haulage market throughout the world. In the UK in 1990, for new trucks above 7.5 tons about 95% are turbocharged; above 16 tons rating it is virtually 100%! The high specific output and low specific fuel consumption outweigh the disadvantages of a narrower usable engine speed range, lack of low speed torque, and poorer transient response compared with naturally aspirated engines.

Obtaining more power out of truck engines has been a strong driving force for the development of turbochargers. A typical modern engine is this Iveco-Ford 'TurboTech' 13.8 litre six cylinder unit. It develops a maximum power output of 377 bhp at 1,800 rpm. [Iveco-Ford]

The mass production of turbochargers to meet the truck market needs made it feasible to consider using turbochargers for passenger automobiles. New computer-aided design techniques, used in conjunction with a new theoretical understanding of how turbo machines work, and with the new manufacturing techniques, made it possible to produce more efficient yet smaller units.

While experts agree that a large percentage of the diesel engines fitted to passenger cars in the future will be supercharged, this is not the case with the spark ignition gasoline engine, which already has a high power density without being supercharged. Its speed range is usually greater than the diesel engine resulting in greater difficulties in matching a turbocharger and obtaining a satisfactory transient response, and the exhaust gas temperature is considerably higher than for the diesel. In order to achieve low fuel consumption at constant driving speeds, the reduced compression ratio of the supercharged spark ignition engine and the increase of the gas exchange losses in the part load range due to the back pressure of the turbine, are usually compensated for by a higher transmission ratio. The 'turbo lag' associated with earlier installations leads to a high-speed driving mode with a subsequent increase in actual fuel consumption on the road. The reasons for the success of supercharged spark ignition engines for automobiles cannot be economic ones!

The growth of the supercharged automobile market

At the time of the big surge in production of turbocharged cars there had been a great deal of publicity about the use of turbochargers in top-class motor racing, so the market research people saw a fashion opportunity. In addition, the technology had reached the point which made it both technically and financially feasible to add turbochargers to top-of-the-range models. As a result, people were prepared to pay the extra to be able to say they drove an automobile model which was turbocharged just like an Indy car. Even the word

Supercharging is now commonplace on many small cars, in order to keep a lively performance while still meeting emissions control regulations. This Volkswagen 1.3 litre G40 Polo uses the revolutionary G supercharger. *[Volkswagen]*

'turbo' developed its own sexy image! But this fashion view does not account for the great amount of research still being undertaken into all types of supercharging and the appearance of turbochargers on ever smaller vehicles.

The great driving force has come from another source – air pollution control regulations. Legal limitations on the amounts of certain pollutants in the exhaust gases of all vehicles in the major using and manufacturing countries have forced manufacturers to look anew at all the possible design developments. As the regulations are gradually tightened, so ever more obscure ideas are forced forward.

The diesel engine could meet the early restrictions most easily and, with its small fuel consumption, it was potentially an attractive substitute for the traditional spark ignition gasoline engine. The passenger car user will always measure the 'sociability' of the diesel engine against that of the gasoline engine, and it had two major drawbacks – it was noisy and, for a given engine size, under-powered. It was also usually more expensive. Design and manufacturing improvements have produced diesel engines which are now nearly as quiet as gasoline engines and are comparable in cost. Turbocharging was the answer to the other major disadvantage, allowing an engine of the same power output as the gasoline version to be used in a car.

A great deal of research was focused on improving the fuel systems and combustion conditions of gasoline engines in order that they should be able to meet the pollution limits laid down in the regulations. While this was going on another possibility existed. Smaller engines

do not emit as many pollutants, so why not fit smaller engines? A good idea, but not one which was very well received by the users; they had become too used to having a good power/weight ratio for dealing with today's complex traffic conditions. Adding a turbocharger was the possible answer. Certainly, the power could be restored to the smaller engine and, although the emissions did increase again, the net benefit was substantial. The smaller engines had additional benefits. The overall vehicle weight was reduced and it was much easier to fit them into the crash safety zones which were also being imposed by regulations.

New tighter emissions control regulations are due to come into force by the end of 1992 which will have an impact not only on the gasoline-powered passenger car market but also on the diesel-powered truck market. Complete electronic control systems, some form of supercharging, fuel injection systems, exhaust gas recirculation and catalytic converters are going to become the norm on virtually all vehicles. Research is continuing into the development of new operating cycles for engines and the possibilities for new fuels.

Turbocharger systems can now be supplied for use

The twin-turbocharged racing engine used in the Sauber-Mercedes Sports Car Championship entry. *[KKK]*

on any size of engine from 0.5 litre upwards, and with boost pressures up to 7 bar. The limits now are the mechanical and thermal loads on the engine. Nevertheless, turbochargers have some unpleasant habits when used in passenger cars, which has tended to limit their acceptability for the less sporty vehicle.

Now that the use of supercharging is being forced by the emissions control regulations, manufacturers are looking at other ways of achieving the forced induction whilst avoiding some of the snags of the turbocharger. In the case of passenger cars, improved driver 'feel' while accelerating, particularly at low speed, is a marketable feature, so that the fuel efficiency problems of some superchargers can be acceptable. A new era in the application of supercharging is starting in the automotive industry.

The structure of this book

It is intended that this book will provide the descriptive and technical background to all of the above topics. The early chapters look at the history of the mechanically driven supercharger, the developments of the gas turbine which led to the turbocharger, some of the new generation of superchargers, and some key developments which are likely to significantly affect the future.

Then, the more technical part of the book starts off with a brief summary of basic automotive design principles and the principles of supercharging. This theoretical background is necessary in order to understand many of the design issues discussed later in the book. Do not worry; it is all kept fairly simple! The less technically minded reader could skip these chapters if desired. Because of its importance in forcing supercharging developments, exhaust pollution and the associated techniques for minimising it are given a chapter to themselves.

The next few chapters focus on turbochargers, how they work, their performance characteristics, how they are designed and how they are manufactured. This is then followed by consideration of the associated issues which are affected by supercharging; the design of exhaust and inlet systems, and the provision of charge air cooling and other cooling needs. The need for boost control mechanisms and how control is achieved are then covered in the next two chapters. This is followed by consideration of how superchargers are integrated into the engine design with a focus on fuel and ignition changes, and then follows discussion of complete engine control systems with the sensors and actuators which are needed.

The penultimate chapters of the book look at the different vehicle characteristics which are needed, depending upon the application and how this is related to supercharging, and at the procedure for adding a supercharger to an engine design. Finally, consideration is given to the after-market of suppliers who will help to create engine versions different to the manufacturer's standard. Three complete examples are given of turbocharger conversions to different engines, including detail of all the steps which had to be carried out.

At the end of the book you will find a number of appendices which contain various useful bits of information which may help anyone interested in undertaking practical work with supercharged engines. A list of most of the current production engines which have forced induction systems of some type, together with the vehicles in which they have been fitted, is provided in Appendix A.

From time to time within the text you may come across a small number in square brackets, like this –[42]. This indicates an entry in the 'References' section at the back of the book, where you will find listed many technical papers and other books which provided source information for this book. Entries in this list can give you further information if you want to explore some topic in more detail.

Numerous specialist words are used in this book and are generally explained when first introduced. For those which are not, and as a general convenient reference, a 'Glossary' of specialist terms is also provided at the end of the book.

1

Development of supercharging

In Paris in 1878 Dr Nicholaus August Otto successfully demonstrated the first four-stroke cycle internal combustion engine[35]. He had invented it barely two years earlier, though the concept was formulated by Beau de Rochas, a French architect, in 1862. By 1896 Rudolf Diesel had filed his first patent for using a supercharger with his compression ignition engine, and in 1901 Sir Dugald Clark discovered that if he used a device to increase artificially the volume of air charge entering a cylinder, the engine produced more power. At about the turn of the century, Rateau in France developed the centrifugal compressor, and in 1902 Louis Renault patented a system in which a centrifugal fan blew air into the mouth of a carburettor. It was all happening very quickly.

In 1907 Lee Chadwick in the USA, working with J. T. Nicholls, developed the idea of putting the carburettor under pressure to increase volumetric efficiency[4]. Initially an 8-inch diameter single-stage centrifugal compressor was used, driven at five times engine speed by a flat belt from the flywheel. Because the results were so good, the next development was to install a three-stage blower driven at six times engine speed by a 2-inch wide leather belt. Three impellers, each with 12 blades, were employed, all of 10-inch diameter, but of varying widths to provide the three-stage compression which fed the carburettor with pressurised air.

On 30 May 1908, Chadwick's car was entered in the Great Despair hillclimb in Pennsylvania and won. This was the first competitive event in which a blown car was entered. Over the next two years the car won many events, the most notable being the 200-mile road race at Fairmont Park in 1910. Replicas of this car, which was capable of well over 100 mph, were sold to the public and it became the first catalogued car to

exceed that speed. In Europe, in 1911 and 1912 Sizaire and Birkigt in Paris carried out experiments with centrifugal blower and piston type displacers respectively. In the USA there was not much further development until that done by Miller and Duesenberg in 1923.

During the 1914-18 war supercharging was developed a lot further for use with aero engines in the continuous attempts to gain altitude for the fighters and bombers[1]. Initial developments centred on the 'Roots'-type positive displacement blower, but this was quickly replaced by the potentially more efficient centrifugal compressor. Because of the need for the high speed of the compressor, step-up gear drives had to be used and there were a lot of problems with these early systems, mainly due to rotational inertia. Spring drives, various flexible drives, fluid couplings and centrifugal clutches were all tried at some time.

The main line of development of aircraft superchargers in Europe continued with mechanical drive. The Rolls-Royce Griffon aero engine set the trend for a long line of engine developments by using a three-speed gearbox system to drive a two-stage centrifugal supercharger. In the USA the use of geared centrifugal compressors for aero engines changed around 1925 as a result of General Electric's development of a practical turbocharger.

In 1921 a supercharged six-cylinder Mercedes 28/95 car driven by Max Sailer won the Coppa Florio race[39]. As a result of this first success, Mercedes designed a supercharged 1.5-litre sports car which competed in the Targa Florio. All the early Mercedes systems employed a Roots type blower mounted vertically and driven by bevel gears from the nose of the crankshaft, feeding pressurised air to the carburettor. The blower drive incorporated a cone clutch connected to

the throttle so that the drive to the blower was only engaged at full throttle. It provided a relatively modest boost of approximately 0.5 bar but obtained up to 50% increase in power.

Fiat were the first to supercharge a Grand Prix racing-car in 1923, when they ran a 2-litre car fitted with a Wittig vane-type supercharger. Following Mercedes practice, the charger was fitted with a hinged flap arrangement which allowed the engine to run naturally aspirated until supercharging was required, and it used a pressurised carburettor. Because of mechanical and lubrication problems and low efficiency, they soon changed to the Roots type blower with a charge air cooler before the carburettor. Mercedes themselves entered a supercharged car in the Indianapolis 500 that year as well. By the spring of 1924 both Sunbeam and Alfa Romeo also appeared with Grand Prix cars supercharged with Roots type blowers driven directly from the nose of the crankshaft. The Alfa Romeo P2 straight

In 1923 Mercedes produced this 2 litre four cylinder supercharged engine which developed 120 bhp at 4,500 rpm. It was fitted with a Roots type supercharger driven from the front of the crankshaft via a clutch linked to the throttle. Cars fitted with this engine competed successfully in the 1924 Targa Florio and Coppa Florio races. *[National Motor Museum]*

In 1936, Auto Union introduced this supercharged racing-car which started the trend leading to the dominance of Grand Prix motor racing by Mercedes and Auto Union by 1939. The rear-mounted V-16 engine was fitted with a vertically mounted Roots-type supercharger. *[National Motor Museum]*

eight delivered a then incredible 135 horsepower at 5,500 rpm.

In the USA, following a lapse of 12 years since Chadwick's work, the Duesenberg engine appeared in 1924 and won the Indianapolis 500 race. It had a 2-litre engine with a centrifugal compressor, installed with the impeller at right-angles to the line of the crankshaft. This was the first supercharging system to suck air through the carburettor, and it was subsequently shown to give an improvement when compared with positive displacement blowers due to fuel cooling. There also began the widespread use of alcohol fuels in racing. With the exception of Mercedes, who persisted in downstream carburettor positioning until 1937, the practice of mounting the carburettor in front of the supercharger became normal.

During the years 1925-38, the Grand Prix formulae led to virtually all racing engines being supercharged; there was a steady increase in power, coupled to increased boost pressures and the use of alcohol fuel. By 1938-9 Grand Prix racing was completely dominated by the enormously powerful Mercedes and Auto Union cars. The Auto Union contender had a 6-litre engine delivering 520 horsepower at 5,000 revolutions per minute, running on methanol fuel, with a compression ratio of 9.2:1 and a boost pressure of 1.8 bar. The Mercedes M125 produced 646 horsepower. Both Mercedes and Auto Union used two-stage supercharging with Roots blowers, and in 1939 were getting up to 2.65 bar pressure on 3-litre engines.

After the war when motor-racing resumed in 1947, Formula 1 Grand Prix was 4.5 litres unsupercharged or 1.5 litres supercharged, and many of the pre-war supercharged designs competed successfully. In 1950-51 the unsupercharged Ferrari engine became dominant and the decline of the supercharged cars started. The only significant attempt to continue with supercharging came with the ill-fated V16 BRM car which used a Rolls-Royce aircraft-type two-stage centrifugal supercharger. At 5,000 rpm the 1.5-litre engine produced only 100 bhp, but at 8,000 rpm this had increased to 330 bhp, backed by a similar rapidly rising torque curve, a characteristic which made it extremely difficult to drive!

In 1952 the Grand Prix formula changed to 2 litres unsupercharged and 500 cc supercharged and normal pump fuel. This marked the end of the blown cars in Grand Prix motor-racing for 23 years, until turbochargers appeared on the scene.

This review so far has focused on four-stroke cycle, spark ignition gasoline engines, but the two-stroke cycle and diesel engines have both made use of some forms of supercharging. The two-stroke engine potentially has twice the power output of a four-stroke engine for the same displacement, although in practice this is not fully achievable. The major disadvantage is that it has no natural induction capability and needs some form of forced charging of the cylinders. This has simultaneously to overcome the exhaust gas back pressure and drive out the products of combustion.

The provision of this 'scavenging' pressure has been a complicating factor for the design of all two-stroke engines. As a result, the use of this cycle has tended to be restricted to applications where the overall reduction in size provides a compelling argument to balance the other difficulties. Two-cycle spark ignition gasoline engines are typically applied to light motor cycles, marine outboard motors and portable tools such as chain saws. The two-stroke cycle is also used for many of the very large diesel engines installed in ships for propulsion. Here, obtaining the maximum power-to-weight ratio and the maximum efficiency is crucial when horsepower ratings in excess of 40,000 are not unusual.

All of the superchargers referred to in this brief historic review were mechanically driven in some manner from the engine crankshaft. The drive has been direct or using a gearbox, or has been driven by shaft, chains or a variety of different types of belts. Some form of compliance had to be included to absorb the inertia loadings accompanying the frequent engine speed changes in automobile applications. Modern installations usually use V-belts or internally toothed belts, with drive ratios typically ranging from 0.8:1 (supercharger to engine speed) to 2:1. Higher drive speeds are not normally practicable due to drive and supercharger limitations. The large superchargers used on drag racers can require as much as 250 horsepower driving power, needing a belt of 3 to 4 inches in width. Electromagnetic clutches are now used instead of mechanical ones where the supercharger is not required all the time.

Mounting the compressor in a position which allows a practicable drive system has always been one of the limiting factors for supercharging systems. Some experiments have been carried out with a hydraulically driven boost compressor which gives much greater flexibility in mounting, and in controlling the amount of boost.

Types of compressors

Given time and resources, practically any one of the countless pumping devices available today may be developed into a supercharger, though they may not all be equally suitable or efficient. Those that have been used for automotive applications can be grouped into the two broad categories of positive displacement and kinetic energy compressors. There are many different types of positive displacement blowers or compressors, but they all have the key characteristic that all the charge which enters the supercharger must pass through the engine[35][42].

As automotive engines have nearly always been reciprocating types following the basic Otto or Diesel cycles, it was natural that early supercharging developments should look towards reciprocating piston compressors. Two-stroke engines were obvious early candidates when it was realised that crankcase compression had limitations.

Harry Ricardo proposed a reciprocating piston

compressor for two-stroke engines at the turn of the century, providing for this purpose additional cranks on the engine crankshaft. An updated version of this concept was used in the British Trojan two-stroke engine in the post 1945 period. DKW in Germany used a similar design for a two-stroke racing motor cycle engine, achieving specific power outputs of up to 140 bhp/litre and even 200 bhp/litre on alcohol fuel, a spectacular performance unfortunately unmatched by comparable reliability. Later engines featured a separate chain-driven compressor crankshaft.

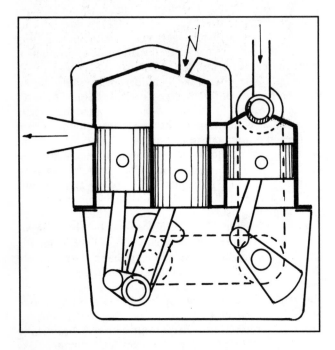

Schematic of the DKW two-stroke racing motor cycle engine with separate scavenging and supercharging cylinders. The crankshafts were coupled together by chains and to the rotary inlet valve. This engine achieved a specific power output of 200 bhp/litre on alcohol fuel.

Stepped pistons, that is with two diameters, have been variously proposed for two-stroke engines. One such development, the Templewall engine, was pursued at the Norton-Villiers-Triumph Motorcycle Company in the early 1980s.

There were some applications of the reciprocating piston compressor to four-stroke cycle gasoline engines; Birkitt fitted this type of blower to Hispano cars in 1911, and Mercedes tried a three-cylinder radial charger in the early 1920s, but quickly changed to vane and finally Roots types which were such a feature of pre-1939 Mercedes racing and sports cars.

In 1848, G. Jones in Birmingham, England, invented a blower which was based upon two lobed rotors meshing together. The same idea was re-invented and commercialised by P. H. & F. M. Roots of Connersville, Indiana, USA, in 1866, and the Roots blower and its variants has been probably the best-known and most widely used type of mechanically driven supercharger until turbochargers became established. It has been used for all kinds of two-stroke and four-stroke gasoline and diesel engines, as well as industrial compressors and for pressurising aircraft cabins. Its popularity has undoubtedly been due to the positive displacement characteristic which ensures adequate discharge pressure over a wide speed range.

The two rotors do not actually touch but are kept in synchronism by externally mounted gears. Air enters at one port, is trapped between a rotor lobe and the casing and is carried around to the discharge port. The Roots type should be referred to as a 'blower' rather than a 'compressor' as there is no change in the volume of the air trapped by a lobe during its transfer from the input port to the delivery port. The discharge to the higher pressure zone causes a turbulent pressure equali-

Working principle of the Roots blower. Air is trapped between the rotating lobes and the outside casing and is carried round from inlet to outlet. The diagram shows a two-lobe version. *[Lancia]*

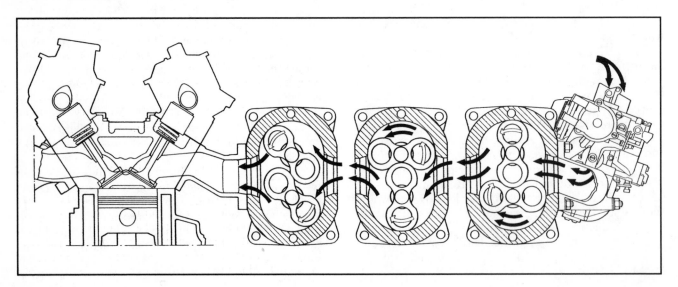

sation at that point and this is the source of the poor compression efficiency of the Roots blower.

Because the only rotating contact is between the synchronising gears, which usually run in their own lubrication chamber, the frictional losses of the type are low. Nevertheless, due to the compression difficulties the overall efficiency can often be below 50% which gives excessive heating of the charge air. The basic design had only two lobes per rotor, but three-lobe and four-lobe versions are not uncommon. The cross-section of the lobes has been mostly cycloidal, but involute and other more complex shapes have been used.

Modern version of the classic Roots supercharger. The cutaway portion shows the synchronising gears which couple the two rotors. [Eaton]

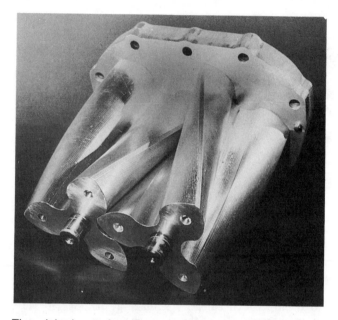

Three-lobed rotor for a Roots supercharger. Combined with the twist given to the lobes, this arrangement gives reduced pulsations in the delivery pressure and reduced noise compared with the two-lobed type. [Eaton]

The pressure tends to increase slightly relative to speed due to the diminishing significance of the leakage path cross-sectional area/time factor. The volumetric efficiency consequently tends to rise with speed, but it is the performance at low speed which is most appreciated. Very high pressure ratios are difficult to achieve because of the increased leakage around and between the lobes.

The Roots blower has a very distinctive noise beat due to the fluctuating discharge as the lobes pass the delivery port, so General Motors introduced the idea of using helically shaped rotors to get a smoother delivery and reduce the noise. Versions of these blowers, originally manufactured for use as scavenge pumps on two-stroke diesel truck engines, have been widely adopted on drag racing cars where their ability to deliver high torque from low speed more than compensates for any inefficiencies.

Manufacturers of Roots type blowers over the years have included Fiat, Mercedes, Auto Union, Rolls-Royce, GMC, Lysholm, Whitfield, Marchall Nordec, Marshall Drew, Wade Engineering, Eaton and many more.

A very large class of compressors is referred to as rotary piston types. There are literally thousands of configuration possibilities, which have been researched and patented over the years. Not all these designs may have been equally viable or efficient, but they have included the work of many notable engineers such as Elija Galloway (1834), Sir Charles Parsons (1852), Cooley (1919), Wallinder and Skoog (1921), Fixen (1934), de Lavaud (1938), Mailard (1943), Cozett, Renault-AMC, Wankel, and many others. Rotary piston machines are generally true compressors, in which the volume of a chamber changes between the inlet and outlet giving an internal pressure rise.

When Felix Wankel started the development work which led to his successful rotary engine, he found the variety of rotary piston machines, proposed since Ramelli in 1588, so bewildering that he devised a classification system similar to the classification of chemical elements which allows the prediction of elements which have not yet been discovered[12]. Unfortunately it does not provide a lead for qualitative assessment of particular configurations, but it has led a number of engineers to examine possibilities not previously considered. Wankel's own format was used as a supercharger for some NSU record-breaking motor cycles.

A very formidable group of machines are the intersecting axis rotary piston compressors, where the axes of the moving elements/housing are not parallel and may be oscillating. The possible configurations of such designs are so complex that they challenge the skills of the most proficient design engineers. Three designs have surfaced so far; the best documented is described by Clarke, Walker & Hamilton[15]. Although used in numerous

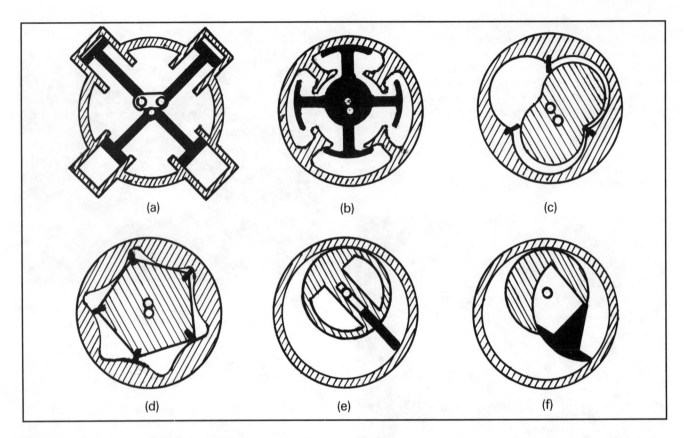

(a)   (b)   (c)

(d)   (e)   (f)

So many different types of compressors have been proposed that Felix Wankel produced a classification system for the thousands of potential designs. Here are six different examples from Wankel's classification which have been developed

(a)   Parsons 1852   (d)   de Lavaud 1938
(b)   Lind 1914   (e)   Ramelli 1588
(c)   Cooley 1903   (f)   Turboflex

part, for example as in the Roots blower, is impracticable.

A close relation to the rotary piston machine is the vane-type compressor; indeed, in some cases it is difficult to decide which category a machine belongs to. The main characteristic of the vane-type is a number of sliding vanes which divide the housing into compartments whose volume changes as the vanes are carried around by a rotating element.

industrial applications, the manufacturing cost of these machines has meant that they have never seriously been adopted for automotive applications.

It is necessary to appreciate the importance of effective sealing arrangements when considering rotary piston engines and high-pressure compressors. The sealing systems of such machines are as indispensable as piston rings are for reciprocating piston designs. However, it is worth noting that piston rings are incomplete sealing elements because they provide unavoidable leakage paths at their splits; hence two or more rings are fitted to every piston. In contrast to this, it is possible to devise a 'complete' sealing grid for some rotary piston machines, the Wankel for example. Such a sealing grid consists of a number of elements suitably linked together to block any leakage path. An effective and complete sealing grid can only be provided between two components – one rotor and its housing – or between two moving parts. Intermittent sealing against a housing and a second moving

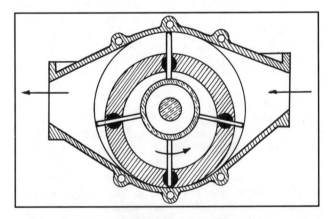

The Centric vane-type pump, compressor or engine. First produced in 1911 by Oerlikon in Switzerland as an internal combustion engine, the Centric became a popular automobile engine supercharger.

The vane-type compressor seems to have fascinated inventors and engineers since Ramelli in 1588, and a great many designs have found their way into patent specifications and practical applications. Examples are Oldham Franchot (1861), Wittig (1900), Oerlikon (1911), Zoller (1925), Cozette, Arnott, Centric, Reveal, Power-plus, Shorrock, Constantine, and Judson.

The Centric supercharger was first produced by Oerlikon in Switzerland in 1911 as an internal combustion engine. This design differs from more conventional sliding vane compressors by having its vanes rotatably attached to a shaft, whilst the rotor is eccentric relative to the housing and the shaft. The vanes slide in trunnion blocks, equally spaced and contained by the rotor, to accommodate the cyclic variations of the angles between the vanes.

Many vane types were produced in the 1920-39 period for automobile use. The Shorrock survived until the 1970s and the type is still widely used for industrial compressors. More recently, Bendix introduced their Rotocharger vane-type mechanical supercharger which has a bypass system to allow the engine to run unsupercharged when not needed.

One of the big objections to many past designs of vane-type compressor has been that the sliding vanes have needed a lubrication supply, resulting in oil contamination of the engine charge air. Modern materials technology now gives the possibility of finding a way round this problem.

In 1784, Cameron, an employee of James Watt, the father of the steam engine, patented a helical engine. It consisted of a rotor with a deep right-hand helical vane over 180° changing to a left-hand helix over the remaining 180° round the shaft to join with the start of the right-hand helix. This rotor was contained in a cylindrical bore, closed at both ends, and a sealing block was

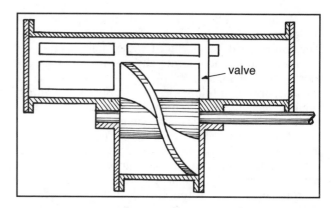

In 1784, Cameron, an employee of James Watt, patented this steam engine with a helical piston fitted with a sliding valve. It was the first of many designs to make use of helixes.

fitted calliper fashion over the vane and was free to move to and fro in response to shaft (ie helix) movement. The sealing block doubled as a sliding valve to control the flow of steam.

This idea of using one or more helixes within an enclosure has since been used as the basis of a number of different compressor designs. The most successful has been the Swedish Lysholm design based on two meshing helixes. These compressors are now firmly estab-

Operating principle of the Lysholm screw compressor. The two rotors turn at different speeds. In the example shown, the 'male' rotor has four lobes, and the 'female' has six flutes, and they are geared together to rotate at the 6/4 ratio. Because of the relative movement of the two rotors, the volume of air trapped between one lobe and the meshing flute reduces along the length of the unit, causing a true compression process. [Fleming Thermodynamics]

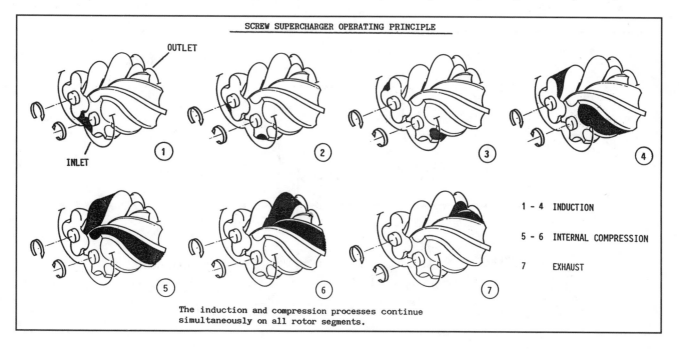

SCREW SUPERCHARGER OPERATING PRINCIPLE

OUTLET

INLET

1 2 3 4

5 6 7

1 - 4   INDUCTION

5 - 6   INTERNAL COMPRESSION

7   EXHAUST

The induction and compression processes continue simultaneously on all rotor segments.

lished and manufactured by several companies. The design is compact and gives an impulse-free discharge. The rotors must be machined within tight limits as it is impossible to incorporate any positive sealing. For most industrial applications oil is the main sealant, needing a separator to follow the compressor, although dry running versions have been produced which can be used as superchargers for gasoline engines.

While at first sight this type of supercharger may look superficially like the Roots type, the significance is the difference between the two rotors. The 'male' rotor has four lobes and the 'female' rotor has six flutes. The gearing between the rotors is such that their speed has the same 6/4 ratio. As can be seen from the diagram, the effect of this arrangement is that a volume of air trapped between one lobe-and-flute pair is pushed forward and compressed as the rotation proceeds.

An interesting application of the Lysholm-SRM compressor was for the 'differential supercharged' diesel truck engine developed by Perkins. In the DDE 6.354 engine, the output was taken through an epicyclic differential gear which drove both the compressor and a high ratio (3.6:1) hydraulic torque converter. As the torque load on the engine increased, so the speed of the compressor relative to engine speed would increase giving a very good torque back-up characteristic. When this engine was applied to 28-34 ton trucks it was possible to get a successful design using only two forward and one reverse speeds in the gearbox.

The Perkins DDE 6.354 'differential supercharged' truck diesel engine used a Lysholm screw compressor driven from an epicyclic differential gearbox. This shared the engine output between the supercharger and a torque converter output gearbox. As the torque load on the engine increased, so the speed of the compressor relative to engine speed would increase.

All the supercharger designs considered so far have been positive displacement types where the air is clearly being pushed forward into a higher pressure zone. The 'kinetic energy' compressors, on the other hand, convert the mechanical drive energy into the kinetic energy of fast-moving gas. This kinetic energy is then converted by a suitable ducting arrangement, a 'diffuser', into the required pressure energy. The theory of operation of such devices is very complex and, until the ready availability of high-speed digital computers, progress in their development was very slow and involved a lot of expensive trial and error. The story of Frank Whittle's early development work on his pioneering jet engine design highlights the difficulties encountered at that time.

The only type which has been generally applied for supercharging of internal combustion engines is the turbo-compressor. In this a rotating fan, the 'impeller', draws air into an 'inducer' area and accelerates it to high speed as it passes through the blades of the impeller. There are two main types – radial and axial flow. In the radial flow type, entry is at the centre of a disk-shaped fan and the exit flow is radial at the periphery of the disk. In the axial flow type, the impeller has a series of blades around its periphery and the air flow is parallel to the axis with the acceleration of the air giving a spiral exit flow.

The radial flow centrifugal compressor can readily be designed to obtain quite a high pressure ratio from a single stage, and this has made it the most popular type for automotive applications – it is the basis of most turbochargers today. The axial flow compressor has a much smaller possible pressure ratio per stage but can very easily be built into a multi-stage device with a very high efficiency. Most modern aircraft jet engines use axial flow compressors.

In the centrifugal compressor, the output pressure is proportional to the square of the rotational speed. It

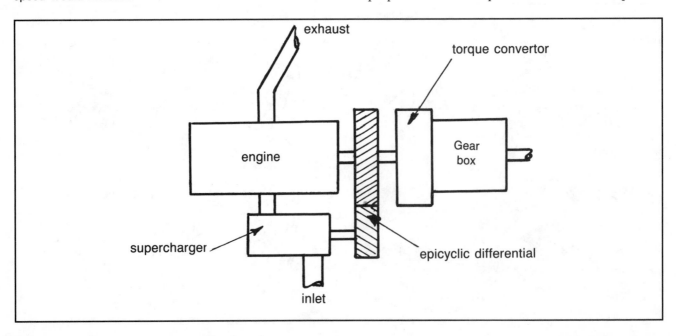

requires a very high speed to produce useful pressure at realistic sizes which means that for use on automotive engines, high-ratio drive gearing is required. With the speed variability required by most such applications, this gearing can present difficulties. As a result, until the advent of the turbocharger the most notable application of centrifugal compressors had been the special cars developed for racing at Indianapolis, where high power at high speed has been more important than speed flexibility.

The air needs of a reciprocating engine are proportional to the speed of the engine. Matching this to the 'speed squared' characteristic of the centrifugal compressor presents many problems, and these are discussed in later chapters. The Paxton supercharger in the 1950s used a variable speed V-belt drive linked to the throttle in an attempt to minimise these matching problems.

With these fundamental problems, why has the centrifugal compressor become such an integral part of automotive supercharging systems today? Because it is very simple to make, very compact relative to the volume of air it has to handle, has low frictional losses and high pumping efficiency, and, probably most important of all, has a characteristic which ideally matches the gas turbine in order to draw its drive power from the engine exhaust gases.

An incidental benefit is the immunity of centrifugal superchargers to back-fire. With large positive displacement compressors, some provision needs to be made to protect them, often by the provision of blow-off valves or weakened fixing bolts. It has been known for the supercharger on a high-performance drag racer to be blown off completely by a backfire!

There are other kinetic energy supercharging techniques using pressure waves and these will be considered in chapters 4 and 12, but the big change to the automotive scene came with the mass production of cars fitted with turbochargers. The majority of these use a combination of a centrifugal compressor with a radial flow gas turbine drawing its energy from the exhaust gases of the engine, and the next chapter looks at how the modern mass-produced turbocharger was developed from the early experiments at the turn of the century.

2

Introduction of the gas turbine

On 30 November 1791, a British patent was issued to John Barber covering the basic principles of the combustion gas turbine system. It described a combustion chamber into which fuel and air were introduced under pressure. This combustion chamber was to be fitted with a nozzle from which the products of combustion would issue onto a turbine wheel. This supplied power to drive a reciprocating compressor for the combustion air as well as to deliver external power. The only difference

In 1791 a British patent was issued to John Barber which covered the essential principle of the gas turbine cycle. It described a combustion chamber pressurised with air, with the products of combustion issuing onto a turbine wheel which drove the air compressor and provided output power. It could never have been made to work with the technology of the time, but Barber clearly understood the concept.

in principle from most later developments was that they would generally use centrifugal compressors and would have the addition of heat exchangers. There is no evidence that John Barber ever tried to build his device, and it almost certainly would not have worked if he had, as the technology of the time was not suitable, but he had clearly grasped the concept of the gas turbine process.

John Barber's work was just one example of the awakening to the possibilities of applying scientific principles to creating new 'engines', and throughout the next hundred years there was a continual outpouring of ideas. Towards the end of the 19th century there were great developments in steam turbine technology and, more importantly, in the theory of their operations. A key element came in 1890 when de Laval in Sweden introduced the convergent/divergent nozzle which could release the theoretical energy from steam.

In 1901 a patent was issued in France to Charles Lemale for a basic gas turbine system design. Working in association with Rene Armengaud, they achieved a working system in 1903. In the USA, in 1902, Sanford Moss had access to a de Laval steam turbine at his university and he used a separately driven compressor with an oil-fired combustion chamber to achieve the first working US turbine driven by combustion products. However, the net power from this set-up was negative[4]!

What was the problem these pioneers were facing? Suppose a gas turbine wheel theoretically delivered 100 horsepower, and suppose the compressor theoretically required 49 horsepower; then there would theoretically be 51 net horsepower. But the turbine wheel might have an efficiency of 70%, so it would actually only deliver 70 horsepower; and the compressor might have an efficiency of 70%, so the net horsepower would come out as (100 x 0.70) – (49/0.70) = 0! The infant technologies were barely able to achieve the essential levels of operating efficiency.

In 1906, the Swiss engineering company Brown Boveri (now part of ASEA-Brown Boveri [ABB]) supplied the first commercial turbo-compressor for use in Armengaud and Lemale's gas turbine research. It needed 328 horsepower to drive it and had an efficiency of about 65-70%. It was of the axial flow type and had 25 stages with the impellers running at 4,000 revolutions per minute. After this, the name of Brown Boveri appears again and again in the history of gas turbine and turbocharger development.

Many of the early successful gas turbine systems were only partial cycles, using hot gases generated as part of other processes, eg, oil refineries. The available materials for building the turbines, which had to withstand great centrifugal forces at high temperatures, generally limited what was achievable. The usual temperature limit was about 600°C. This was one of the design areas where engineers first encountered the phenomenon of high temperature creep.

One of the experimental ideas for producing reliable gas turbine systems was given the name of the 'diesel boiler' cycle. This used a compression ignition reciprocating engine to handle the high temperature part of the cycle as it had more efficient compression and expansion at high pressures. A two-stroke diesel engine, exhausting at a high back pressure (say 4 bar), would drive only its scavenging air reciprocating compressor which was mounted on the same crankshaft. The exhaust, cooled by a large amount of scavenge air, would then proceed to the turbine, all of whose output was net.

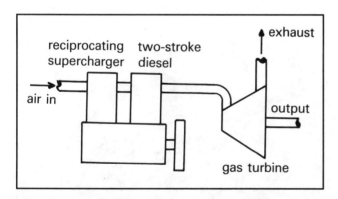

The 'diesel boiler' principle. A two-stroke diesel drives only its scavenging and supercharging compressor but delivers its exhaust at high pressure to a power turbine.

In 1905, Dr Alfred Büchi, a Swiss engineer, filed his first patent for a combined gas turbine and reciprocating engine. This patent is generally accepted as being the foundation of modern turbocharged internal combustion engine developments. In 1909, Büchi first published information on his work, and the first practical tests using exhaust gas turbines in conjunction with internal combustion engines took place in 1911 at Sulzer Brothers works at Winterthur in Switzerland. This used a Diesel engine with supercharging pressures up to 2 bar and combustion pressures exceeding 95 bar, giving a brake mean effective pressure of over 14 bar.

Technology development generally was forced by the First World War between 1914 and 1918. The use of mechanically driven superchargers for military aircraft has already been mentioned in Chapter 1. In 1917, Rateau was experimenting with turbocharging on French aircraft, and in 1918 the General Electric Company in the USA was making tests on a turbocharged Liberty engine[14].

Brown Boveri began building turbochargers as regular production items in 1923. It was easier to get a workable system in large-scale applications where the necessary efficiency criteria could be met with the currently available theoretical knowledge, manufacturing methods and materials technology. Large marine diesel engines were becoming accepted for commercial shipping, and the reduction in size and weight which was achievable using turbochargers more than offset the additional complexities and reliability problems attached to them.

Fuel consumption could be improved with exhaust-gas-driven turbochargers in spite of decreased expansion in the combustion cylinder due to back pressure, since mechanical losses due to friction remain practically constant for cylinders of given dimensions even though the mean effective pressures are greatly increased.

In 1925 Büchi introduced his 'pulse system' based upon using exhaust gas pulses in separate manifolds to enhance efficiency, a technique which is now widely used and is discussed in detail in Chapter 12. In a lecture in 1936, Büchi gave examples of many regular turbocharged aircraft, industrial, marine and locomotive diesel engines in service at that time. In that year the US Navy gave approval for the use of turbocharged six-cylinder 900 bhp, 700 rpm diesel engines in a series of naval vessels.

The high exhaust temperatures associated with gasoline engines still gave problems with the use of turbochargers at this time. By the start of the Second World War, temperatures of 7-800°C and speeds of 22,000 rpm were being handled by General Electric turbochargers used on the B17 Flying Fortress, Lightning P38, Liberator B24, and Thunderbolt P47 aircraft.

The development of jet engines for military aircraft gave a great impetus to the development of the necessary high temperature materials technology, and creep-resistant high-temperature steels suitable for making reliable gas turbine blades soon became readily available.

After the war, when motor-racing started again, not only did the mechanically driven supercharger re-appear, but engineers also turned their attention to the possibilities of using the aircraft-type turbocharger. In 1952 a race-car equipped with a turbocharged diesel engine was entered in the Indianapolis 500, and by the mid-'60s turbocharging was used for USAC and Indy race-cars.

Later, with the change of Formula 1 Grand Prix rules, Renault led the way to an era which became dominated by turbocharged race engines.

The first production passenger car to use turbocharging was the General Motors Oldsmobile Jetfire Turbo Rocket[11]. Its engine was an existing 215-cubic-inch displacement (3.5-litre) 90° V-8 aluminium engine with a 10.25:1 compression ratio running on premium fuel. A boost pressure of 0.34 bar at full throttle gave a 30% increase in torque compared with the standard engine. As soon as the boost started to approach 0.07 bar, a system of water/methanol injection was brought into action using a pressurised tank. A special new horizontal carburettor was developed for the engine and 'wastegate' boost control was employed. The turbocharger ran at speeds of up to 90,000 rpm. The engine was strengthened and changes were also made to the ignition system. The Turbo Rocket engine produced 215 bhp against 156 bhp from the standard engine. Oldsmobile were followed at the beginning of 1975 by Porsche who started production of the 911 Turbo, a high-performance version of the well-known 911 car.

The Turbo Rocket was a fairly limited production vehicle, but in 1978 Buick, Saab and Mercedes all introduced volume production of turbocharged engines for passenger car usage, followed by Chevrolet with a turbocharged opposed six-cylinder engine in the Corvair Monza Spyder.

The standard turbocharged engine today is essentially a compression or spark ignition reciprocating engine with the addition of a forced induction centrifugal compressor driven by a gas turbine which extracts energy from the exhaust gas. It still has a close resem-

blance to the naturally aspirated version. However, over the years there have been numerous attempts to produce 'compound' engines which exploit the combination of internal combustion engine and gas turbine in more complex modes to achieve greater power or efficiency.

The Curtiss-Wright 'Turbo Cyclone' aero engine was developed after the war for use in the Lockheed 'Super Constellation' long-distance passenger aircraft. It was an 18-cylinder radial engine fitted with a gear-driven two-speed centrifugal supercharger; three exhaust gas turbines were all linked to the crankshaft by fluid couplings and the engine developed up to 3,700 hp. It certainly achieved technical and commercial success, but soon yielded to the competition from jet and turbo-prop engines in an era of cheap fuel.

Other highly sophisticated compound engine designs were denied even fleeting commercial applications despite promising high efficiencies and fuel economy. The Napier Nomad[7] aircraft engine was a 12-cylinder horizontally opposed two-stroke liquid-cooled diesel

The Napier Nomad compound aircraft engine developed in the early 1950s. It combined a 41.1-litre 12-cylinder horizontally opposed two-stroke diesel engine with an axial flow three-stage exhaust gas turbine and a 12-stage axial flow supercharging compressor. In its finally developed form, with water injection and some afterburning, it produced a peak effective output of 4,500 horsepower from a remarkably light engine. The turbine/compressor shaft was coupled to the main output shaft through an ingenious continuously variable gearbox. The turbine produced 2,250 horsepower at sea level, of which 1,800 horsepower was needed to drive the supercharging compressor. [Napier Turbochargers]

unit which was compounded with an axial flow three-stage exhaust gas turbine and a 12-stage axial flow compressor, supplying boost air at 8.25 bar, with a pressure ratio of 8.25:1. A charge air cooler was fitted, with water injection, and extra fuel was injected into the exhaust manifold. The effective engine volumetric compression ratio was 31.5:1. This gave an engine of relatively modest weight and overall dimensions producing 4,500 hp, equivalent to 0.83 lb/ hp. In 1955 Geislinger adapted the idea for railway engines.

In any case, the logical final outcome of many compound engine developments would reduce the basic piston engine of such configurations to a gas generator, all power for external work being taken from the turbine. Hence the advantages and limitations of compound engines would be only marginally different from those of gas turbines; indeed, their cost and complexities would be even greater. Computer simulations have recently been used to explore many possible compound cycle engines – diesels with mechanical expanders, turbochargers, mechanical superchargers, etc. These studies have shown no very obvious benefits except perhaps for some special applications. There have also been a number of attempts to introduce the pure gas turbine cycle for automotive use, but none of them have led to production engines, amongst other reasons because of the difficulties in providing a suitable transmission system.

Nevertheless, studies of compound engines still continue, and from time to time significant steps forward are taken. One factor which has influenced this work is the fact that compounding with a downstream power turbine can significantly improve the response characteristic of the turbocharger.

In 1980 Cummins tested their Turbocompound Diesel[36]. This was based on one of their standard NTC400 truck engines, rated at 400 bhp at 2,100 rpm.

It was an in-line six-cylinder unit of 855 cid (14 litres), turbocharged and aftercooled. The turbocompound part consisted of a radial inflow low-pressure turbine, speed reduction gearbox, and a fluid coupling to the main engine shaft. The net result was a 15% improvement in fuel consumption over the reference standard engine after a comparison of over 50,000 miles of vehicle running. The engine delivered 450 bhp at 1,900 rpm with a 15% torque rise to 1,440 lbs ft at 1,700 rpm.

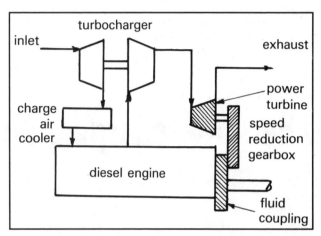

Schematic of the Cummins Turbocompound Diesel truck engine. Based on a standard NTC400 turbocharged 14-litre six-cylinder unit, a power turbine was added which was fed from the exhaust of the normal turbocharger. The power from this turbine was connected via a speed reduction gearbox and fluid coupling to the main engine shaft. The result was an increase in output power from 400 bhp to 450 bhp, with a 15% improvement in fuel consumption.

A fine example of the modern application of the turbocharged engine – the 1989 Lotus Esprit Turbo SE [Lotus]

3

The supercharger renaissance

The mechanically driven supercharger had ceased to be of relevance to production vehicles until recently. It was used for scavenging on some two-stroke diesel truck engines, and was still used in some competitive events, notably drag racing, but serious manufacture gradually ceased and many famous names went out of business. The turbocharger was already widely used in trucks when the need for forced induction in automobiles started to come to the fore, so it was natural that the designers turned to the turbocharger as the means of achieving the smaller, higher-power but less polluting engines that were wanted.

However, now that the market viability of supercharged cars has become established and the opportunities for improved emission controls are clear, the attention of a number of volume manufacturers has turned back to the mechanically driven supercharger. The turbocharger can deliver high maximum power, but it is not so good at low engine speeds and has difficulties in responding to transient demands for power. The mechanically driven supercharger can meet these needs, but has the disadvantages of traditionally lower compression efficiency with associated high air temperature, the need for the mechanical drive, the increase in fuel consumption resulting from the need to provide the drive power for the supercharger, and a higher manufacturing cost.

Emissions control regulations have resulted in the fitting of catalytic converters to the exhaust systems of many automobiles, and the trend indicates that this will become universal within the next few years. However, the exhaust gas back pressure caused by the catalytic converter makes it more difficult to get an adequate pressure drop for an exhaust turbine, and thereby limits the effectiveness of a turbocharger installation; this is

yet another factor influencing the renaissance of the mechanically driven supercharger.

As we will be examining later in the book, the power and torque requirements of the average passenger car are very different from those of the sports or competition car. For a large part of its operating time the engine is well away from the maximum output point. The length of time that high boost is needed is relatively short, so that higher fuel consumption at this time may not make any significant change to the overall fuel consumption. The use of variable slip electric clutches and pressure air bypass valves can give smooth boost pressure control systems comparable to those developed for turbochargers.

Manufacturers' recent developments have been aimed at finding compressor configurations which can be manufactured more cheaply, and which make use of computer-aided design techniques to achieve higher efficiency. Some of these new superchargers are now described in this chapter.

A version of the Lysholm screw compressor has been recently developed as an automotive supercharger by the Scottish design firm of Fleming Thermodynamics and manufactured in England, Australia and Japan with the trade name Sprintex. By applying modern manufacturing and materials technologies it has been possible to produce a compact, lightweight and efficient compressor.

Depending on model size, the Sprintex has a maximum speed of 15,500 rpm, a maximum pressure ratio of 2.2:1 and a maximum volumetric flow rate of 205 litres per second; the weight is 9-15 kg. The adiabatic compression efficiency is in the 75-80% region compared with typical Roots blowers of 40-50%.

A number of specialist tuning firms have developed

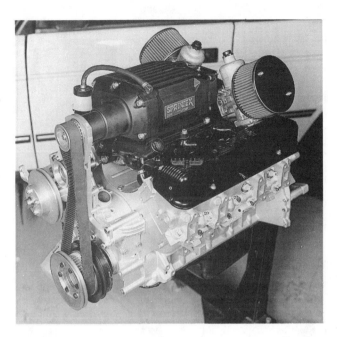

The Sprintex spiral supercharger installed on a Land-Rover engine. [DPR]

applications of the Sprintex to many of the popular production engines, bringing new life to the use of mechanically driven superchargers as an after-market add-on, but it is still a small volume product for specialist vehicles.

The German company KKK (Kühnle, Kopp & Kausch) has been for many years one of the leading suppliers of automotive turbochargers. Recently, in response

A four-cylinder engine on a drag race motor cycle fitted with a Sprintex spiral supercharger. Running on nitromethane, this bike exceeded 200 mph for the standing quarter mile.

Two sizes of the Kühnle, Kopp & Kausch mechanically driven rotating piston supercharger, type Ro. [KKK]

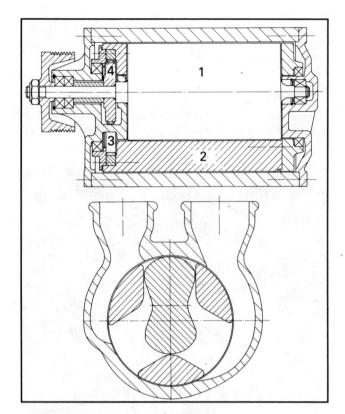

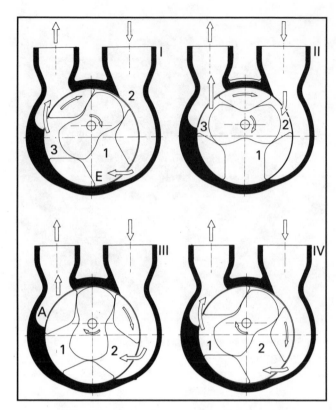

Cross-section of the KKK Ro-charger rotating piston supercharger. *[KKK]*

1 two-lobed rotating piston
2 three-chambered rotating 'cylinder'
3 ring gear to take drive to the cylinder
4 sprocket on piston drive shaft which engages with the ring gear

Operating principle of the KKK Ro-charger rotating piston supercharger. *[KKK]*

I   The inner rotor opens chamber 1 fully, so that a charge of air is drawn in. The position of the inlet edge E defines the charging limit of the chamber 1.

II   In this position, chamber 1 has its maximum volume and the pocket of air has been trapped.

III   The volume of chamber 1 is reduced as the inner piston rotates into it, compressing the air. The position of the outlet edge A defines the degree of compression.

IV   At this position, chamber 1 has started to discharge on the pressure side of the supercharger. At the same time, chamber 2 has reached the position which chamber 1 occupied in stage I. The process begins anew. There are three discharges per cycle.

to the trend to re-examine the possibilities for mechanically driven superchargers, they introduced their Ro-lader series. This uses a rotary piston design originating from amongst Wankel's list. A two-lobed 'piston' rotates eccentrically inside a three-chambered 'cylinder' which itself rotates within the housing. Because of this three-element design, it is not practical to provide any positive sealing between the elements.

At the beginning of a compression cycle, one of the three chambers in the rotating cylinder is open to the air inlet (see illustration). As this chamber rotates until the inlet port is closed, it is at maximum volume. With further rotation, one of the lobes of the inner rotating piston moves into the chamber, starting to reduce the volume and therefore compressing the air trapped within the chamber. By the time the rotating cylinder brings the chamber to the delivery port, the chamber volume will be nearly at a minimum, giving a high delivery pressure. Further rotation drives the remaining air out of the chamber into the delivery port and then the whole cycle starts again.

Models in the range provide for a throughput of

up to 200 litres per second at pressure ratios of up to 2.0:1, speeds up to 12,000 rpm and efficiencies in the 60-65% range. KKK have positioned these superchargers in the market against their own smallest-size turbochargers, suitable for use on gasoline engines up to about 124 kw (166 hp) in power rating, and diesel engines up to about 100 kw (134 hp).

The old faithful, the Roots type blower, has also been given a new lease of life. Lancia introduced a two-lobe version, the Volumex, on the Trevi 2000 model. Following the success of this, it was added to the HP Executive 2000 and Coupe 2000 to give the VX models. These are fitted with a transversely mounted in-line four-cylinder 2-litre engine. The Volumex supercharger is mounted on the side of the engine and is driven by a toothed belt from the crankshaft. The supercharged

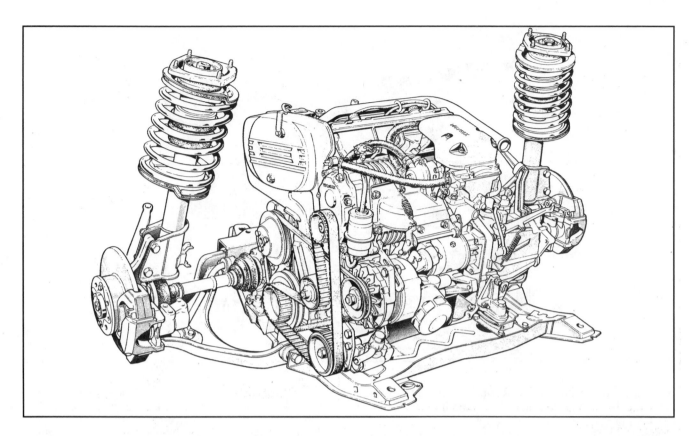

engine delivers 135 bhp compared with 122 bhp from the standard unsupercharged version. The Roots blower gives a smooth and immediate availability of power at low speed, with peak torque being reached at 3,000 rpm.

Lancia's success with the Volumex supercharger prompted them to introduce a novel application of it in the Delta S4 rally competition car. This uses a com-

The four-cylinder engine used on the Lancia Coupe VX. This engine is fitted with a Roots-type Volumex positive displacement supercharger. *[Lancia]*

The engine layout of the Lancia Delta S4 rally car which used a combination of turbocharger and positive displacement superchargers. *[Lancia]*

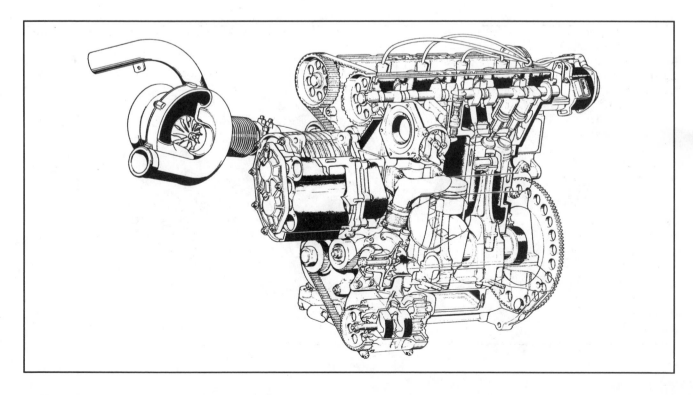

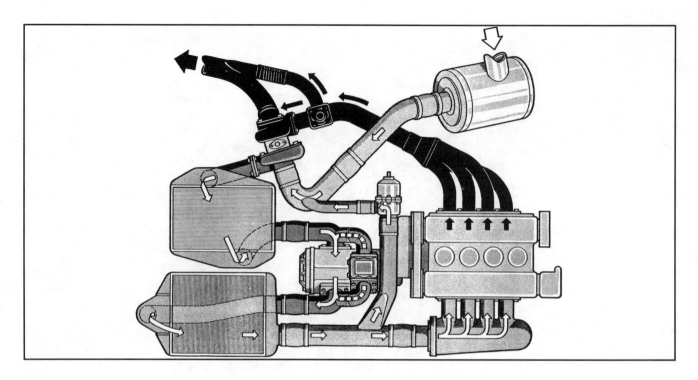

bination of turbocharger and Roots blower. Initially an Abarth experimental out-and-out competition special, a road-going version was developed which was produced in limited numbers in order to achieve Group B homologation. It has a 1.8-litre in-line four-cylinder engine.

A KKK turbocharger, with associated control wastegate, is installed in the exhaust system and a Volumex Roots type supercharger is mounted on the rear of the engine with a toothed belt drive. The inlet air passes from the air cleaner to the turbo-compressor and then to the first of two charge air coolers. The outlet

Schematic of the combined supercharging system of the Delta S4. Air is compressed first through the turbo-compressor, cooled and then further compressed by the Volumex Roots-type supercharger before being cooled again. By-pass valves around the Volumex, from inlet manifold to air suction, and around the exhaust turbine, allow for controlling the boost pressure under all running conditions. [Lancia]

Cutaway view of the Lancia Delta S4 road-going rally car. The rear-mounted engine with the large charge air coolers can be clearly seen. [Lancia]

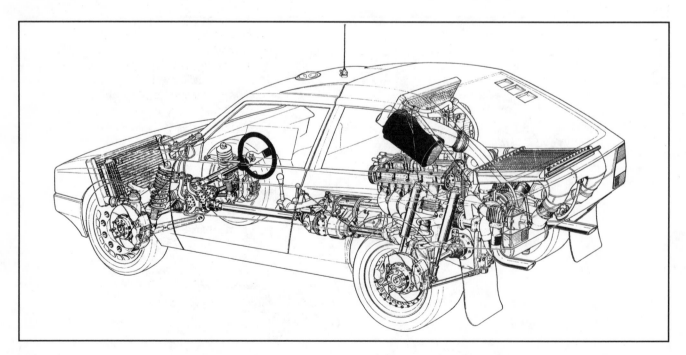

from this cooler is then connected to the positive displacement supercharger. The delivery from this compressor then goes via the second cooler to the inlet manifold. Air by-pass valves are fitted between the outlet and inlet of the Volumex and between the engine inlet manifold and the turbo-compressor inlet.

At low speeds, the positive displacement compressor provides the boost pressure. As the speed increases, its action is decreased until it is eliminated altogether by the by-pass valve, which reduces the amount of power absorbed in driving the compressor. At this point the turbo-compressor takes over to produce the peak boost pressure which can exceed 2 bar.

A joint development between the Eaton Corporation and Ford of America has also brought the Roots type supercharger back into production. Eaton looked at a variety of different possible systems for getting the benefits of supercharging without the disadvantages of the turbocharger. The Roots type has the attraction of having a completely balanced rotating system and a relatively low operating temperature. Its biggest weaknesses in the past have been the problems of reliability at high speed, indifferent compression efficiency and an unacceptably high noise level. Eaton believed that with the benefit of modern computer design techniques and manufacturing methods these problems could be overcome, and a supercharger could be produced which would be acceptable in the environment of a modern passenger automobile.

They chose a three-lobed rotor system, using an involute tooth shape. As a first step towards reducing noise and improving efficiency, the rotors were twisted through 60° into a helical format. This gives nearly constant inlet and outlet volumes while minimising losses in volumetric efficiency due to carryback of the high-pressure outlet air to the inlet.

The Roots type blower does not carry out any compression within itself. The rotors simply convey a volume of air from the inlet port to the outlet port at constant pressure. As the transfer volume becomes exposed to the pressurised system at the outlet port, a portion of the high-pressure air in the outlet manifold backflows into the supercharger so that the local system pressure equalises. This pressurised volume is then sealed from the inlet by the meshing of the rotors as they rotate back to the inlet section.

This pulse pressure equalisation generates noise at three times the speed of rotation. Computer simulation of the effect of different port shapes enabled the designers to dramatically reduce the noise until it was not discernible above the general vehicle noise. During the course of the port development programme, it was discovered that the low-speed volumetric efficiency depended on the degrees of rotation from the closing of the inlet to the point at which the trapped air volume was opened to the discharge port. As the ports were widened to increase the flow area, the seal time was reduced, as was low-speed flow. Along with a decrease in low-speed flow, the outlet temperature increased with

decreased seal time. Thus a trade-off had to be made between large area ports for high-speed flow and small ports for better low-speed performance. Further shaping of the ports helped to partially resolve this problem.

The absence of internal compression is an advantage when pressure control is considered. The traditional ways of achieving this with mechanically driven superchargers are either to provide some form of disengagable or controlled slip clutch in the drive, or to use a by-pass valve to dump excess pressure. With true compressors, the latter arrangement has the disadvantage that the work put into compression is dissipated again in the by-pass valve, wasting fuel. With the Roots type, the outlet pressure is the same as the inlet pressure if it is isolated from the pressurised system, and a by-pass valve can be used with only the minimum of pumping friction losses. Eaton engineers designed a special valve which is actuated by a vacuum feed adjacent to the throttle body, and this allows recirculation of the air when supercharging is not needed.

In 1984 Ford and Eaton started working on applying this supercharger to boost a 3.8-litre V6 engine. The whole engine design had to be reviewed to handle the greater power and torque, involving changes to crankshaft, connecting rods, valves, pistons and transmission. It was decided that a charge air cooler was needed, but this presented problems when it was mounted on the vehicle body in the normal manner – it was found to act as an amplifier for the residual supercharger noise. Eventually the cure was found by mounting the cooler on the engine itself. A poly V-belt drive system was adopted for the supercharger and auxiliaries, as the supercharger alone required 45 horsepower at full boost.

In 1989 the supercharger came on the general market, installed in the Ford Thunderbird Super Coupe and Mercury Cougar XR7 automobiles. The 140 horsepower and 292 Nm of torque from the naturally aspirated V6 engine of the standard Thunderbird jumped to 210 horsepower and 428 Nm of torque at 2,600 rpm in the Super Coupe supercharged version. The supercharger is a nominal 1.5-litre unit driven at 2.6 times crankshaft speed to a maximum of 15,600 rpm. At 4,000 engine rpm, the supercharger system can provide up to 0.82 bar of boost pressure.

The problem which is posed by designs such as the Volumex and Eaton Roots types, and the KKK Rolader, is the very high precision mechanical engineering required, which is reflected in the manufacturing unit costs. With increasing manufacturing volumes these should come down but they are still a long way from the low costs being achieved currently with small turbochargers. Recently Volkswagen introduced their G-lader in an attempt to break out of this constraint.

The G-lader is a new design of mechanical supercharger based, yet again, on principles known since the beginning of the century, with the original patent being granted in 1905 to a Frenchman, L. Creux. A G-shaped spiral blower element (hence the name) is moved eccentrically within another similar but fixed spiral. The

The components of the Volkswagen G-lader mechanically driven supercharger. At the top of the picture are the two fixed halves of the casing showing the twin G-spirals. Below left is the oscillating blower spiral which is sandwiched between the two casings, and below right the coupled shafts which give the blower its motion. *[Volkswagen]*

Cutaway view of the Volkswagen 1.3-litre engine fitted with the G40 supercharger driven by a belt from the crankshaft. *[Volkswagen]*

blower spiral is rocked by another eccentric control shaft in such a manner that inlet and outlet ports are uncovered at appropriate moments as the volume of space between the spirals varies. There is a duplicate chamber, operating out of phase, to give a smoother, higher-volume delivery.

The G40 version (using 40 mm wide spirals) fitted to the Polo Coupe gives a maximum boost pressure of

0.72 bar, and at rated speed (10,200 rpm) it supplies 96 litres of air per second.

The larger G60 version (with 60 mm wide spirals), when installed on the 1.8-litre engine of the Golf, gives approximately 30-50% more torque in the lower and medium speed ranges compared to the turbocharger version. At engine speeds from 2,400 to 5,700 rpm, a torque of more than 200 Nm is available. Without this supercharger, Volkswagen consider that at least 2.5 litres capacity would be required to achieve so much torque.

4

The coming trend

It was noted in the Introduction that automobile manufacturers are still looking at many different techniques which may help to produce more efficient, low-pollution engines. Most of these are still just laboratory experiments, but some are well down the development path and may be seen in production vehicles in the near future. In this chapter we look at a few of these developments which are related to supercharging, just to give a flavour for what may happen.

There are numerous practical difficulties in using conventional turbocharging systems on the very high output diesel engines needed for large trucks:

- low turbocharger efficiency at very high pressure ratios;
- high peak cylinder pressure;
- low boost at low engine speed;
- poor starting and light-load running with low engine compression ratio;
- insufficient compressor range at high-pressure ratios;
- slow turbocharger acceleration.

Variable valve timing has been used to reduce cylinder pressure and/or temperature, and this is discussed in Chapter 17. Another idea which has been explored by a number of companies is the augmentation of exhaust gas energy by re-heating it in an auxiliary combustion chamber interposed between engine and supercharger. Various such schemes have been proposed over the past 50 years or so which aimed at increased power output, fuel economy, a reduction of polluting emissions, or to meet some particular problems. By providing a secondary air supply to such an exhaust reaction chamber any residual hydrocarbons in the exhaust gases can be completely burned.

Outstanding amongst these projects, which have completely rethought the combination of the turbocharger and reciprocating engine, is the Hyperbar system[19]. This was developed in France, originally as part of a project to produce a very high output engine for driving AMX tanks. It uses a separate gas turbine complex with its own combustion chamber as well as the traditional turbocharger connections to the engine. All turbo-compressors are rotary speed-related machines and the engine is a volumetric machine, and they are difficult to mate. The Hyperbar system is based upon the maintenance of the operational point of the compressor in the neighbourhood of the line of best yield.

A very high pressure ratio turbocharger is used, running near to the compressor's surge limit, and it is combined with an extraordinarily low compression ratio diesel engine. A control valve is mounted between the compressor and the combustion chamber/turbine, in a by-pass pipe in parallel with the engine, which is adjusted to absorb the excess volume delivered by the compressor over that taken in by the engine, while maintaining the necessary scavenging ratio.

There are a number of distinct operational phases for the Hyperbar system. Initially, the gas turbine and combustion chamber combination is started in self-maintaining mode as a free-running gas turbine cycle. This makes use of an electric starting motor on the turbocharger which is decoupled once the unit is running. Then the diesel engine is started in the normal manner with an electric starter and runs in an idling state with the engine contributing no energy to the turbine (the available boost pressure from the gas turbine unit makes it possible to start the engine despite its very low compression ratio).

As the engine comes under load it has three phases of running:

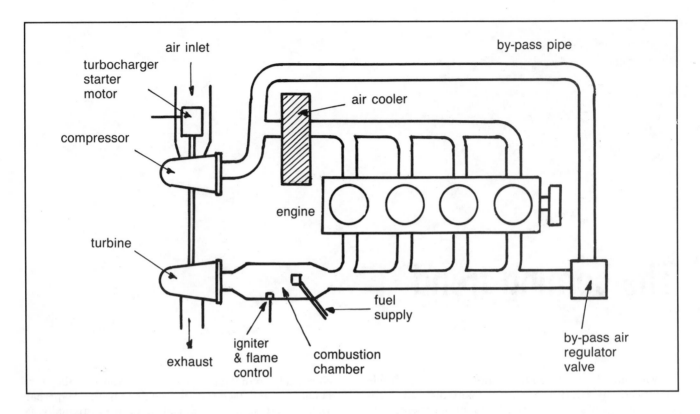

air inlet

by-pass pipe

turbocharger
starter
motor

air cooler

compressor

engine

turbine

fuel
supply

exhaust

igniter
& flame
control

combustion
chamber

by-pass air
regulator
valve

Schematic of a Hyperbar engine. This combines a low compression ratio turbocharged diesel with a separate combustion chamber. The turbocharger can run in gas turbine mode with the combustion chamber to provide good boost pressure for starting the diesel. The balance between the engine and the bypass direct to the combustion chamber is adjusted to keep the turbocharger running in its peak efficiency state with varying engine running conditions.

(a) A phase of constant supercharging pressure. This phase corresponds to the power range 0-20% of maximum power, during which the engine is gradually substituted for the combustion chamber as the source of gas for the turbine.

(b) A phase of variable supercharging pressure. Between 20-100% power, the engine behaves like a combustion chamber with the controlled pressure drop of the gas turbine, running like a normal turbocharger installation.

(c) The high-torque phase with maximum supercharging pressure maintained by increasing separate fuel burning.

These different operating phases allow the compressor and turbine to be held in their high-efficiency working states while still giving maximum flexibility in the operation of the diesel engine. A penalty paid for this is the inevitable minimum fuel consumption of the combustion chamber when idling.

The Hyperbar engine uses a supercharging pressure of the order of 10 bar with the geometric compression ratio in the range 5-10:1. The volumetric compression ratio of the engine is a function of the

supercharging pressure and of the allowable maximum pressure, which is limited to about 140 bar at present. The lowering of the compression ratio from the 15:1 typical of conventional diesel engines to 9:1 causes a fall of about 400°C in the peak temperature in the cylinders, which in turn tends to reduce the emission of nitrogen oxides.

The engine is characterised by the absence of smoke at all speeds, a lowering of the cycle temperature and heat losses to cooling water, a lowering of the temperature of the piston, cylinder head and liner, and a reduction of all exhaust gas emissions.

On a direct-injection Poyaud diesel, nitrogen oxide emission has been reduced from 13 gms/hp-hr at the standard 15:1 compression ratio, with 300 horsepower, to 6 gms/hp-hr at 9:1 compression ratio and 600 horsepower on the Hyperbar version. The carbon monoxide emission has also been reduced due to the higher air/fuel ratio permitted.

In a conventional engine working with higher cylinder pressures, the supercharging air must be cooled from about 200°C to 60°C to keep down the maximum cylinder temperatures. This will require either bulky air/air coolers or a separate low-temperature water circuit. In the Hyperbar engine, the air emerges from the compressor at temperatures above 350°C, entering the engine at about 100°C. The amount of heat to be removed per horsepower is therefore about twice as much, but the temperature difference is about three times as much between the cooled air and the atmosphere, allowing the use of more compact coolers.

In 1977, Dr Brian Lawton, of the Royal Military

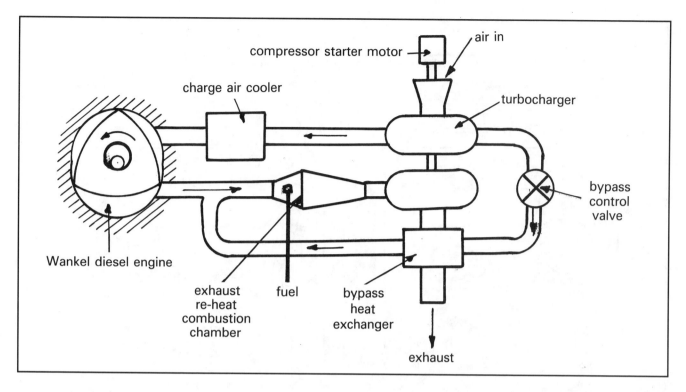

compressor starter motor

air in

charge air cooler

turbocharger

Wankel diesel engine

bypass control valve

exhaust re-heat combustion chamber

fuel

bypass heat exchanger

exhaust

Lawton's Wankel-type turbocharged diesel engine which makes use of an exhaust re-heat system to operate successfully with the low compression ratio (6:1). This engine has a power/bulk ratio of 44.08 bhp/cu ft.

College of Science in Britain, developed a technically and commercially viable turbocharged Wankel diesel with reheat, against a background of complete failure by notable diesel engine manufacturers in Europe and Japan[35]. It has only a 6:1 compression ratio for the diesel part and achieves a bhp/bulk ratio of 44.08 bhp/cu ft which compares most favourably with 16.25 bhp/cu ft for an advanced turbocharged reciprocating piston diesel renowned for its compact proportions.

The Lawton engine has a swept volume of 2.116 litres, an effective overall compression ratio of 18:1, a brake mean effective pressure of 15.3 bar, a maximum combustion chamber pressure of 98.6 bar, an output shaft speed of 4,000 rpm, a boost pressure of 4.6 bar, an air/fuel ratio of 42:1, a brake horsepower per rotor of 200 maximum, and a specific power of 51.98 bhp/litre.

In a similar manner to the Hyperbar engine, the combination of the turbocharger, heat exchanger and auxiliary combustion chamber, together with the necessary by-pass valve and piping, form an effective external combustion engine, which is indispensable for starting the very low compression ratio diesel engine. The characteristic speed/torque and power relationships of the Lawton engine make it very suitable for road vehicle use.

Some research has been taking place into the feasibility of building completely uncooled internal combustion engines[42]. There are numerous theoretical

benefits from such a design. Most of the energy saved by reducing the heat transfer to the cylinder walls and cylinder head is delivered to the exhaust in the form of a higher exhaust temperature. This makes compounding more attractive because of the available surplus turbine power. The removal of the cooling fan and the water pump, with their associated losses, and avoidance of the need for radiator space, are additional attractive features. Efficiency benefits of up to 23% have been predicted. However, at present, materials difficulties are the main problem, although ceramics are being considered for cylinder liners and pistons.

Like many automobile manufacturers, Lancia occasionally produces a 'concept car' which brings together a number of new ideas which may be developed for future models. In 1986 they showed their 'Experimental Composite Vehicle' ECV2 which included an interesting twin turbocharged engine, using a 'modular turbocharging' approach. The 1.8-litre Abarth Triflux engine had four valves per cylinder, two inlet and two exhaust. Each exhaust valve was connected to a separate manifold, each with its own KKK 'K24' turbocharger. The two turbo-compressors were connected to two separate charge air coolers feeding a common inlet manifold. Each exhaust turbine was associated with its own pressure controlling wastegate, but in addition another pneumatically operated valve could completely close off the exhaust from one turbine.

At low speed this valve remained closed, completely blocking the flow from one set of exhaust valves. All the gas flow from the engine would be passed through the one turbocharger, giving a very fast response. As the engine speed rose, the electronic control system

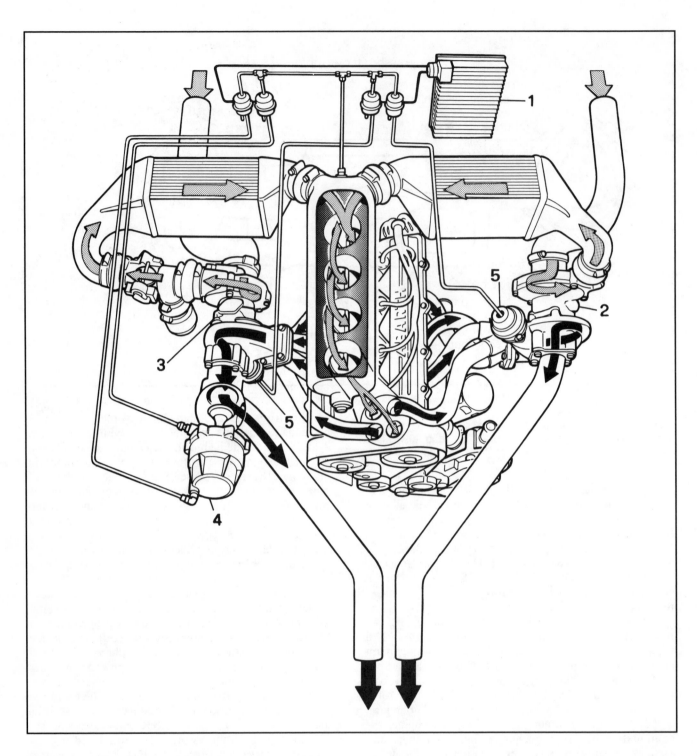

Schematic of the Lancia modular turbocharging system. Each set of the twin exhaust valves is connected to a separate exhaust manifold feeding twin turbochargers (2 and 3). A cut-off valve (4) closes off the exhaust from the turbocharger (3) at low speed so that the maximum gas flow keeps up the speed of the turbocharger (2). The electronic control system (1) brings the second turbocharger into action as the engine speed rises. Thereafter, boost pressure is controlled by the two exhaust bypass wastegates (5). *[Lancia]*

would open the valve to bring the second exhaust system into action to handle the increased gas flow.

Pressure wave supercharging

So far in this chapter, attention has been focused on the use of the exhaust gas turbocharger in its most familiar form, but with new ideas in its application. However, there is another completely different method of using the energy of the exhaust gases to provide forced induction – pressure wave supercharging.

All such systems exploit not only the kinetic energy of the exhaust gases, created by the rush of gases out of the cylinders when the exhaust valves or ports are suddenly opened, but in addition they take advantage of pressure waves in the exhaust system. These waves move at the speed of sound and promote, together with their reflections and resonance effects, rarefaction or compression in properly tuned systems to assist with the induction or exhaust processes.

One attempt by Sendyka to produce a completely static system is illustrated, and the use of exhaust pulses to improve turbocharger efficiency is discussed at length in Chapter 12.

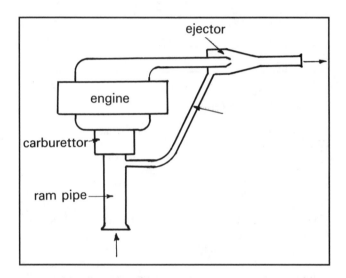

Working principle of the Sendyka pressure wave charging system. Exhaust pressure waves, acting through an ejector in the exhaust system, transfer suction waves to the inlet ram pipe. The momentum of the resulting inlet air movements causes a supercharging effect at the inlet valves.

In 1910 Burghard invented a rotary machine to exploit pressure waves, but neither the technology nor the theoretical understanding was then available which could have made it work. 1909 and 1928 saw Brown Boveri working on the Holzwarth turbine in which the fuel was not injected continuously, as in the conventional gas turbine, but intermittently, as in the diesel engine. In 1940/42 Claude Seippel invented a pressure wave machine, which he named Comprex, which formed the high-pressure stage of a gas turbine system[29][33].

The development by Brown Boveri of Seippel's early work into today's highly efficient automotive Comprex pressure wave supercharger is a classic example of the benefits which high-speed digital computers have brought to engineering companies. The theory underlying the workings of the pressure wave super-

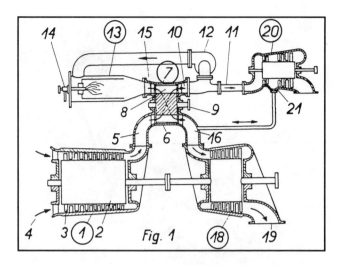

In 1940-42 Claude Seippel invented a pressure wave machine, which he named Comprex, as the high-pressure stage of a gas turbine system. This is one of the illustrations from his 1940 patent. [ABB]

charger is so complex that the development and design would have been impossible without the availability of huge computation and modelling capabilities.

The introduction of any new ideas into automotive mass production lines can take many years, dependent not only on proving the idea and the manufacturing technology but also on market plans. Comprex has moved through the stages of being an interesting idea, to manufacturing trials, then limited-edition vehicle production, to being generally available in a showroom model. The completely different characteristics of Comprex compared with the turbocharger have caused a lot of rethinking in the automotive industry, and the continuing acceleration of developments is already opening up a multiplicity of new applications. Because of this, no apology is offered now for examining the Comprex pressure wave supercharger in some detail as an indication of what may be happening in the future.

The pressure wave process does not depend on the pressure and flow fluctuations within the manifolds as caused by the engine cylinders, but makes use of the physical fact that if two gases having different pressures are brought into direct contact, equalisation of pressure occurs faster than mixing. This is especially so if the gases are guided in narrow channels, the working channels or cells.

Externally, the Comprex looks a little like a turbocharger, with inlet pipes at one end and exhaust pipes at the other end of a cylindrical housing. In addition there is a shaft at the air end driven from the engine, usually by a toothed belt. Internally, the working circuits are open-ended channels arranged on a rotor which is kept in continuous rotation between the two end casings by the belt drive from the engine crankshaft. Between the casings and the rotor faces there is no contact, but the gap is kept very small in order to minimise

The Comprex pressure wave supercharger, model CX93. The air inlet and outlet can be seen at the left; the exhaust chambers are at the right. An integral wastegate is fitted. *[ABB]*

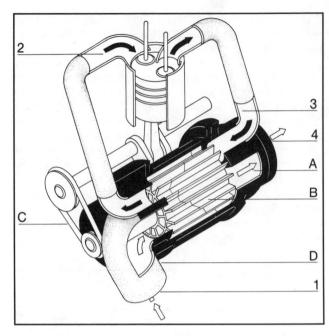

Schematic arrangement of engine and Comprex supercharger. *[ABB]*

(A) gas housing
(B) rotor
(C) drive belt
(D) air housing

(1) fresh air inlet
(2) compressed air to engine
(3) exhaust gas from engine
(4) exhaust gas outlet

leakage. The belt keeps the rotor at a speed proportional to the engine speed, but transfers no energy except to overcome bearing friction and inertia.

One casing, the air casing, comprises a flow passage connected to the fresh air intake filter and another passage connected to the engine inlet manifold. The other one, the gas casing, contains the gas inlet passage connected to the exhaust manifold and the gas outlet passage connected to the tailpipe. Within the casings the passages lead to port openings provided in the rotor side inner face of the casings. Through these ports gases can flow into or out of the rotor channels. The exhaust gas inlet port is made small enough to cause sufficient pressure rise in the manifold (eg 2 bar) when the engine is operated at rated power.

As the rotor makes a revolution, the ends of each channel are alternately closed or opened to a flow passage. In the actual Comprex units, each of the passages (1-4 in the diagram) ends in two ports displaced relative to each other by 180°. Thus every rotor passage undergoes two complete cycles during each revolution of the rotor. For explanation, it is appropriate to represent the circular motion of the rotor channels by a straight motion. The diagram shows the sequence of events occurring during one cycle (or half a revolution) with the channels moving in a downward sense.

The channel starting at the top, closed at both ends and full of fresh air at about atmospheric pressure, is first exposed to the exhaust gas inlet (3). Very soon afterwards its opposite end is connected to the charge air outlet (2). Both ends are then closed again. Next, the gas outlet port (4) is reached, followed on the opposite side by the fresh-air inlet port (1). These latter ports are made much wider than the first ones in order to allow

time for complete scavenging of the channels. When the channel is closed again, it is already filled with fresh air and ready for the next cycle.

The shaded area indicates the extent to which the exhaust gas enters into the rotor channels. The additional examples on the diagram, labelled 'a' to 'p', show how the pressure waves propagate within the rotor channels as the various ports are opened and closed. Steps 'a'-'f' occur while the high-pressure exhaust passage (3) is connected to the rotor. Since the penetration speed into the cells of the exhaust gas is slower than that of the pressure waves, the cells close before the exhaust gas reaches the high-pressure inlet passage (2), step 'g'.

After completing the supercharging work, the cells open into the low-pressure exhaust passage (4). The pressure difference causes the exhaust gas to start flowing out and, at the same time, expansion waves are generated, propagating toward the inlet side. These expansion waves let air in through the low-pressure inlet passage (1), steps 'h'-'m'. This inflow and outflow continues even after the exhaust gas has been completely emitted, leading a part of the fresh air directly into the exhaust passage, steps 'n'-'o', giving a clear scavenge, and the rotor cells containing only fresh air when step 'p' is reached.

Turbochargers lack boost capability at the low-speed end and normally would overshoot the limits if no wastegate were used. Comprex, however, typically

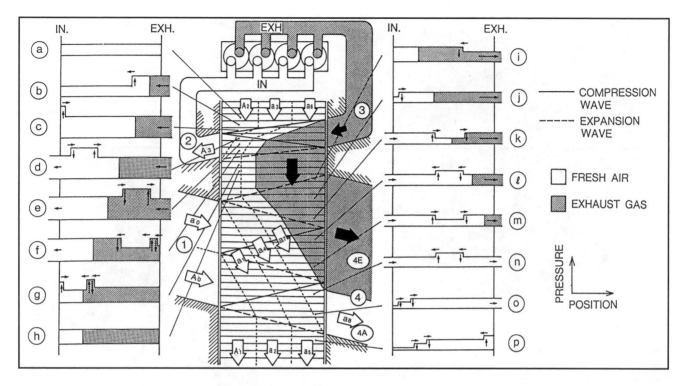

Working principle of the Comprex pressure wave supercharger, showing pressure propagation and the working gas flow. High-pressure exhaust gas (3) enters the rotor cells which are full of air and drives the air out to the high-pressure inlet manifold (2). As the rotor moves past the passage openings, the high-pressure gas and then the high pressure air channels are closed, followed by the low-pressure gas passage (4) opening. The pressure waves resulting from the exhausting of the rotor cells draw in fresh air from the low-pressure air passage (1) as it is exposed by the rotor movement. *[ABB]*

produces higher boost over the entire speed range. The difference is most conspicuous at low engine speed and becomes quite apparent during transient operation. In a Comprex charger, since the energy exchange takes place without any intermediate mechanical carrier (unlike the conventional turbocharger which requires a shaft between turbine and compressor) the change in the thermodynamic state of the exhaust gases is transmitted to the charge air within milliseconds. The quantities that determine the time factor in this cycle are merely the speed of sound and the time taken to fill volumes between the supercharger and engine.

The charge air pressure of the pressure wave supercharger when ideally matched varies in proportion to the mass flow, whereas that of the turbocharger theoretically obeys a square law. This simplifies many of the engine matching problems.

During initial starting, the exhaust gas can pass back through the Comprex charger and extinguish the initial combustion. A temporary by-pass is therefore provided at the inlet to handle this. The charge air duct is closed by a flap valve and fresh air is drawn in by

the engine from the air filter via a non-return valve. As soon as the charge air pressure from Comprex exceeds about 0.15 bar the starting flap is opened.

The typical rotor speed of the Comprex pressure wave supercharger is about 30,000 rpm compared with a turbocharger at 140,000. This requires the belt drive to give about 4-5 times engine speed. The rotor shaft is mounted in the air casing on a self-lubricated rolling bearing. Lubricant pipes are not needed, avoiding a source of risk and oil leaks; the bearing operates in the sub-critical speed range.

The characteristics of Comprex require that pulse operation of the exhaust system (see Chapter 12) cannot be used. A special larger-volume exhaust manifold is needed to ensure that a steady pressure is maintained at the Comprex gas inlet port. In addition, it is rather sensitive to back pressure in the exhaust mufflers and piping, and a larger cross-sectional area is likely to be needed compared with the equivalent turbocharger.

During ABB's (ASEA-Brown Boveri) development of Comprex into a product suitable for mass production, a special iron-nickel alloy had to be developed and a special foundry had to be built to produce the rotors with wall thicknesses of 0.5 mm. Low expansion alloys are used for the mantle and the rotor to minimise axial clearances. One of the characteristics of the early design was excessive noise due to the passage of the rotor channels past the ports, but after computer modelling tests a multiple-fluted rotor was designed which cancelled out this sound generation. There are normally 70 channels, arranged in two concentric rows.

The driving power transmitted by the belt is low, and over wide regions of engine operations, the gas flow

The rotor of a Comprex pressure wave supercharger. The offset between the two rows of cells helps to suppress air noise as they move past the gas passages. *[ABB]*

Volkswagen Passats and then a pilot production series of 700 Opel Senators.

Now Mazda have gone into full production with the Capella[66]. This has a four stroke in-line four cylinder overhead camshaft diesel engine, of 1.998-litre capacity, delivering 60.3 kilowatts of power (81 hp) at 4,000 rpm. The following changes were made from the

A Comprex-supercharged Mazda diesel engine, model RF-CX. This 2-litre engine produces 82 bhp at 4,000 rpm. *[ABB]*

moment overcomes the slight losses caused by windage and bearing friction, so that a small quantity of power even flows back over the belt to the engine. The rotor will continue to run in the unlikely event of the belt breaking. The belt drive's biggest disadvantages are that it constrains the mounting of the Comprex and is another thing to go wrong.

Because of the higher charge temperatures, charge air cooling with Comprex in the low speed range is more necessary and provides far greater benefits than with turbochargers.

Owing to the exhaust gases and charging air being in direct contact during the energy exchange in the cell wheel, it is possible for the exhaust gas to recirculate internally into the charge air. The amount of this recirculation can be accurately controlled within wide limits to conform with emissions control regulations (see Chapter 7).

With Comprex the high temperature of heat transfer from output to input makes its use with gasoline engines a more difficult problem. As a result, ABB have focused all their early developments and production on diesel-engined vehicles. Nevertheless, one early version was fitted to a Ferrari racing-car in 1981. It was entered for the Long Beach Grand Prix but the rotor shaft kept breaking under severe acceleration during practice and it never actually raced[39].

The first passenger car fitted with a Comprex pressure wave supercharger was a Mercedes test automobile in 1974; then in 1979 an Opel Rekord started testing, together with a small fleet of Mercedes vehicles. This was followed later by a demonstration fleet of 50

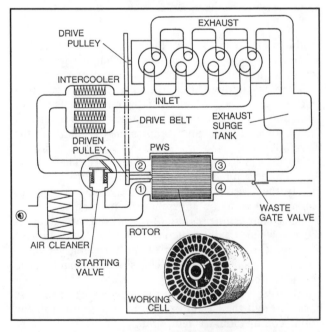

Schematic diagram of the Comprex supercharging system fitted to the Mazda Capella automobile. *[ABB]*

naturally aspirated version: the compression ratio was reduced from 22.7 to 21.1, and inlet valve timing was changed from 39° to 15° after bottom dead centre. A belt-driven Comprex unit was installed, with a speed of 4.25 times engine speed, together with a starting valve and a surge tank in the exhaust manifold. Pressure control was achieved using a wastegate which is integral with the gas housing. The early closing of the inlet valve gives the same effective compression at start up as the naturally aspirated version with the higher compression ratio.

The resulting maximum torque and output are 53% and 34% higher respectively than those of the original naturally aspirated engine. The car has an improved acceleration such that it is equal to one fitted with a gasoline engine of the same swept volume.

The performance characteristics obtained have been better than the turbocharged version of the same engine. The high charging pressure and charging efficiency even at light load have reduced the emissions of smoke and hydrocarbons in comparison with the turbocharged engine. The nitrogen oxide emissions are higher at light load than the turbocharged version because of the inlet valve timing change, but they are still better than the naturally aspirated engine.

The power taken through the drive belt for a Comprex installation can increase rapidly during load transients because the inertia of the rotor is large. The belt drive constrains the placement of the charger, complicates the application and coerces the speed characteristic. However, the first pressure wave supercharger invented by Claude Seippel in 1942 did not need a mechanical drive. It was designed as the upper stage of a gas turbine system, and because it operated under

The Mazda Capella 2-litre diesel was the first mass production automobile to be fitted with the Comprex supercharging system. *[ABB]*

steady state conditions the pressure wave machine could be driven solely by the gas pre-whirl. It was found that the automotive Comprex would also free-run once it had been brought up to speed so it was natural that ABB would try to produce a version without the belt-drive constraint, by making minor modifications to some of the port shapes. In the free-running version the gas flow acts on the edges of the rotor channels to provide a turbine effect and keep the rotor spinning[67].

The engine of a passenger automobile traverses the entire speed range in first gear under load within 2-3 seconds. When accelerated flat out, this occurs within 1 second. The supercharger must follow this rapid rise in engine mass-flow and build up the boost pressure sufficiently rapidly to ensure that the combustion during these fast transients occurs without air shortage.

The free-running Comprex, like the turbocharger, lags in rotor speed build-up during engine transients, but unlike the turbocharger this does not affect the build-up of boost pressure, merely changing the amount by which the rotor cells are filled. A paradoxical situation arises where the boost air supply from the free-running but lagging Comprex is an improvement compared to the belt-driven version.

During a fast acceleration any parasitic power consumption is deleterious because it reduces the air surplus and thus increases the smoke emission. A free-running Comprex can partly draw the required energy for its own acceleration during the less critical concluding phase. The speed range which the free-running pressure wave supercharger must span is narrower than the engine speed range, and the rotor acceleration need not be in step with the engine. It may lag, and hence the power consumption during acceleration hardly exceeds 100 watts. The initial reserve of surplus air supply at acceleration commencement is much higher than a conventional turbocharger, a mechanically driven

The CCX102 free-running Comprex pressure wave supercharger (top) which weighs 6.70 kg, compared with the original type CX102 shaft-drive unit (bottom) which weighs 9.46 kg. *[ABB]*

supercharger, or even the original belt-driven Comprex.

A compact DC electric motor in the hub, with an overriding needle clutch, is used to spin the Comprex up to 2/3,000 rpm before the main engine starts. The run-up time is less than the normal diesel pre-glow starting time.

In this new design, the cell wheel is made from extruded silicon nitride ceramic. The low thermal expansion of this material enables even smaller axial clearances, reducing losses. Its lower density reduces the weight and inertia of the rotor to improve free-running

characteristics, while its high strength combined with the lower density results in smaller stresses.

Without the belt drive, the free-running Comprex can be placed anywhere on the engine, and the absence of the shaft allows an axial inlet duct for the air. With the prior electrical spinning up to speed there is no longer any problem with exhaust gases getting back to the inlet during engine starting, so that the starting valve in the inlet duct can be omitted.

Initial testing of the new free-running Comprex pressure wave supercharger has been carried out on a 2.5-litre 190D Mercedes car.

A new approach to mechanical supercharging

The previous chapter discussed the attractions of mechanically driven superchargers for passenger automobiles, where good response at low speed can outweigh additional fuel costs. However, the designs which have generally been studied are not only expensive to manufacture but also suffer from a further general disadvantage – as they operate at relatively low speed they have to be bulky in order to handle the necessary volume of air throughput.

The centrifugal compressor used in standard turbochargers is cheap to make and, because of its high rotation speed, is very compact for a given air flow. The Hyperbar work demonstrated that if a turbo-compressor can be kept operating in a narrow range close to its peak efficiency, the engine/compressor combination can produce remarkable performance.

If, therefore, a suitable variable-speed drive system could be developed which could keep a turbo-compressor near to constant speed with widely varying engine speed, it would give the possibility of a very efficient and compact supercharging system. A number of manufacturers are working on this approach and some interesting developments are likely to become public during the next few years.

5

Basic engine principles

To help the general reader who has not studied engineering thermodynamics, this and the following chapter introduce a few principles which form the basis for many supercharging design decisions[14]. Do not worry, it is all fairly painless! It may seem a bit odd introducing these topics now, when there have already been four chapters which make some passing reference to them, but would you have read so far if this had been at the start of the book?

Firstly, in order to bring some consistency to the book, it is appropriate to define the system of measurement units which has been adopted. After all, there is a great choice between such things as horsepower, PS-DIN, kilowatts, foot-pounds, kilogram-metres, Newton-metres, pounds per square inch, bar, degrees Celsius, degrees Fahrenheit, etc. etc. Because this book is being published initially in the UK, the final choice has been based on the more common usages amongst automotive engineers in the UK, bent a little by the author's prejudices.

To help with the flow of reading, general values given in the text may have two common variants quoted; specific data schedules provided by manufacturers will use the measurement units they use themselves. Otherwise the following selection has been made:

Engine power output – horsepower (hp) or brake horsepower (bhp).

Engine torque – Newton-metres (Nm).

Speed – revolutions per minute (rpm).

Pressure – bar.

Temperature – degrees Celsius (°C) or degrees Kelvin (°K).

Engine displacement – litres.

Appendix D includes the conversion factors between all the different units of measurement that you may encounter.

Heat and mechanical work are theoretically mutually convertible, one into the other. Work can always be completely turned into heat, but the converse is not always true in practicable systems. However, the principle of the conservation of energy must always apply. In an isolated thermodynamic system, the total energy of the system remains constant – the sum of chemical (fuel), heat and mechanical work energy transfers must always be constant. This law of thermodynamics constrains many of the possible processes of the internal combustion engine.

Much of the discussion during the remainder of this book is concerned with the behaviour of gases, either air or products of combustion. The associated gas theories were developed using the idea of the 'perfect gas'. Fortunately, in the areas of interest to us, air behaves generally as a perfect gas and even the normal exhaust gases are a reasonable approximation unless one is getting into very detailed design work.

The temperature of a gas is a measure of the speed of movement of the atoms within the gas. As the temperature is gradually lowered this atomic movement becomes slower and there is a temperature at which movement would cease altogether; this is known as the absolute zero temperature. The early Fahrenheit temperature scale and the later Celsius scale were based on the freezing and boiling points of water, 32 and 212 for Fahrenheit and 0 and 100 for Celsius. On the Celsius scale, absolute zero temperature would be –273.15°C. The Celsius and Fahrenheit scales are not practicable for use when calculations must be done relative to absolute zero temperature, so two absolute temperature scales are used – degrees Kelvin, which has increments the same as the Celsius scale, and degrees Rankine, which matches the Fahrenheit measurements. Thirty-two degrees Fahrenheit is 491.67° Rankine.

The common measurements of gas pressure are relative to the normal atmospheric pressure, but in a similar manner to temperature, measurements need to be made relative to absolute zero pressure, a perfect vacuum. Against this, the normal atmospheric pressure is approximately one bar.

The basic perfect gas equation, on which all the other variations are based, states that the product of absolute pressure and volume of the gas is equal to its absolute temperature multiplied by a constant which depends upon the measurement units used. This is usually summarised as $PV = RT$.

There are four types of processes carried out on the gases within an internal combustion engine: constant volume, constant pressure, isothermal, and adiabatic. In constant volume processes, because of the basic gas equation, any change of temperature must be associated with a change of pressure. Similarly, in a constant pressure process, changes of temperature must be accompanied by a corresponding change of volume. An isothermal process is a constant temperature one; any change of pressure or volume must change the other. The adiabatic process is one in which the heat of the gas remains constant; there may be a work transfer but no heat transfer. This type of process is one of the most common within internal combustion engines, and is characterised by the requirement that the product of pressure and volume, raised to the power of γ remains a constant. The factor γ (the Greek letter gamma) is the ratio of the specific heat value for the gas measured at constant pressure to that measured at constant volume; for air it is about 1.402.

Another important characteristic of the compressible gases with which we are dealing is the way that they behave when flowing through pipes and nozzles. Ernst Mach, the Austrian physicist, demonstrated in the late 19th century that important compressible flow variations were not a function of simple flow velocity but of the ratio of flow velocity to the speed of sound wave propagation in the fluid under consideration. In his honour, this ratio is called the Mach number. The use

of dimensionless parameters such as the Mach number is considerable in supercharging design, and for good reason.

The speed of sound is equal to the square root of the product of the gravitational acceleration, the gas specific heat ratio, the gas constant and the gas static absolute temperature at the point where the gas flow is measured. For any given gas, such as air, all of the above factors, except temperature, are practically constant, and the Mach number is proportional to the square root of the absolute temperature. The molecular theory of gases shows that absolute gas temperature is directly proportional to the mean kinetic energy of the molecular motion. Hence the square of the Mach number is the ratio of flow kinetic energy to the internal energy of the fluid. This relationship is of profound influence in both theoretical and applied gas dynamics. It allows, through the usage of dimensionless ratios, the elimination of size, and shows that, at the same Mach number, flows through geometrically similar passages experience similar aerodynamic forces and energy losses.

In later discussions we will be referring to 'nozzles' and 'diffusers'. The nozzle is an orifice, usually with a change of area which allows flow of a gas from a high pressure to a lower pressure zone. Because of the fixed relationships of the gas equations, the reduction of pressure will be accompanied by an increase in volume resulting in an increase of velocity. The diffuser deals with the inverse situation, slowing down the velocity of gas and raising its pressure. The diagram shows typical nozzle and diffuser shapes for subsonic flow velocities.

If the difference in pressure across a nozzle becomes great enough, the velocity at the throat reaches the speed of sound which applies in that gas at that pressure and temperature. When we enter into a supersonic flow state (the Mach number exceeds 1), the flow characteristics

Relationship of Mach number and nozzle/diffuser shapes. For subsonic conditions (a), Mach number less than 1, a speed-increasing nozzle converges while a speed-decreasing diffuser increases in area. In supersonic flow (b), Mach number greater than 1, the shapes are the opposite way around. The de Laval convergent/divergent nozzle (c) can achieve gas acceleration well beyond the speed of sound by changing shape as the gas speed reaches Mach 1.

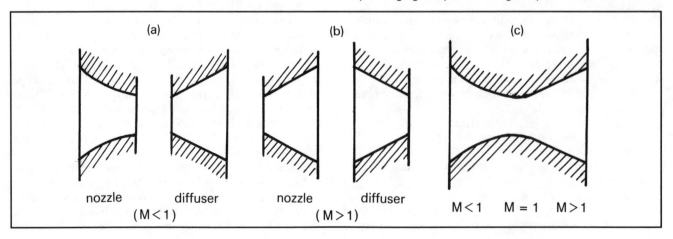

(a)   (b)   (c)

nozzle   diffuser   nozzle   diffuser   M < 1   M = 1   M > 1
(M < 1)   (M > 1)

become inverted. This behaviour caused the crashes of many early attempts at supersonic aircraft as their control surface behaviour inverted at the sound barrier. In the case of the supersonic nozzle, the area must increase progressively in order that velocity may increase; similarly, the diffuser reduces in area. One of the great contributions of the Swedish engineer de Laval was the invention of the convergent-divergent nozzle which made possible the development of practical turbines where the gas velocities exceeded the speed of sound.

Engine operating cycles

Let us now look at how today's internal combustion engine operating cycles developed from early theoretical ideas. A French physicist, Sadi Carnot (1796-1832), was the first to study the performance of an ideal heat engine in which the cycle consisted of four operations, two being isothermal and two adiabatic. The diagram shows these four operations plotted on a graph of pressure against volume, with heat being added at high temperature at one part of the cycle and later abstracted at another part of the cycle:

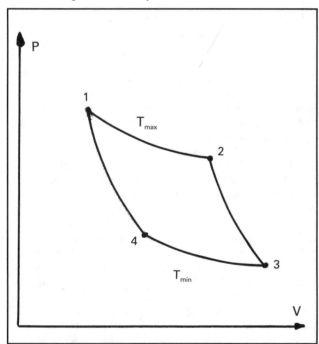

Air standard pressure/volume diagram for the Carnot theoretical engine cycle. It comprises isothermal expansion of the working fluid with heat input at T_{max}, adiabatic expansion, isothermal compression with heat rejection at T_{min}, and adiabatic compression.

1-2 Isothermal (constant temperature) expansion of the working fluid at the temperature of the hot source, T_{max}, accompanied by heat absorption from the source.

2-3 Adiabatic expansion with a temperature drop of the working fluid from T_{max} to T_{min}, the temperature of the cold sink.

3-4 Isothermal compression at the temperature of the cold sink, T_{min}, accompanied by heat rejection to the sink.

4-1 Adiabatic compression with a temperature rise of the working fluid from T_{min} to T_{max}.

Carnot introduced the concept of the 'air standard efficiency' for an engine cycle, based on air as the working fluid throughout. Combustion can be replaced by external heat addition and a hypothetical recirculation of exhaust gas to the inlet passes via a heat abstraction process. The air standard efficiency for the Carnot cycle is then given by $1-(T_{max}/T_{min})$.

From Carnot's work came the realisation that the efficiency of any reversible cycle engine operating between two energy reservoirs is independent of the nature of the working fluid and depends solely on the temperature of the reservoirs, a fact which is at the root of many design decisions concerning the development of all heat engines, including internal combustion ones.

In 1816 a Scottish clergyman, the Reverend Robert Stirling of Dumfries, invented another engine cycle which matches the Carnot cycle for efficiency. The more practicable Stirling engine keeps re-appearing on the

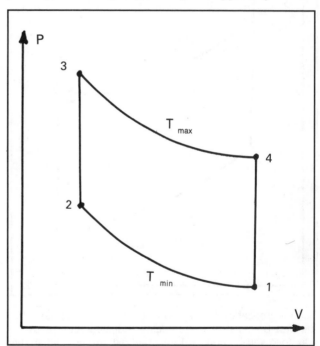

The more practicable Stirling cycle used constant volume transfers through a regenerative heat exchanger combined with isothermal expansion and compression. The possibilities of this cycle are still being researched by automobile manufacturers.

engineering scene. It uses externally applied heat rather than internal combustion, so can use many different heat sources, and several automobile manufacturers have been working on applications of the Stirling cycle as a possible way of dealing with emissions control problems.

The prime characteristics of a Stirling engine are

a hot space, with external heating, a cold space with some form of cooling, and a regenerative heat exchanger through which the working fluid is passed. The four stages of the Stirling cycle are as follows (see diagram):

1-2 Isothermal (constant temperature) compression in the cold space with external heat abstraction at the temperature T_{min}.

2-3 Constant volume transfer from the cold space to the hot space with internal heat addition from the gas movement through the regenerative heat exchanger.

3-4 Isothermal expansion in the hot space with external heat addition at T_{max}.

4-1 Constant volume transfer from the hot space to the cold space with an internal heat abstraction through the regenerative heat exchanger giving a temperature drop $(T_{max}-T_{min})$.

Now let us look at the more familiar cycles which are the basis of modern internal combustion engines. The theoretical cycle put forward by August Otto which led to his first working gasoline engine is shown in the

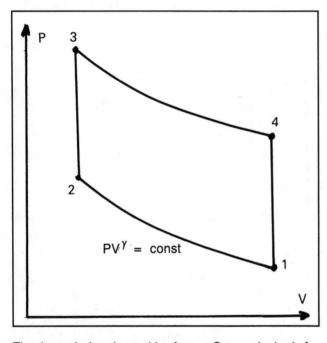

The theoretical cycle used by August Otto as the basis for the first practical gasoline engine. Adiabatic compression was followed by constant volume heat addition, adiabatic expansion and constant volume heat abstraction.

next diagram. Again, the cycle has four phases:

1-2 Adiabatic compression.
2-3 Constant volume heat addition.
3-4 Adiabatic expansion.
4-1 Constant volume heat abstraction.

The air standard efficiency of the Otto cycle, its 'thermal efficiency', is given by $1 - (1/r_v)^{\gamma-1}$, where $r_v = v_1/v_2$, the 'volumetric compression ratio'.

Rudolf Diesel's version of an internal combustion engine cycle is shown in the next diagram. The four

phases of this cycle are:

1-2 Adiabatic compression.
2-3 Constant pressure heat addition.
3-4 Adiabatic expansion.
4-1 Constant volume heat abstraction.

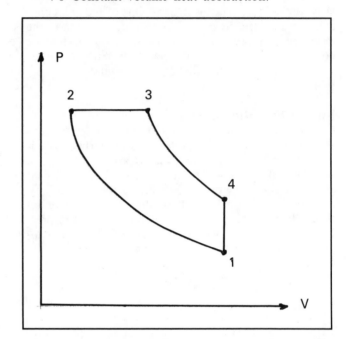

Rudolf Diesel's version of the internal combustion engine cycle. Adiabatic compression was followed by constant pressure heat addition, adiabatic expansion, then constant volume heat abstraction.

The air standard efficiency of the Diesel cycle is given by $\eta_{th} = (r_c^{\gamma}-1)/r_v^{\gamma-1} + \gamma(r_{c-1})$, where r_v is the compression ratio as in the Otto cycle, and $r_c = v_3/v_2$, the change in volume during the combustion process.

Practical four-stroke engines today use a cycle which is a combination of the Otto and Diesel cycles, and this is illustrated in the next diagram which shows the pressure/volume characteristic for an ideal naturally aspirated engine. Point 1 is the beginning of the stroke at bottom dead centre. Process 1-2 is the compression stroke; 2-3 is the part of the combustion process occurring instantaneously at constant volume at top dead centre; 3-4 is the rest of the combustion process occurring at constant pressure while the piston is moving down the cylinder; 4-5 is the continuation of the expansion process following the end of combustion. At point 5 the exhaust valve opens, allowing the pressure to fall back to the ambient level. The intake and exhaust strokes are not shown but would be represented by a horizontal line of changing volume but no effective change of pressure.

Useful work is obtained during processes 3-4-5 since the pressure acting on the piston is aiding its outward movement. Against this must be set the work required to compress the gas in the cylinder, process 1-2. The net

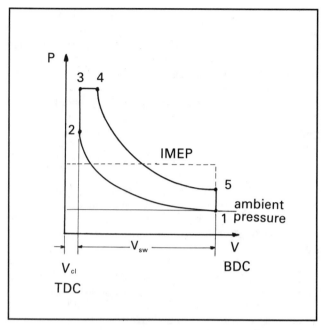

The ideal air standard pressure/volume diagram for the dual combustion cycle which is the basis of the modern internal combustion engine. The compression stroke is adiabatic, followed by heat input at constant volume, then further combustion at constant pressure, adiabatic expansion, and then finally constant volume expansion as the exhaust valve opens.

1-2 compression
2-4 combustion
4-5 expansion

work done $= \int PdV$
             $=$ area 1-2-3-4-5-1
V_{sw} = swept volume
V_{cl} = clearance volume
$(V_{sw} + V_{cl})/V_{cl}$ = compression ratio

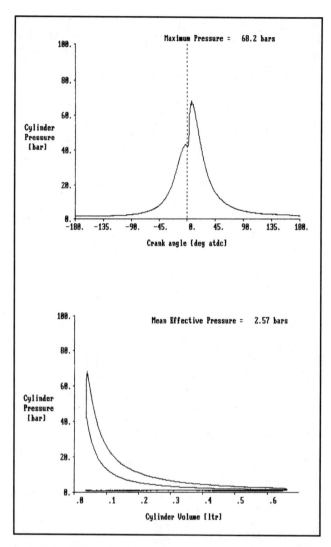

Actual indicator diagrams from a test engine. Cylinder pressure is plotted against crank angle in one diagram and cylinder volume in the other. *[UMIST]*

work output (expansion minus compression) is given by the area inside the diagram 1-2-3-4-5-1. For a four-stroke engine, the area inside the diagram multiplied by half the engine speed gives the power output.

On steam engines and early internal combustion engines a special 'indicator' mechanism could be screwed into a port in the cylinder head for test purposes. This had a spring-loaded drum with a length of string wrapped around it which was connected somewhere to the connecting rod. As the engine operated the drum would oscillate backwards and forwards as the cylinder volume changed. A form of spring-loaded pressure gauge mechanism was coupled to an arm at the end of which was a pencil which contacted the drum surface. A small piece of paper would be clipped to the drum, and when the engine ran the pencil movements on the oscillating drum would plot the actual pressure/volume diagram for the engine. Today, such test measurements are made

electronically and recorded by computer, but the resulting P/V diagram is still referred to as an 'indicator diagram'.

The comparison of the air standard efficiency to be expected from a particular engine and that actually obtained by measurement gives the 'diagram efficiency'. Calculation of the effective power from actual measurements gives the 'indicated horsepower' for the engine. On the pressure/volume diagram it is always possible to define a pressure such that the area below that pressure line is equal to the area included in the actual drawn engine line. This 'indicated mean effective pressure' is the value which would produce the same net work as the actual engine pressures if it operated uniformly throughout the working stroke.

In the illustration, the change in cylinder volume between point 1, bottom dead centre, and point 2, top dead centre, is known as the swept volume (V_{sw}). The remaining trapped volume at point 2 after compression is known as the clearance volume (V_{cl}). The ratio of the total cylinder volume ($V_{sw} + V_{cl}$) to the clearance volume (V_{cl}) is the engine's 'compression ratio'. In later discussions of supercharging, this ratio will often be referred to as the 'geometrical compression ratio' to distinguish it from the 'effective compression ratio' produced by supercharging.

The compression ratio has a critical effect on the efficiency of the internal combustion engine and we will be seeing in later chapters how this affects supercharging issues. The following figures give an example of the change of the air standard efficiency with compression ratio:

Comp ratio	3	4	5	6	7	8	10	15
Efficiency	35.6	42.6	47.5	51.2	54.1	56.5	60.2	66.1

Of course, not all the actually indicated horsepower is available at the output shaft. There are a variety of engine losses which have to be taken into account, primarily the friction and pumping losses. It may also be argued that some of the engine auxiliaries need also to be taken into account – it would not usually be practicable to operate without the cooling water pump, for example. The final usable output from the engine shaft in a vehicle is what is of most interest. Under test conditions this will be measured on a dynamometer test bed, or 'brake'. As a result, the usable power is normally referred to as the 'brake horse power' (bhp) and the equivalent mean cylinder pressure referred to output performance is known as the 'brake mean effective pressure' (bmep).

If the indicated horsepower is determined and the brake horsepower is measured, the difference between the two represents the engine losses, and the ratio of the two values is the 'mechanical efficiency' of the engine. In many cases only the brake horsepower is known; this requires a different approach to estimate the losses.

The Morse test can be readily applied to a spark ignition gasoline engine. Measurement of the output power is carried out on a dynamometer and one of the spark plugs is disconnected. The power will of course drop due to the loss of work from the affected cylinder, but in addition the remaining cylinders will have to carry the pumping and friction losses associated with the idling cylinder. Repeating this test on each cylinder in turn can give a reasonable approximation of the total losses.

For a diesel engine it is more difficult to carry out a Morse test, so a 'Willans line' test may be used. If a series of fuel consumption rate measurements are made at constant speed and gradually reducing power, the resulting values can be plotted on a graph. Extrapolating backwards to zero power (not a measurable value on the dynamometer), it will be found that a residual fuel consumption value is shown, which has a correspondence to the engine's losses.

All the pressure/volume indicator diagrams so far used have been based on distinctly definable gas processes (adiabatic, isothermal, etc). In real engines these forms are only approximated, and one of the illustrations here shows a measured indicator diagram from a test engine.

Now, looking at the overall energy balance of an internal combustion engine, we can see that there are inputs of heat energy in the air drawn in and the fuel burned. There are heat outputs to a supercharger charge air cooler (if fitted), to the inlet manifold, cylinder walls and head, exhaust manifold and turbocharger (if fitted), and finally to the released exhaust gases themselves. In addition there is the mechanical work available at the output shaft. From the first law of thermodynamics, we know that the total of the heat inputs must balance the total of the heat outputs plus the work output.

The theoretical cycle diagrams used so far have not included the suction and exhaust strokes appropriate to the four-stroke engine. They could equally well apply to the two-stroke engine with the added advantage of twice the net power output because of the omission of the two idling strokes. However, the attraction of the two-stroke cycle fails when brought up against the realities of how to achieve it.

The four-stroke engine has a distinct intake stroke during which the piston moves away from the cylinder head, drawing the fresh charge into the cylinder. The two-stroke engine has no such suction stroke; when the inlet port or valve is open, the piston is already moving to reduce the cylinder volume, opposing filling. The two-stroke engine is not self-aspirating and needs some form of compressor to charge the cylinder. The four-stroke engine also has an exhaust stroke, and again the two-stroke has no such positive expulsion. A lot of gas leaves by expansion into the manifold when the exhaust valve or port opens, so long as cylinder pressure exceeds that in the manifold; the remaining gas fills the cylinder. In a four-stroke engine this residual is pushed out during the exhaust stroke, but the two-stroke needs scavenging by an incoming fresh charge.

Compression versus spark ignition

The discussion earlier showed how the distinction between the true Otto and Diesel cycles has been blurred in modern engines. Nevertheless, we do still use the name diesel to distinguish the class of engines which use compression ignition from those which use spark ignition. What then are the main differences between these two types?

In the diesel engine, air alone is drawn into the cylinders and compressed sufficiently that the temperature of the air after compression exceeds that required to ignite the fuel. The fuel is injected only when combustion is required; burning is relatively slow as the fuel mixes with the air. The power of the engine is regulated just by changing the fuel supply; excess air mass is always acceptable. The diesel engine needs the compression ratio to be high enough to give reliable cold starting.

In the gasoline engine, the fuel and air are pre-mixed. Compression is of a homogeneous mixture with ignition by spark at the desired point. The rate of combustion depends on heat and mass transfers from the burning area to the remainder of the charge and is accompanied by a temperature increase due to continued compression. The fuel/air ratio is critical, and power regulation is achieved by changing the total charge density in the cylinder. Self-ignition has to be avoided by keeping the compression ratio low enough and using a fuel with a high self-ignition temperature. If the compression ratio were very high (as in the diesel engine) and self-ignition occurred before the plug sparked, the almost uniform mixture would all ignite at the same time. The resulting explosion can fatally damage the engine. Self-ignition, or pre-ignition as it is often called, can occur due to hot spots forming on spark plugs, valves, deposits on pistons, etc.

The rate of flame propagation in an internal combustion engine is governed by local turbulence, heat transfer between the burning and unburned regions, compression heating of the unburned gas due to the piston motion and expansion of the burning mixture, air/fuel ratio, and the heat transfer to the surrounding walls (which will slow down the combustion process). The part of the charge still not burning, the 'end gas', may reach ignition temperature before the flame front gets to it. The resulting explosive combustion is called 'detonation' or 'knocking'. Rapid knocking combustion generates intense pressure wave actions in the combustion chamber and very high local heat transfer rates to the piston and cylinder head walls.

The knock resistance of fuels is measured in terms of the octane scale which compares a fuel against the knock-resistant properties of the petroleum compound iso-octane. Steps which can be taken to minimise the onset of detonation are to keep the compression ratio down, reduce the maximum distance of the spark plug from the extremes of the combustion chamber, and keep the end gas cool by high wall surface area relative to the combustion chamber volume.

As we will see later, the onset of detonation is one of the most serious limiting factors when introducing any form of supercharging into an engine design. In an example engine, the compression ratio of 9:1 had to be reduced to 6.7:1 for a boost pressure of 0.5 bar if no other changes were made in any other knock-controlling parameters.

For combustion of normal fuels a supply of oxygen is needed, usually obtained from air which is drawn into the engine. But air does not only contain oxygen, it also contains a large proportion of nitrogen plus some other gases. Only 21% of air, by volume, is oxygen. For combustion purposes it is the mass of oxygen that matters, not its volume, and by weight air contains 23.3% of oxygen. This means that when sizing air intake passages, etc, you need to remember that every kilogram of oxygen needed by the engine has to carry with it 3.29 kilograms of nitrogen whose volume is 79% of the total.

Considering a simple four-stroke naturally aspirated engine, the initial assumption is that during the inlet suction stroke a volume of air (or air/fuel mixture) is drawn into the cylinder equal to the swept volume of the cylinder. In practice, this is not true. There will be a pressure drop through any air filter, another through the carburettor or throttle valve, and more pressure drops due to inlet manifold, port and valve restrictions. In addition the cylinder will contain the residual exhaust gases from the last cycle. At the very least this will amount to the equivalent of the cylinder clearance volume, but if there have been exhaust valve and exhaust pipe restrictions, the amount of residual gas can be substantial.

The net result of all this is that the effective volume of oxygen available in the cylinder at the end of the inlet stroke is less than the amount which could be anticipated from the bore and stroke of the engine. This reduction in cylinder filling is known as the 'volumetric efficiency', and a typical value might be 80%. By tuning the intake, exhaust, etc, it is possible to get more than 100%, but generally only at one speed. Techniques for achieving this are discussed in Chapters 12 and 13.

Now, after that very potted engine thermodynamics course we can move on to the real subject of this book – supercharging.

6

Supercharging principles

So far we have been considering the basic engineering thermodynamics of naturally aspirated engines. Let us now look at the implications of what this book is all about – supercharging. The first supercharging applications just set out to remove the inefficiencies of induction in the naturally aspirated engine, but this very quickly changed to building up a positive 'boost' pressure on the intake. The supercharged engine starts off with its charge air at a higher pressure and density. As a result more fuel can be burned because more oxygen is available from the higher density, even though the volume is the same, giving more power from the engine.

The accompanying indicator diagram shows the change when supercharging is added to an engine. The naturally aspirated cycle is shown by the dotted line 1-2-3-4-5, with compression starting from point 1 at ambient pressure. If supercharging is added, the starting point (6) is lifted above the ambient pressure by the amount of boost. Compression then follows to point 7, where combustion begins. Because of the larger available mass of air, more fuel is burned and the resulting maximum pressure achieved (8) is much greater, and combustion will continue longer to point 9 before adiabatic expansion down to point 10 where the exhaust valve opens.

The major contribution to the area of the diagram, and thus the output power, is in the region of low cylinder volume and high pressure. The portion at the large volume end contributes little to the useful output, but it determines the size of the engine. The supercharged version of the diagram is fatter in the high-pressure/low-volume zone, with a corresponding increase in mean effective pressure.

The higher pressures shown may not be acceptable mechanically for a given engine. Increasing the clearance

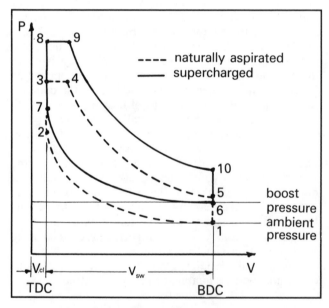

Comparison of supercharged and naturally aspirated cycles having the same compression ratio.

volume, thereby reducing the geometrical compression ratio, can give the same maximum cylinder pressure as a naturally aspirated engine, but this still gives a greater mean effective pressure and greater power output.

If r_1 is the maximum permitted unsupercharged compression ratio for an engine without detonation, r_2 is the allowable supercharged compression ratio, P_1 and P_2 are the supercharged and unsupercharged intake pressures (bar absolute), then:

$$r_2 = r_1 \times (P_1/P_2) \times 0.73$$

In the range of low boost, say 0.3-0.6 bar, the effect

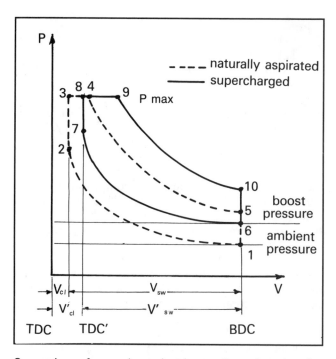

Comparison of supercharged and naturally aspirated cycles having the same maximum pressure but different compression ratios.

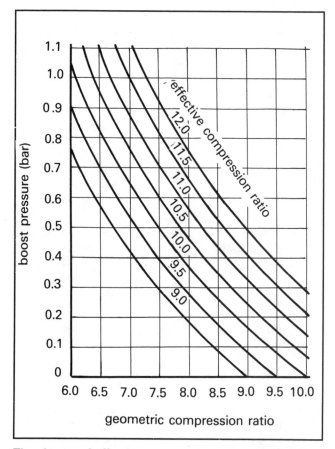

The change of effective compression ratio with changing boost pressure.

of every 0.26 bar of boost is to increase the effective compression ratio by 1 approximately. For example, a geometric compression ratio of 9.0:1 and a boost of 0.6 bar gives an effective compression ratio of 11.3:1[25].

A naturally aspirated engine compresses the charge air from practically ambient conditions of specific charge air volume to its final compressed volume given by the engine compression ratio. For the supercharged engine this compression is shared by the charging compressor and the engine. The density ratio or compression ratio (this is a volume ratio not a pressure ratio) handled by the compressor is a very important first design characteristic and is given by the ratio of the air density at intake manifold conditions to the air density under ambient conditions. In a very first approximation, the brake mean effective pressure is proportional to the density ratio unless limited by the mechanical or heat loads of the engine.

Ignoring for the moment any inefficiencies in supercharger functioning, supercharging an engine can improve the fuel consumption. Consider a naturally aspirated engine and a similar supercharged engine with double the indicated power output (double the work per cycle at the piston). The supercharged engine will be using double the amount of fuel used by the naturally aspirated one. However, frictional losses are speed rather than load related, so they are not going to change significantly between the two engines. As a result, the supercharged engine will produce more than twice the net power output of the naturally aspirated engine; the overall efficiency will be higher.

All of these discussions have, of course, so far ignored the power consumed by the supercharging compressor. For the mechanically driven supercharger this directly reduces the net power available from the engine. For the turbocharged engine, at first sight it looks as if this power can be obtained free by using energy otherwise lost out of the exhaust pipe.

The next pressure/volume indicator diagram shows what would happen if the stroke of the engine was extended so far that the adiabatic expansion of the exhaust gases was able to continue right down to ambient pressure at point 8. The available exhaust energy for turbocharging consists of two parts[42]. Firstly the 'blow down' energy of the adiabatic expansion from point 5, where the exhaust valve actually opens, to ambient pressure at point 8; the area 5-8-9. In addition, the work done by the piston in displacing the remaining exhaust gas, area 9-10-11-13 in the case of the four-stroke engine, can also potentially be obtained. If the turbocharging system enables the intake pressure to exceed that in the exhaust pipe, piston pumping during the intake and exhaust processes may be turned from a debit into a small but significant bonus. More details of how this energy can be transferred to the turbine of a turbocharger are given in Chapter 12.

The fuel economy of a turbocharged engine is influenced by the same factors as the normally aspirated engine. It was shown earlier that the basic air standard

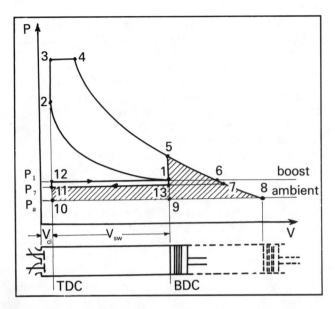

Work available from an ideal exhaust process. The stroke of the piston is assumed to be extended to allow adiabatic expansion of the exhaust gases down to ambient pressure.

thermal efficiency of an engine is very much dependent on the compression ratio. Unfortunately, turbocharging normally makes a reduction of the engine geometric compression ratio necessary; a high boost pressure usually means a low geometric compression ratio. In practice, fuel economy is likely to deteriorate by about 3-6% if the compression ratio is reduced by one point.

At high or at full load the specific fuel consumption of a turbocharged engine is superior to the consumption of a similar normally aspirated engine. However, today's fuel economy regulations tend to judge engines and cars by their low-load fuel consumption. At idling and low-load conditions, the influence of engine displacement has more effect on fuel economy than the influence of compression ratio. For the same required power, the turbocharged engine can have a smaller displacement, giving a net benefit. For example, a particular 2.2-litre turbocharged engine with equivalent characteristics to a 3-litre normally aspirated engine had an improvement of 20-30% in fuel consumption even after allowing for an increase in consumption of 10% caused by the reduced compression ratio.

A factor which affects the benefits of any form of supercharging is the temperature rise in the charging compressor. As the pressure rises the temperature will also rise (remember, the basic gas law). Increased pressure means increased charge density, the objective of supercharging, but the increased temperature will increase volume and thereby reduce the density, undoing some of the good work.

Most supercharging compressors approximate to an adiabatic compression process following the gas laws discussed earlier. If T_1 and P_1 are the inlet absolute temperature and pressure, and T_2 and P_2 are the outlet

values then:

$$T_2/T_1 = (P_2/P_1)^{(\gamma-1)/\gamma}$$

This gives: $T_2 = T_1 \times (P_2/P_1)^{0.286}$

As an example, if the inlet air temperature is 20°C (absolute temperature 293°K) and the inlet pressure is 1 bar absolute, then for a boost pressure of 1.1 bar (absolute pressure 2.1 bar) the theoretical outlet temperature will be:

$$T_2 = 293 \times (2.1/1)^{0.286} = 293 \times 1.236 = 362°K$$
(89°C)

The temperature rise of 69°C calculated above is the theoretical value in an ideal compressor working with air, but 100% adiabatic efficiency is as likely as perpetual motion! The actual temperature rise is given by the ideal temperature rise divided by the compressor adiabatic efficiency.

This will very much depend upon the type of compressor and its operating regime, but if we had an adiabatic efficiency of 70%, the actual temperature rise through the compressor would be:

69°/0.7 = 98°C

The degree of boost which is needed from a supercharging compressor depends upon the application. The following table suggests some values for boost pressure (bar) and target requirements[39]:

Application	Max boost	Requirements
Car/van (gasoline) road use	0.3-0.5	Max low-speed torque, 35% power increase
Car/van (diesel) road use	0.7	Max low-speed torque, 35% power increase
Mild competition rally, etc)	0.5-0.7	Max low & mid-range power, 40-50% power increase
Competition autocross, hillclimb, sprint, etc	0.7-1.7	Good mid-range & top-end power with quick throttle response up to 170 bhp per litre
Competition circuit (gasoline)	1.0-1.7	Max top-end power racing compatible with reliability; up to 250 bhp per litre
Competition drag racing (methanol)	1.0-3.0	As much power as possible using special fuel blends, 350 bhp per litre

Mechanical versus turbo supercharging

In the historic review earlier in the book it was seen how the early applications of mechanical supercharging became replaced by the upsurge of turbocharger applications, and then how this has been followed more recently by a re-appearance of engine-driven superchargers for some vehicles. Let us now look at some of the design factors which have influenced the choice of mechanical supercharging or turbocharging.

The constant improvements of passenger car aerodynamics and increasing vehicle weight experienced in the course of the last few years have intensified the demand for high torque at low engine speeds while giving maximum power output second priority[25]. This is reflected in the following figures for two Porsche automobiles with the same top speed but developed some years apart:

Model	Top speed	0-100 kph	Power
911 Turbo 1975	260 kph	5.4 secs	221 kw
944 Turbo S	260 kph	5.9 secs	184 kw

The engine of a powerful passenger automobile, when accelerated flat out in first gear, can go through the full speed range within a second, and the supercharger must follow this rapid rise in engine mass flow. Indeed, the supercharger must build up the boost sufficiently rapidly to ensure that combustion during these fast transients occurs without air shortage.

Urban test cycles exhibit strong changes in engine speed and load, the steps frequently proceeding from a very low level; periods with steady state conditions do not exist except during idling. Speed changes of more than 1,000 rpm per second and load steps of more than 5 bar per second in bmep are not a rarity. The road performance quality of the vehicle is evaluated on the basis of such situations and not of the statistically predominating number of changes of lower amplitude.

In the following, there must be a distinction between low-pressure 'pressure charging' as used on normal road cars (0.3-0.6 bar) and maximum power supercharging with the boost up to 6 bar as used in competition cars – only the former is considered here.

The turbocharger has several attractions in addition to its ability to make use of the wasted exhaust gas energy. Turbo machines have a very large 'gulp' capacity relative to their size. The mean piston speed of a reciprocating engine which determines the total cylinder volume and therefore the size is limited for mechanical reasons. Furthermore, a factor of four or two shows up for the four or two-stroke cycle engines because only one stroke is used for aspirating air. The centrifugal compressor runs uninterruptedly and is only limited aerodynamically by the speed of sound and can be very compact relative to the engine size. The requirement to drive it at very high speed is easily met by the equally compact exhaust-driven turbine.

However, the combination of a volume machine (the engine) with a speed machine (the turbocharger) presents a number of matching difficulties and leads to

such things as the dreaded 'turbo lag'.

Unlike a turbocharger, the boost pressure delivery of a positive displacement supercharger is almost linear over the normal engine speed range. Nevertheless, if high boost is needed at low speed, some form of boost limiter at high speed will still be needed just as for the turbocharger. The classic Roots blower has a poor adiabatic efficiency compared with the centrifugal compressor, but some of the more refined modern supercharger designs can match the turbocharger's compressor efficiency.

A comparison issue which is difficult to quantify is the psychological one of vehicle 'feel'. Despite what the theoretical engineers and pro-turbocharger lobby may say, in sheer 'get up and go' and general all-round performance on the road, as opposed to the drawing-board, the mechanically supercharged engine compares very favourably with the turbocharged one.

Porsche conducted some interesting comparative tests with one of their engines, the 2.5-litre, four-cylinder 16-valve in-line version fitted in 944S models since 1987. For mechanical supercharging, the compression ratio was reduced from 10.9 to 9.0 by increasing piston bowl depth. The engine had electronic fuel injection and ignition systems[74].

A Roots blower was used for the tests. The compressor efficiency drops to less than 40% at speeds of more than 5,500 rpm, and requires drive powers of up to 50 hp (37 kw) at 6,000 rpm. Compared with the turbocharged engine, 47-68% higher torque was obtained

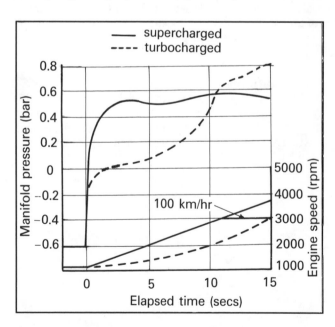

The results of tests carried out by Porsche on a 2.5-litre 944S to compare the behaviour of the standard turbocharged engine with one fitted with a Roots type positive displacement supercharger. Rapid opening of the throttle gave a high boost pressure much more quickly with the mechanically driven supercharger, accompanied by a rapid rise in engine speed.

in the low and middle speed range, and the nominal power was up by 17%. Above 3,000 rpm, the turbocharged engine has up to 19% higher torque. The fuel consumption of the mechanically supercharged engine was 13% up at low speeds and 10% up at high speed compared with the turbocharged engine. In the middle range, both are about the same.

During performance measurements with the vehicle, the acceleration times with the mechanically supercharged engine could be reduced by 10% to 40% compared with the turbocharged engine, depending on the chosen initial speed and gear (see the accompanying graph).

It is possible to define three areas in the engine characteristic curves which pose different demands:

A Normal driving, when the engine runs mostly in the naturally aspirated engine range. Boost pressure will be of no use as it must be throttled off; an exhaust turbine should present as large a hole as possible.

B Acceleration, when high torque is needed. Fuel consumption is of less importance as the engine only operates briefly in this region. A small turbine nozzle area and the highest possible overall turbocharger efficiency are desired.

C Where the vehicle runs steadily over longer time periods on freeways and inclines. Here the supercharging device must be efficient.

For region A a disengageable mechanical supercharger can meet the requirement, and in region B it will eliminate the 'turbo lag'. In B and C, however, maximum torque is reduced by the driving power needs of a mechanical supercharger.

Diesel differences

Much of the previous information has applied to any type of supercharged engine, but it is worth looking now at some of the significant differences between diesel and spark ignition gasoline engines when supercharging is applied.

The fuel/air mixture ratio for a gasoline engine is critical and must lie within a narrow range around what is known as the 'stoichiometric' value. In the diesel engine, with its separate direct fuel injection, it is only necessary to ensure that there is enough air to match the amount of fuel being injected; excess air above this minimum is generally beneficial. Indeed, if this excess drops below a certain limit, the efficiency decreases rapidly. Above the limit, output performance almost immediately follows the driver's command. While in the lower-load range the supercharged diesel engine has more excess air than a naturally aspirated one, in the course of a load step the pressure ratio must be adjusted in order that the air excess does not drop below the minimum permissible value; for example, if the bmep increases from 3 to 9 bar, the charge air pressure must rise from 1.2 to 1.8 bar.

This excess air gives a number of benefits. It keeps down the maximum cylinder and exhaust temperatures, thereby allowing greater performance to be obtained from the construction materials used, it simplifies supercharger control systems, and it can be used to provide a scavenging flush of air through the cylinder at the end of the exhaust stroke to remove the last traces of exhaust gas.

The diesel cycle does not suffer from detonating combustion, thanks to the progressive fuel injection process. As a result, high boost pressures are quite acceptable even though they are being added on to the already high peak pressures natural to diesel engines. Current technology sets a limit of about 140 bar for maximum cylinder pressure, determined not only by mechanical strength limits but also by the difficulties of getting an efficient fuel injection pump to work against such very high pressures.

An especially annoying characteristic of the diesel engine is the hard 'pinging' noise in the no-load and part-load ranges of the engine while cold. Supercharged engines run quieter the higher the supercharging rate or the degree of preheating.

7

Exhaust pollution control

The pollution of the environment caused by motor vehicles became a major issue during the 1970s and '80s and has had an enormous influence on the design and marketing of automobiles. The US Environmental Protection Agency's Clean Air Act has been followed by similar legislation from the Economic Commission for Europe and has accompanied a trend towards reduced lead content in gasoline. Unless designers can meet these increasingly tough laws their work will just not be sold.

What are the particular elements of pollution which are affected by this legislation? The exhaust gases of an automobile contain the nitrogen included in the original intake air, together with the carbon dioxide (CO_2) which results from the complete combustion of hydrocarbon fuels. In addition, in practical engines, there are also unburnt hydrocarbons (HC), carbon monoxide (CO) as a result of incomplete combustion, and oxides of nitrogen (NOx) produced in very high temperature reactions. In the exhaust gas of a diesel engine, because of the progressive type of combustion, there will also be soot particles (Pm) and heavy hydrocarbons. All of these last five items are covered by the legislation as being damaging to health and are subject to strict limitation.

The latest European standard (ECE15+EUDC) which has to be met by 1992 is very similar to the US Federal 1987 test. The tests involve typical driving cycles during which the amounts of the polluting emissions are measured. There are two standards, one for Type Approval and a slightly relaxed one for production cars. For Type Approval, the maximum allowed for diesel particulates is 0.19 grams per kilometre, 0.97 gm/km for HC + NOx (which are combined for legislation purposes), and 2.72 gm/km for CO. The equivalent figures for production line vehicles are 0.24 for particulates, 1.13 for HC + NOx, and 3.16 for CO.

Carbon dioxide (CO_2) is not yet explicitly controlled even though it is now widely recognised as one of the causes of the climatic 'greenhouse effect'. Proposals have been presented to the US Congress for such a limitation, with a maximum of 250 grams per mile proposed for 1995, dropping to 170 grams per mile in the year 2003.

In addition to the gaseous pollution problems, pressure is starting to rise to reduce the noise pollution caused by vehicles, especially heavy trucks, and this is another topic which is exercising engineers' minds.

Designers of conventional gasoline engines, faced with all these stringent requirements, have had to apply complex and often expensive techniques to get the necessary emissions reduction with retained driveability, while barely maintaining previously established performance levels.

The resulting power units and their ancillary equipment of increased bulk and weight have suffered increases in brake specific fuel consumption (bsfc) of between 10 and 30%. Faced with this already complex and somewhat unsatisfactory situation, what possible reasons can there have been for the addition of a further component, the turbocharger, whose air delivery characteristics are not ideally suited to the operational requirements of the four-stroke reciprocating spark ignition vehicle engine?

Mechanical supercharging or turbocharging does not worsen emission problems; it can indeed make some significant improvements. This has been one of the major factors which has caused the growth in the supercharged vehicle market. The experience so far with supercharged engines has shown that the measures required for emission control are generally the same as for normally aspirated engines. The Porsche 911 Turbo was the first production turbocharged automobile to receive an emission certification from the US Environmental Protection Agency.

Diesel engines have an advantage in that their excess air reduces combustion temperatures and the associated NOx generation. The excess oxygen also reduces hydrocarbons and carbon monoxide. They do, however, have their own problem of sooty smoke generation.

The following table gives the results obtained when the ECE+EUDC tests were run on three different versions of the Volkswagen Golf vehicle – 1.6-litre gasoline-engined Driver, 1.6-litre standard diesel, and the 1.6-litre turbocharged Umwelt diesel:

Vehicle	CO	NOx	HC	Pm	CO_2	Fuel cons
	gm/km	gm/km	gm/km	gm/km	gm/km	lt/100 km
Gasoline	6.608	2.360	1.471	n/a	162.21	7.565
Diesel	0.54	0.675	0.147	0.179	152.69	5.728
Turbo diesel	0.307	0.547	0.084	0.159	163.66	6.115

The overall benefits of the diesel compared with the gasoline engine are clear, and the improvement obtained by turbocharging the diesel can also be seen. The increase in fuel consumption and carbon dioxide for the turbocharged car compared with the standard diesel are a direct result of the greater power available from that engine (6 bhp more).

Emissions control techniques

A variety of different techniques have been used to reduce emissions, either singly or more usually in combination. These include reducing the engine size, reducing the compression ratio, producing 'lean burn' combustion conditions, adding exhaust oxidising reactors, fitting catalytic converters, recycling exhaust gases, fitting particulate traps on diesel engines, and providing complex closed-loop control systems. The following paragraphs look at each of these techniques and see how supercharging affects the issue.

Just reducing the size of the engine inevitably reduces the amount of pollutants produced. A supercharged engine will have a smaller displacement to achieve the same performance, while the exhaust gas volume in the idling range and in the range of low partial load is smaller than for the normally aspirated engine.

Reducing the compression ratio is another way to reduce pollutant generation. Normally, the geometric compression ratio of a supercharged engine is lower than that of an equivalent naturally aspirated engine. At a compression ratio of 6.5:1, the HC-emissions are about half of the value measured at a ratio of 8.5:1. The NOx emissions decrease to about 60 to 70% at corresponding values. As we have seen, the supercharged engine runs for much of its life in the naturally aspirated zone,

so the total pollutant volume emitted during tests is reduced.

Designers have spent a lot of time trying to produce satisfactory 'lean burn' gasoline engines. The objective of such an engine is to create the combustion chamber conditions which burn just the right amount of fuel with just the right amount of air and produce complete combustion with no unwanted side reactions. While this objective has been nearly reached in laboratory conditions, it is a much more difficult job to achieve it in production engines in a manner that will remain effective throughout the vehicle life. Nevertheless, some interesting steps towards the ultimate objective have already seen the production line.

Supercharging can help with 'lean burn' engines. The compressor turbulence produces a better fuel/air mixture, and can assist in getting better cylinder distribution of the mixture. For the same power, combustion temperatures can be reduced. The peak compression pressure is not raised much but the indicator diagram is fatter to get the extra power.

Running with a rich fuel/air mixture in a gasoline engine can reduce NOx emissions but at the expense of increased unburnt hydrocarbons and carbon monoxide. Such an engine can be fitted with an 'exhaust gas reactor' which is essentially a high temperature chamber which adds sufficient air to complete the combustion process correctly. This rich mixture operation can give good power and driveability and is compatible with high boost operation[23].

Low levels of NOx pollutant production are inherent in the rich mixture combustion conditions prevailing in the engine cylinders, and little or no NOx is generated in the oxidising reactor which operates in the 650 to 1,000°C range. The rate of non-catalytic oxidation of the hydrocarbons in the exhaust reactor is a function of the square of the reactor system pressure, which can be significantly higher for a turbocharged engine. Carbon monoxide conversion rates are also improved by increased system pressure while the exhaust turbine takes advantage of the energy release occurring in the reactor, and the overall thermal efficiency of the system is potentially better than that of a conventional rich mixture, emissions-treated unit.

The best known technique for dealing with exhaust gas pollution is the fitting of a 'catalytic converter'. These are already compulsory in some countries and will soon be generally fitted. A catalyst is a chemical which encourages a reaction between other chemicals without actually becoming involved in the reaction and being used up. The usual ones used are the expensive rare metals platinum, palladium and rhodium. The catalyst is deposited on the surface of a fine honeycomb of ceramic or metal. Typically this has a surface area in all the honeycomb cells of about 250,000 square feet, all packed into a stainless steel box about the size of an average exhaust muffler. The operating temperature of the catalyst is critical and must remain above about 300°C for the reactions to take place.

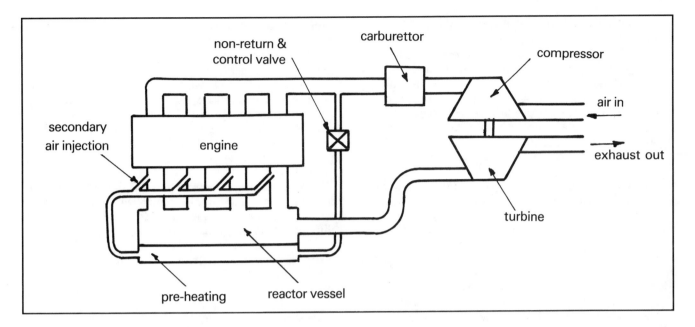

Schematic of an engine with an exhaust thermal reactor. The carburettor is adjusted to feed a rich mixture to the engine which minimises detonation and NOx generation. A controlled supply of air is bled from the input through a pre-heater and is injected at the exhaust ports. This causes the remaining fuel components and carbon monoxide to be completely oxidised in the thermal reactor chamber.

There are two main types of catalyst – the simple oxidation one and the three-way catalyst. The oxidation catalyst converts carbon monoxide to carbon dioxide, and the hydrocarbons to carbon dioxide and water. The three-way catalyst also reduces the nitrogen oxides to nitrogen and oxygen, the latter being used in the oxidising of the CO and HC.

In order for the three way catalyst to function correctly, the fuel/air ratio is critical. The Greek letter lambda (λ) is used to identify the correct balance point. A gasoline engine running at a λ value of one is operating at the ideal air/fuel ratio of 14.6:1. If $\lambda = 1.2$, the engine is running rich; $\lambda = 0.8$ would be a weak mixture state. It is essential for a car which is fitted with a three way catalytic converter to run so that the operating conditions lie in a very small window around the $\lambda = 1.0$ state. A simple carburettor-fed engine with no special controls will only have about 70% of the pollutants removed by the catalyst because of the degree of variability in practical operations.

Up to 90% removal can be achieved by introducing 'closed loop' engine management systems which actually measure the oxygen content of the exhaust gases before the catalyst, and adjust the fuel system to maintain the correct lambda value. For a three-way catalyst to reduce NOx there must be no excess oxygen. A diesel engine invariably runs with excess air so the three-way type cannot be fitted, and the simple oxidation catalyst

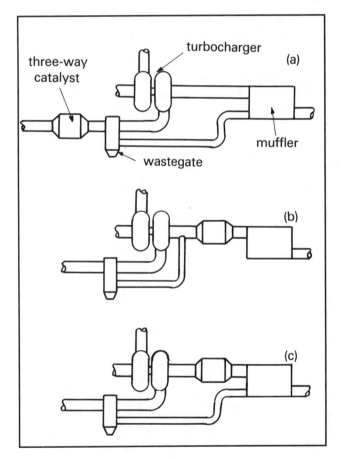

Alternative positions for a catalyst relative to the exhaust turbine of a turbocharger

(a) between the engine and the turbine;
(b) after the turbine, with full gas flow;
(c) after the turbine, but with the wastegate gas flow bypassing the catalyst.

alone must be used if needed. This oxidises the CO and HC but does not affect the NOx.

To work effectively, catalytic converters need to run at a working temperature in excess of 300°C, and a quick engine warm-up is important. As a result of installing a catalytic converter, this need for a high exhaust pipe temperature and the back pressure caused by the catalyst honeycomb give a tendency towards higher fuel consumption.

There are different possibilities for arranging the catalyst when installed on a turbocharged engine. If it is placed close to the engine, before the turbine, it will give a quick warm-up for the catalyst. However, the turbine rotor can be damaged by small particles coming off the ceramic material, which normally are not damaging to the catalyst function. A catalyst based on a metallic substrate would probably allow a position upstream of the turbine, although the 'turbo-lag' is still worsened. Installed after the turbine there is no danger of turbocharger damage, but catalyst warm-up is slower. There is also the possibility of letting the wastegate exhaust by-pass the catalyst, thereby reducing the thermal load on the catalyst.

In the diesel engine, by contrast with the gasoline engine, the objectives of optimising the fuel economy and exhaust gas emissions do not stand in conflict with one another. Improved utilisation of the fuel energy results directly in lower emissions of the main product of combustion, CO_2. Diesel engine HC and CO emissions are generally very low, so they do not require exhaust gas treatment, but all diesel engines emit relatively high amounts of NOx and under certain operating conditions generate visible particulates.

A very effective way to reduce NOx in diesel engines is to recirculate a portion of the exhaust gas back into the charge air. This easily enables the NOx concentration to be reduced to 30% of its initial value before any detrimental secondary effects occur. Exhaust gas recirculation is also used on some spark ignition gasoline engines.

An exhaust gas recirculation (EGR) valve installed in the hot pipe can only be controlled indirectly (eg by vacuum) because of the heat. Because the pressure differential for EGR on turbocharged engines is often hardly sufficient, a throttle valve on the turbocompressor intake is frequently required. For both mechanical and turbo superchargers, EGR to the compressor intake side is not desirable because of the dangers of contamination of the compressor. However, since supercharging can be restricted to the upper load range and EGR to the lower load range, it is possible to combine EGR with a mechanical supercharger.

A requirement of the pollution control regulations is that the blow-by gases which reach the crankcase cannot just be vented direct to the atmosphere and are usually now returned to the engine air intake. Such engine blow-by systems, even after oil separators, always have some residual oil. With exhaust gas recirculation, the entire air inlet system gets contaminated unacceptably, including the supercharger, the charge air line and the inlet ports in the cylinder head; also the air cooler if fitted. The usual solution is to use a bleed from the

Comparison of exhaust gas recirculation systems for Comprex supercharged, turbocharged, and mechanically supercharged engines. *[ABB]*

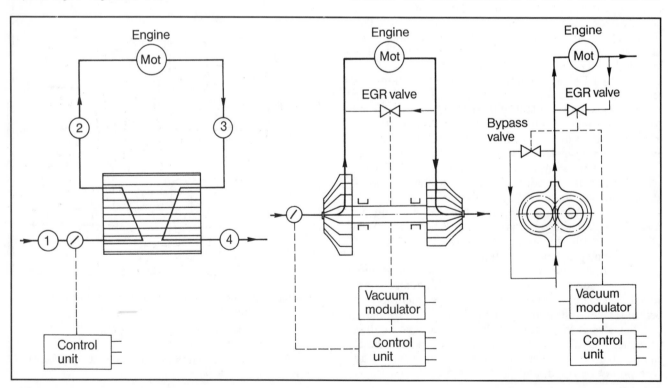

Use of a turbocharger on the smallest cars can give sparkling performance while minimising fuel consumption and polluting emissions. This Chevrolet Turbo Sprint has a turbocharged fuel-injected 1.0-litre three-cylinder engine which gives it a 0-60 mph time of 10.5 seconds. *[Chevrolet]*

boost air supply to operate an ejector system which transfers the blow-by gases direct into the exhaust system.

One of the significant characteristics of the Comprex pressure wave supercharger is the potential direct channel between exhaust and intake. By simply throttling the inlet air supply it is possible to cause the engine increasingly to draw a proportion of its input from the exhaust gases. Exhaust gas recirculation to reduce pollution is thus readily achieved without any additional difficult pipework. Conventional EGR ducts that provide a fully open connection between exhaust and inlet involve the risk of abrasive materials such as scale being transported from the exhaust manifold to the engine intake. With Comprex this danger is avoided as any particles are centrifuged out in the rotor and then entrained by the reverse flow and transported to the exhaust.

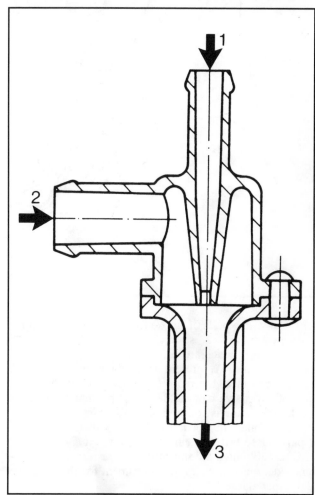

An ejector used to remove crankcase blow-by gases. A small part of the boost air is routed to the ejector (1). This air flows through the ejector nozzle, creating a suction effect at the connection for the hose to the crankcase breather (2). The stream of blow-by gas and air is connected to the exhaust system at (3). *[Opel]*

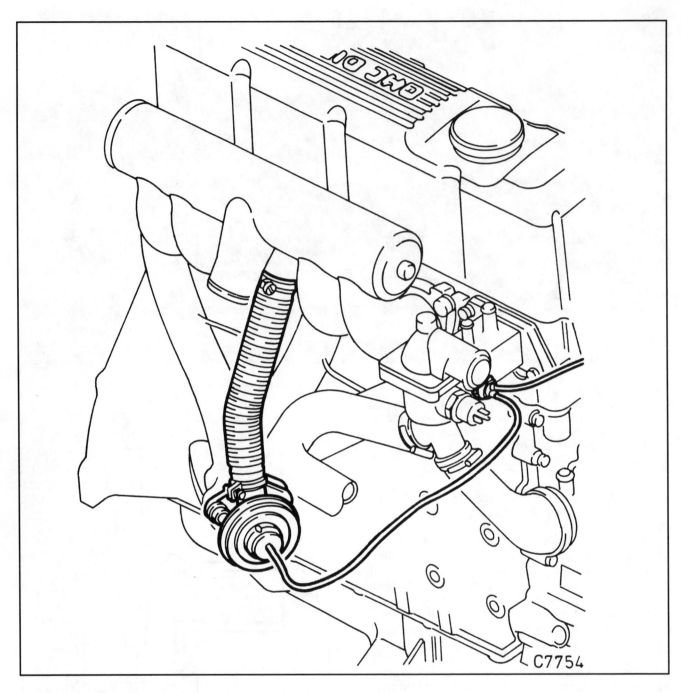

Exhaust gas recirculation valve on a 2-litre diesel engine. [Opel]

The visible puffs of smoke from diesel engines under acceleration are a source of polycyclic aromatic hydrocarbons which are considered to be likely cancer-causing agents. At present most passenger car diesel engines can meet the required limits without the addition of expensive particulate traps, but much research work and testing is continuing to allow for future more stringent rules. In a small turbocharged diesel engine, a particulate trap for emissions control may cause an unacceptably high amount of back pressure on the turbine side; this can be another argument for the mechanical supercharger.

For a given power output, a mechanically super-charged or turbocharged car will tend to produce less noise pollution. The compressor isolates the impulsive intake stroke noises from the air inlet, and the turbine on a turbocharged car does the same for the exhaust. The turbine and compressor introduce their own noises, but these tend to be at higher frequencies and are less bothersome and more easily muffled. Higher boost pressures tend to make diesel engines run more quietly.

8

How turbochargers work

The one type of supercharger which has been most widely adopted for mass-produced vehicles is the turbocharger, and this chapter looks at how they work. Turbochargers fall into two main groups – the simple mass-produced units mainly used for trucks and cars, but also with small marine and aircraft engines, and the larger, more complex, high-efficiency units for medium- and low-speed diesels used for railway traction, electricity generation, industrial and large marine applications.

At the bottom end, a small automobile turbocharger might have a rotor diameter as small as 45 mm and weigh about 3 kilograms. At the top end, a turbocharger used on a large marine propulsion diesel engine could be transmitting as much as 4,000 horsepower through the shaft from turbine to compressor. The focus of this book is, however, on the small automotive types, used mainly on passenger automobiles and small commercial vehicles.

The turbocharger comprises a centrifugal compressor driven by a turbine mounted on the same shaft. There are two different basic principles of working for turbomachines – axial flow and radial flow. In the axial flow machine, the working gas passes through usually several rings of blades mounted alternately on the rotor and stationary casing. Work transfer takes place accompanied by changes of pressure and flow direction through the rings of blades, but all the time the gas moves roughly parallel to the axis. In the radial flow machine, although flow at the hub will be parallel with the axis, in general the gas flow is at right angles to this, either inwards or outwards for turbine or compressor respectively. In a radial flow machine, the rotor may be shrouded or left open on one side. The distinction between axial and radial has become blurred of late with mixed flow types becoming common.

One of the smallest automotive turbochargers on the market, the Kühnle, Kopp & Kausch K03. The whole unit weighs less than 3 kilograms, and the rotor runs at speeds up to 220,000 rpm. *[KKK]*

During the history of turbocharging, the types of compressor and turbine have reflected the general state of the art in those fields of turbomachinery. The first turbochargers used centrifugal compressors of a pure radial type with a shrouded impeller together with axial

Three of the largest turbochargers on the market installed on a Sulzer-type 8RND90M two-stroke diesel engine in the Al Ain power station. This engine has an output of 26,800 horsepower at 122 rpm. At full power, each of the ASEA-Brown Boveri type VTR631-1P turbochargers is transmitting 3,000 horsepower through the shaft between turbine and compressor! *[ABB]*

Basic types of turbo-machines
(a) axial flow
(b) radial flow
(c) mixed flow

turbines. The radial flow turbine had a late start in turbocharging and has been primarily developed for use in the small-size inexpensive automotive turbocharger. Its great advantage is that it maintains a relatively high efficiency when reduced to very small sizes; it can efficiently handle a high expansion ratio, approaching 4:1. The probable general pattern for the future uses unshrouded radial impellers for compressors and mixed flow for most turbines, with multi-stage axial flow for some large turbines.

Let us now look at how the centrifugal, radial flow, compressor works. Swirl-free air, which does not rotate around the axis of the machine, enters the inlet casing, where it is directed into the compressor impeller eye. Since the velocity of the air increases as it approaches the eye, or 'inducer', its static pressure will decrease accordingly. In the impeller the blades impart a swirling motion to the air, and it leaves the impeller tip at high velocity. Work transfer takes place in the impeller and the static pressure of the air increases from the inducer to the impeller tip due to the acceleration. This pressure rise is dependent upon the component of the exit air velocity which is tangential to the impeller diameter (V_c), multiplied by the impeller tip speed (U) and divided by the gravitational acceleration constant (g). The static pressure, then, is $(U \times V_c)/g$.

At the impeller exit, a substantial portion of the work input is in the form of kinetic energy, given by the square of the total air velocity (V) divided by twice the gravitational constant – $V^2/2g$. Therefore another part is necessary – the diffuser, which converts this kinetic energy into a useful rise of static pressure by slowing down the high-velocity air to an acceptable value. The collector or volute then collects the air flow from around the circumference of the diffuser and delivers it to the exit duct.

The impeller blades may be straight or curved. A straight-bladed impeller is easy to make using die-casting or similar techniques, but it has a relatively low efficiency due to shock losses at the inlet. Alternatively the edge of the blades at the inducer can be curved so that air entering the impeller will be at exactly the same angle as the blade.

The compressor blade exit may also be radial or

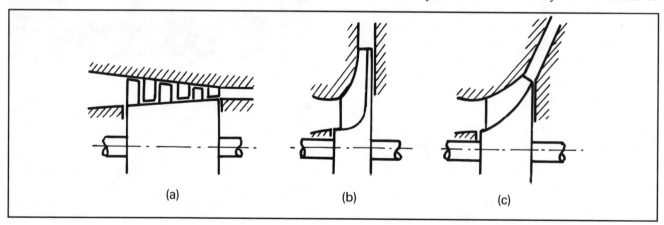

(a)   (b)   (c)

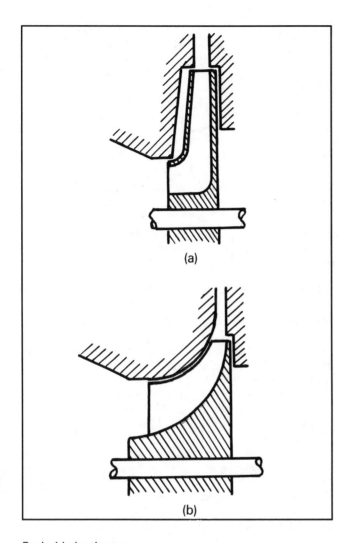

Basic blade shapes
(a) straight radial blades
(b) backward curved blades

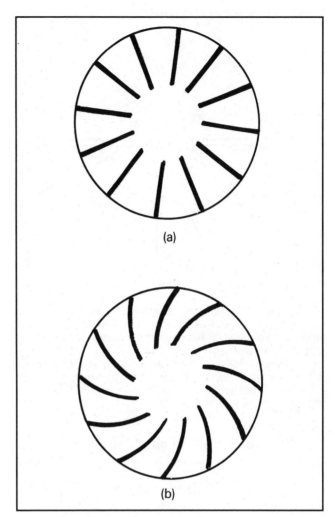

Basic types of compressor impeller
(a) shrouded
(b) unshrouded

backward-curved. The backward-curved blading requires a higher tip speed but the leaving speed is lower, which means that a larger percentage of the overall pressure rise takes place within the impeller itself and the diffuser becomes less important. The curved blades are more difficult to make and are subject to greater bending stresses at their roots. This has two major consequences – the maximum pressure ratio for impellers of similar disk shapes is lower because of the strength considerations, but the operating range is wider and the peak compressor efficiency usually higher. A single model with backward-curved blades can cover a wide range of engine requirements, reducing stockholding requirements.

Shrouded impellers are difficult to make and are likely to be weak. The maximum efficiency is high because of the minimal recirculation from tip back to inlet, but they tend to collect dirt and are hardly ever used now.

The diffuser on early turbo-compressors consisted of a series of divergent nozzles which slowed down the air by expanding its volume. These nozzles became replaced by a ring of blades or vanes which formed the necessary divergent passages. The simplest type of diffuser, though, is the vaneless one. In its simplest form this is defined by two parallel walls. The volume of space between the walls increases as the radial distance from the impeller tip increases, giving the needed slowing down of the air. In some machines the diffuser walls may be shaped to get a non-linear change of area with diameter.

The vaneless diffuser is widely used in automotive turbochargers due to the broad operating range, low cost and good tolerance to erosion and fouling. Its disadvantage, however, is a much lower pressure recovery compared with a vaned diffuser of the same diameter. It works particularly well with backward-curved blades.

Vaned diffusers are usually used with radial blades. Because the air leaves such an impeller with a very high velocity, approaching or even exceeding the speed of

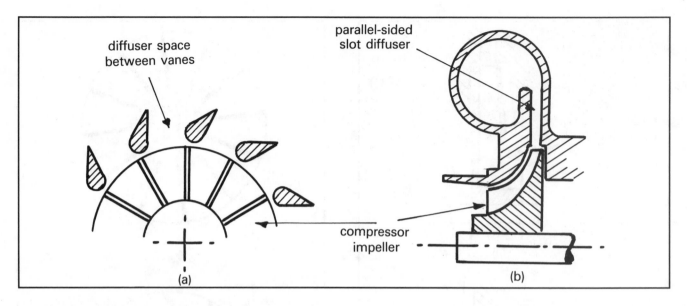

Comparison of vaned and vaneless compressor diffusers
(a)   Vaned diffuser. A series of angled vanes surround the impeller. The spaces between the vanes form divergent diffuser passages.
(b)   Vaneless diffuser. The air leaving the impeller radially passes between two parallel walls formed in the housing. The area of this slot increases in proportion to the radius, thus slowing down the gas flow.

sound, vaned diffusers are often combined with short vaneless diffusers in order to improve the operating range.

Many of the foregoing comments apply equally to the turbine. The early radial gas turbines were truly radial. A turbine of this type has a relatively large wheel diameter for a given set of gas flow, pressure and discharge kinetic energy values. Since small size, weight and inertia are generally desirable, there has been a trend towards more axial flow within the wheel.

The turbine nozzle is the counterpart of the compressor's vaned diffuser, its job being to create a swirling motion of the gas before entering the turbine wheel. In general, the gas increases its velocity while passing through a set of nozzle vanes. Because of weight reasons and also because subdivided exhaust manifolds for best pulse utilisation require small cross-sections for the turbine inlet ports, the inlet velocities to the turbine housing become very high. Sometimes there remains only a relatively small amount of flow acceleration needed from the nozzle passage. In the case of nozzles for radial turbines, this fact becomes even more pronounced and there is little work left for the nozzle vanes. It appears only natural then to dispense with the vanes entirely. In this case the turbine housing has to be shaped properly so that it can take over the nozzle's function and produce the necessary initial swirling motion.

The vaneless turbine is probably the most common amongst the smaller automotive versions as it is cheap to manufacture, is reliable, and has acceptable efficiency.

There is, however, one function which still makes a set of nozzle vanes an attractive option. If the vanes are made to pivot, the area between the vanes can change, thus changing the power characteristics of the turbine, and we will see later how important the issue of turbocharger power control is in any vehicle installation.

Tests on a truck engine showed that providing 12 vanes to a standard turbine achieved 20% higher power at maximum torque and an improvement of 4% in the fuel consumption. The benefits are most apparent at part-load, high-torque conditions, and as only a limited time is spent running under these conditions, the total fuel savings are not very high.

The moving nozzle vane, or 'variable geometry' turbine, is used for some larger turbochargers, but reliability and cost issues have mitigated against its wider adoption for small machines. The linkages to operate the vanes are liable to seizure as a result of the continual temperature cycling without any lubrication and usually need some form of power servo to actuate them. Numerous attempts have been made to gain the benefits of the multi-vane approach, but using simple one- or two-stage movements. Some examples are illustrated in Chapter 15 which use single- or double-flap vanes to change the apparent turbine throat area, including one where the vane slides horizontally. Generally, these have been limited to diesel engine exhaust temperatures (500-650°C), and expensive metals or ceramics have needed to be used.

A technique which has been used by both Volvo and Porsche, on truck diesels and high-performance passenger cars respectively, provides two turbochargers of different sizes. By controlling the sequence in which these are used, the equivalent of a two-step variable geometry turbine can be obtained.

The power of a gas turbine is dependent on the mass flow of gas through it. As well as temperature and pressure, this mass flow will be a function of the nozzle area. When working with radial flow vaneless (or nozzle-

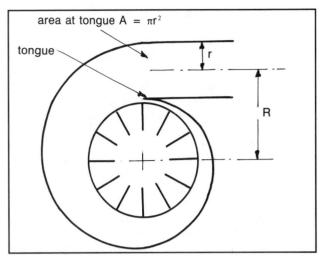

area at tongue A $= \pi r^2$

tongue

r

R

A 'variable geometry' turbine with the turbine housing removed. The ring of nozzle vanes are all arranged on pivots and are coupled by a mechanism which can rotate them on the pivots. This varies the space between the vanes and thus the total area available for the gas flow. Because of the gas pressure on the vanes, a strong servo motor is needed to move the mechanism. In the photograph the vanes are half open. [KKK]

Simple diagram of the A/R principle. The area at the tongue of the turbine inlet is divided by the radius to the centroid of the area to give a parameter which is indicative of the 'swallowing capacity' of the turbine. The principle shown applies where the turbine housing entry is circular in cross-section. Appendix B gives the detail for determining A/R under all conditions.

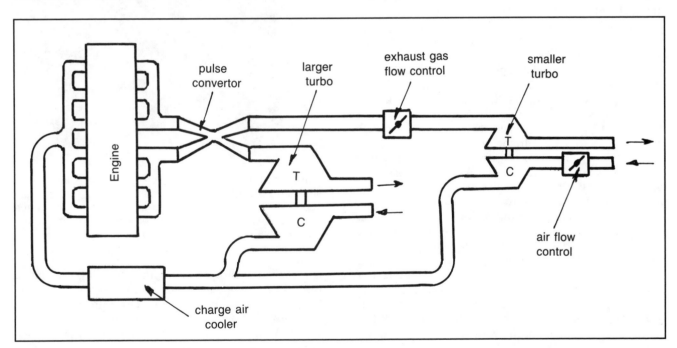

The Volvo two-stage turbocharging system used on truck engines. The larger turbocharger is always active, while adjustment of the air flow and exhaust gas flow valves by the control system varies the contribution made by the second-stage turbocharger. This arrangement gives rapid turbocharger response at low engine speeds while still leaving maximum supercharging available for high-power and high-speed operation. The pulse converter in the exhaust system ensures that the energy of the exhaust pulses is shared between the two turbines.

less) turbines there is obviously no measurable nozzle area and a substitute must be found. This is usually referred to as the 'A/R' value for a particular turbine housing.

An A/R 'nozzle' rating is computed using the principle of continuity of flow and the requirement that the volute feeds the turbine wheel tip with a free vortex flow field. The free vortex law is based upon the principle of the conservation of angular momentum. In order to satisfy this constant angular momentum requirement, the tangential velocity must vary inversely with the radius. Thus, from the inlet throat of the housing the tangential velocity component is accelerated down to the turbine wheel tip. In order to obtain optimum turbine efficiency with a 90° radial inflow turbine wheel design, it is a requirement that the tangential velocity component of the gas approaching the wheel tip has approximately the same magnitude as the wheel tip peripheral velocity. Thus, depending upon the diameter of the wheel and its design rotational speed, different magnitudes of the tangential velocity vector are required.

The detailed calculations for A/R are given in Appendix B; it is sufficient to say here that the 'radius to the dynamic centre' is calculated. This locates that point which divides the scroll area such that half the flow passes above and half below that radius. The gas velocity at the dynamic centre radius is the mean value of the flow velocity. The total area of the entry port is divided by the radius to the dynamic centre to give the A/R rating for a particular turbine rotor/housing combination.

Typically, a 'family' of nozzle-less radial flow turbine scroll housings are designed for use with a common turbine wheel. The manufacturing cost differences between different size housings for the same rotor size are negligible, and the housings are sized in increments of A/R to facilitate engine application. Increasing A/R numbers imply increasing flow capacity or 'nozzle' area, and are used to vary incrementally the turbine flow characteristics for specific applications. The speed of the turbine depends upon the A/R value as well; the larger the nozzle area, the slower the turbine will run. If a housing is used with a larger R, A must be increased to maintain the same A/R characteristic. Change an A/R of 0.7 to 0.9 and the turbine will run slower.

Turbines are not so sensitive to engine matching problems as are the compressors. As a result, there are usually more compressor variations than turbine ones in a particular manufacturer's model range.

In a later chapter we will be looking at the design of exhaust systems, and it will be seen that there are benefits to be derived from providing multiple feeds to the turbine. Often these will all just merge into a single turbine entry port, but multiple port designs are not uncommon. Turbines with as many as four entry ports have been produced, but two is now usually the limit. The turbine casing can be split circumferentially, but this tends to give uneven torque with the rotor 'windmilling' for part of its rotation. The more common method

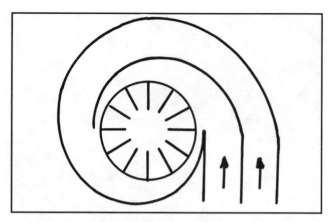

Diagram of a circumferentially split turbine housing.

The Garrett TBP4 turbocharger as used on diesel trucks, showing an axially divided turbine housing. The straight vaneless diffuser in the compressor housing and the water-cooling passages around the turbine end bearing are also clear in this photograph. *[Garrett]*

is to split the flow axially with a dividing wall inside the volute casing which separates the two gas flows all the way down to the blade tip. This thin wall can give problems when subjected to the high temperatures of the gasoline engine exhaust, and as a result is more commonly found in diesel engine applications.

9

Supercharger performance

Compared with the straightforward characteristics of a positive displacement machine such as the normal internal combustion engine, the behaviour of turbomachines is much more complex, with significant changes dependent upon the square of the operating speed. This combination of a volume machine with a speed machine influences directly the matching of turbochargers to engines, and involves consideration of the aerodynamic gas flows through both compressor and turbine.

By contrast, the characteristics of mechanically driven superchargers are more straightforward, particularly as there is no complication from the necessity to think about any involvement of a turbine. We will, therefore, look first at the more difficult turbocharger situation, and then compare the mechanically driven supercharger characteristics afterwards.

The concept of the Mach number has been described earlier and has been applied to compressors and turbines and verified by countless experiments. In the testing of turbomachinery, it has been established that if two Mach numbers, one related to the flow and the other related to the peripheral speed of the machine, are held constant, then energy input, work output, fluid energy losses and efficiency are constant. The performance spectrum or 'map' of a particular machine is obtained by varying these two Mach numbers and plotting the results. For convenience, several constants are usually omitted from these dimensionless ratios such that apparently dimensional values are obtained. Typically the peripheral speed Mach number becomes the ratio of rotational speed to the square root of the inlet absolute temperature, and is usually indicated by $N/\sqrt{T}$.

The dimensionalising of the flow Mach number is not so obvious, but it can be demonstrated that the parameter is proportional to the specific heat ratio and

Mach number. The mass flow rate (M) in unit mass per unit time, the total absolute temperature (T), the gravitational acceleration (g), the gas constant (R), the absolute total pressure (P), and a characteristic flow area (A), constant for a given machine, are all involved in the calculation. For a specific machine this can all be reduced to $(M\sqrt{T})/P$.

If a judicious selection is made of the reference conditions, the performance maps can be approximately simplified to the extent that actual speed and flow rate are presented rather than more abstract parameters. When this is done, the resulting quantities are sometimes referred to as 'corrected speed' and 'corrected flow', leading the uninitiated to think that someone has been manipulating the data to achieve some unspecified purpose[42].

A typical compressor map is illustrated which plots lines of constant corrected speed, pressure ratio and adiabatic efficiency versus corrected flow rate. These are usually measured under standard SAE reference conditions. Cross plotting is used to interpolate between the speed lines and to construct the contours of constant efficiency which give this performance presentation an appearance similar to a topographic map. Note that the speeds given are those of the turbo compressor and not the engine on which it is installed.

The pressure ratio is obtained from the outlet total absolute pressure divided by the inlet total absolute pressure, and represents the actual pressure ratio from compressor inlet to outlet devoid of any ducting losses. Total pressure is the sum of the measured static pressure plus the dynamic head. Dynamic pressure is directly related to the flow velocity, or kinetic energy, and represents the additional pressure obtained if the gas could be reduced to zero velocity without losing any energy. Thus,

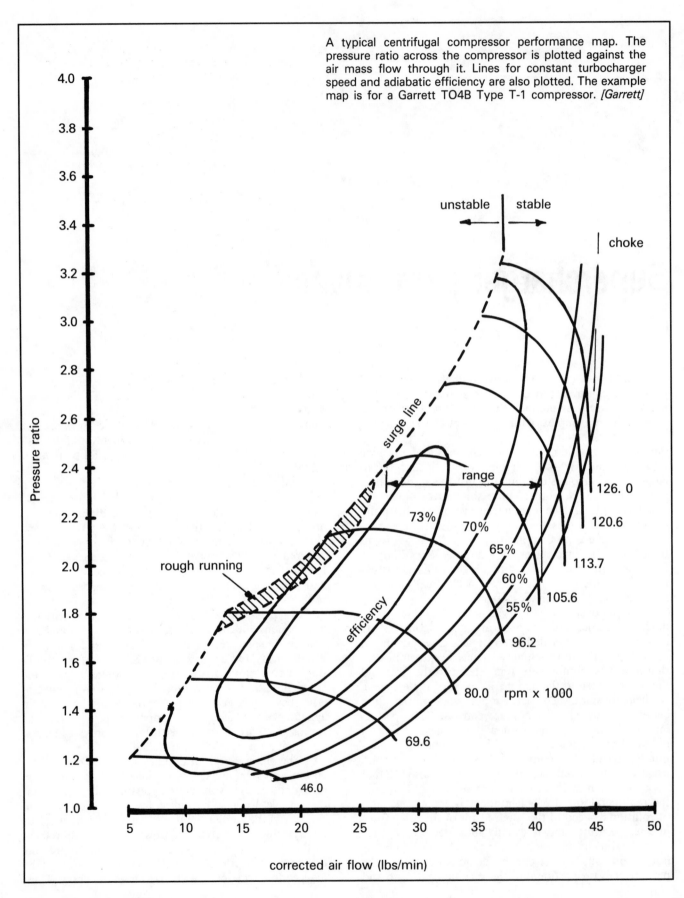

A typical centrifugal compressor performance map. The pressure ratio across the compressor is plotted against the air mass flow through it. Lines for constant turbocharger speed and adiabatic efficiency are also plotted. The example map is for a Garrett TO4B Type T-1 compressor. *[Garrett]*

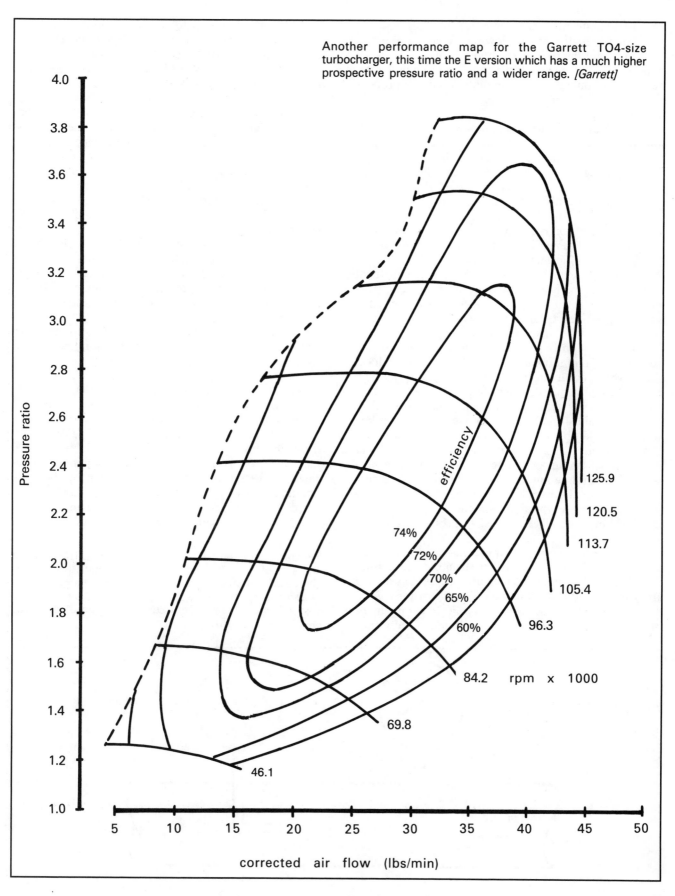

Another performance map for the Garrett TO4-size turbocharger, this time the E version which has a much higher prospective pressure ratio and a wider range. *[Garrett]*

efficiency

125.9

120.5

113.7

74%

72%

70%

65%

60%

105.4

96.3

84.2   rpm x 1000

69.8

46.1

Pressure ratio

corrected air flow (lbs/min)

at zero velocity total and static pressures are equal.

Total pressure, at one flow measurement point, is used to permit the resulting compressor map to be easily applied to actual engine duct sizes. At a given flow rate, velocity and duct area vary roughly in inverse proportion, and the dynamic head is proportional to velocity squared.

Compressor efficiency, because we are dealing with a highly compressible gas, must be defined more rigidly than the simple definition of work out divided by energy input, although the concept is the same. The reference point is the ideal adiabatic compression which changes the pressure with no heat lost or gained, but therefore an inevitable rise in temperature. If this 'perfect' temperature rise is compared with the actual higher temperature rise obtained in practice due to energy losses, the 'adiabatic efficiency' is obtained.

There are essentially three areas on a centrifugal compressor map. The central area is the stable operating zone. In the low-volume flow area at the left, the surge line defines an area of pressure and flow where the compressor is unstable. When the mass flow rate through a compressor is reduced while maintaining a constant pressure ratio, a point is reached at which local flow reversal occurs in the boundary layers. If the flow rate is further reduced, complete reversal occurs. This will relieve the adverse pressure gradient until a new flow regime is established at a lower pressure ratio. The flow will then build up again to the initial condition and this flow instability will continue at a fixed frequency and can in some circumstances be quite violent. The narrower the operating range of the compressor, the sharper the surge, but the broader the range, the lower is the peak efficiency. A typical automobile compressor has a 2:1 flow range, usually measured at a constant pressure ratio of 2.0.

When a turbo compressor is connected to an engine inlet manifold, the volume of the manifold is often not sufficient to damp out the pressure fluctuations arising from the periodic suction strokes of the pistons. As a result, even though the mean mass flow rate might be greater than the surge line obtained under steady flow compressor calibration tests, the minimum mass flow rate at the pulse peak may cause surge to develop, and an allowance needs to be made for this possibility.

The area to the right of the map is associated with very high gas velocities. When the flow rate reaches the velocity of sound at some cross-section, for example the throat of the impeller eye or the entry to the diffuser, 'choking' can occur. When this happens, the compressor speed can rise substantially with little increase in the mass flow rate.

The vaned and vaneless diffuser types of compressor will have distinctly differently shaped maps (see accompanying illustrations). The vaned diffuser type generally has a higher efficiency but a much narrower stable operating zone.

The internal combustion engine likes its charge air at the highest density at the lowest pressure. This points to the importance of compressor efficiency in keeping down the exit temperature and the desirability of charge air cooling. Low compressor efficiency requires a higher boost pressure to get the necessary volume, which also means higher temperatures. High compressor efficiency also reduces blade tip speed and therefore mechanical stress.

The behaviour of the turbocharger with increasing altitude is an important factor in its favour. Altitude effects are obviously important for aircraft engines, but can also be important for automotive engines which have to operate in mountainous countries. The density of air drops to 74% of the sea level density by the time 3,000 metres (10,000 feet) is reached, and for a naturally aspirated engine the output power will drop by the same amount, or even a little more. When a turbocharger is fitted, at wide open throttle the intake manifold pressure is almost the same regardless of altitude up to the

Illustration of the total gas pressure concept. The gauge at the side of the tube just measures the static pressure of the gas. The gauge whose inlet faces into the gas stream is also affected by the dynamic pressure of the moving gas and will show the total pressure – the sum of the static pressure and the dynamic pressure.

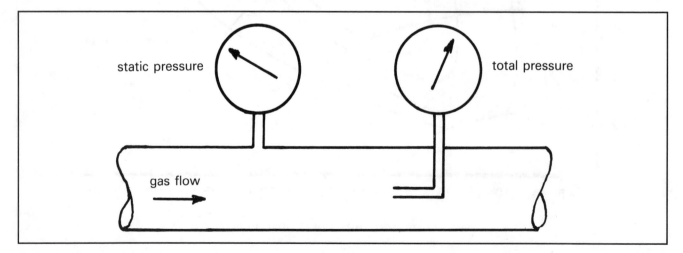

static pressure

total pressure

gas flow

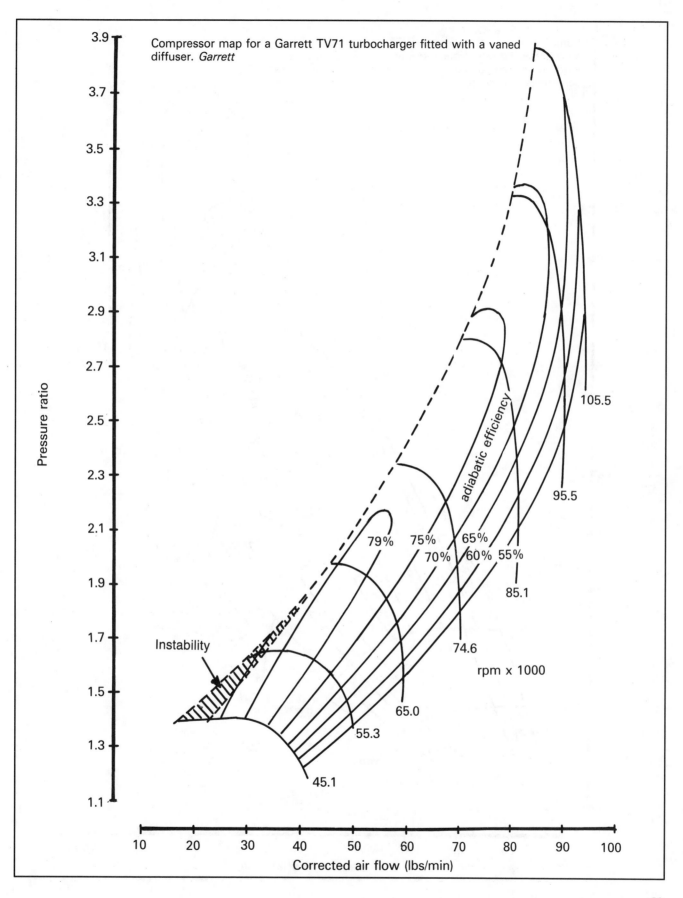

Compressor map for a Garrett TV71 turbocharger fitted with a vaned diffuser. *Garrett*

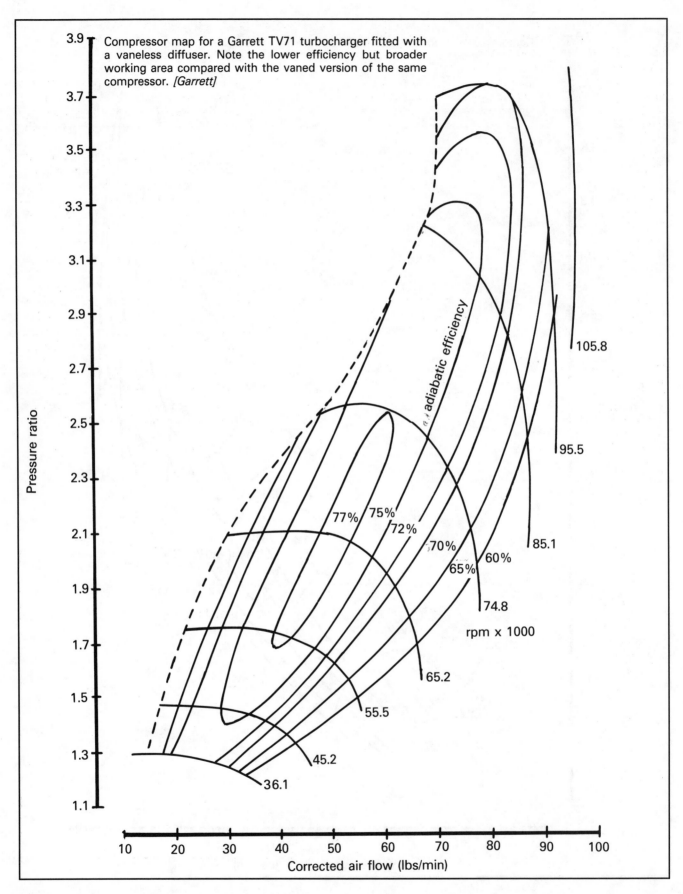

Compressor map for a Garrett TV71 turbocharger fitted with a vaneless diffuser. Note the lower efficiency but broader working area compared with the vaned version of the same compressor. *[Garrett]*

limits of the turbocharger capacity – the ambient pressure drops from one bar at sea level to 0.69 bar at 3,000 metres altitude. If a constant boost pressure of 0.69 bar is maintained, the absolute manifold pressure at sea level is 1.69 bar, and at 3,000 metres it is 1.38 bar. So while only 74% of the sea level power would be available when naturally aspirated, the figure becomes 82% when turbocharged.

In most automotive turbocharger installations there is an excess of turbine power which is thrown away at sea level by the operation of the boost pressure limiting systems. This means that this excess power can be used to compensate for the loss of air density. In addition, as a further compensation there will be a tendency for the turbine speed to rise with increasing altitude. As a rough rule of thumb, the turbocharger speed will increase approximately 2% per 300 metres of altitude[26].

A typical turbine performance map is illustrated which plots lines of constant corrected speed, corrected flow and overall 'turbine' efficiency versus total-to-static turbine pressure ratio. The discussion about compressor performance generally applies to turbines with a few notable exceptions.

A total-to-static pressure ratio is usually used because the exit conditions of the turbine cannot be predicted by the manufacturer. If the total discharge pressure were used this would give a higher nominal efficiency, but makes the assumption that the discharge kinetic energy would be recovered downstream of the turbine with zero loss.

The mechanical losses in the compressor/turbine combination are not readily measurable in a normal test situation. The compressor energy balance and efficiency can be measured and in the normal configurations this must absorb all of the turbine output. As a result, the turbine performance is usually debited with the rotor bearing losses. The quoted turbine efficiency is therefore the product of the true turbine efficiency and the mechanical efficiency.

Reference has already been made to different turbine A/R values being obtained by using a range of different housing shapes with the same rotor assembly. In addition, manufacturers will produce a range of rotor assemblies with varying 'trim' sizes so that turbochargers can be matched to almost any vehicle size. The accompanying illustration shows the working pressure ratio/mass flow limits recommended by KKK for their K-series turbochargers. Superimposed on the chart are the corresponding values for their R-series mechanically driven superchargers, showing how both types are related by the manufacturer to engine power output.

Performance map for a Garrett T025 turbine, with 62 trim and 0.53 A/R. The flow/pressure ratio curves at the different turbine speeds can hardly be separated and can be approximated by a single curve appropriate for the correct matched flow. The efficiency/pressure ratio curves are plotted separately so that the effect of turbine speed can be seen. [Garrett]

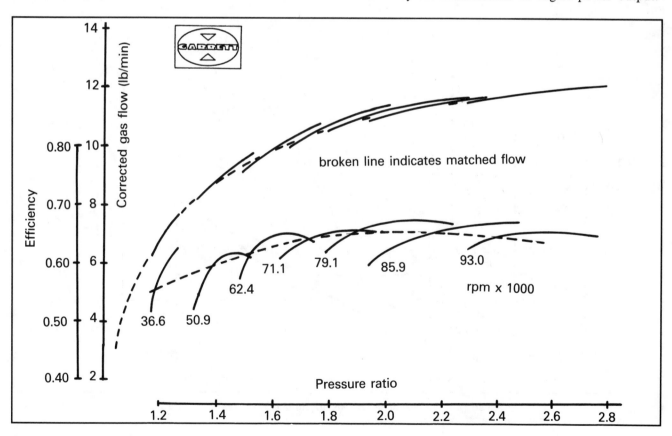

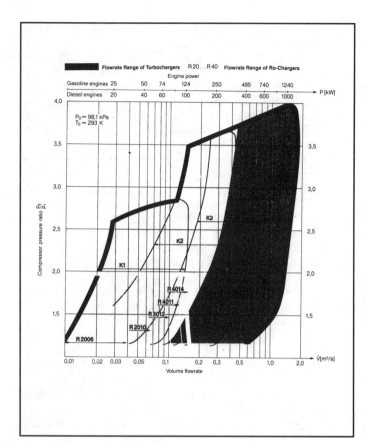

Overall operating ranges for the KKK families of
turbochargers and rotating piston superchargers, showing
the preferred applications for different engine sizes. *[KKK]*

Mechanically driven superchargers

A compressor map for a KKK R20 rotating piston
positive displacement supercharger is shown as an
example of the completely different characteristics of
the mechanically driven supercharger compared with
the turbo-compressor. The same parameters are plotted as are used for the centrifugal compressor maps
but the different shape of the curves is very clear; the
surge and choking zones are not applicable on such
a machine.

The use of the mass flow as the reference
parameter for the traditional turbocharger compressor map has resulted from it being the most useful
value when relating the compressor to both turbine
and engine. For mechanically driven, positive displacement superchargers, the speed of rotation of the compressor is a parameter which conveniently can be
directly related to the engine. As a result, many supercharger manufacturers use this as the basis for their
published data sheets.

The accompanying illustrations show drive speed
versus volume flow and pressure ratio, and drive speed
versus power consumption and pressure ratio for a

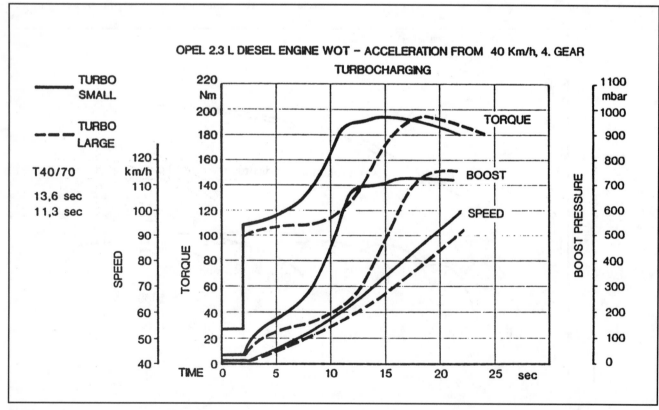

Graphs showing the different speed of response of an engine to sudden wide-open-throttle conditions when fitted with
alternative large- or small-diameter turbochargers. *[Opel]*

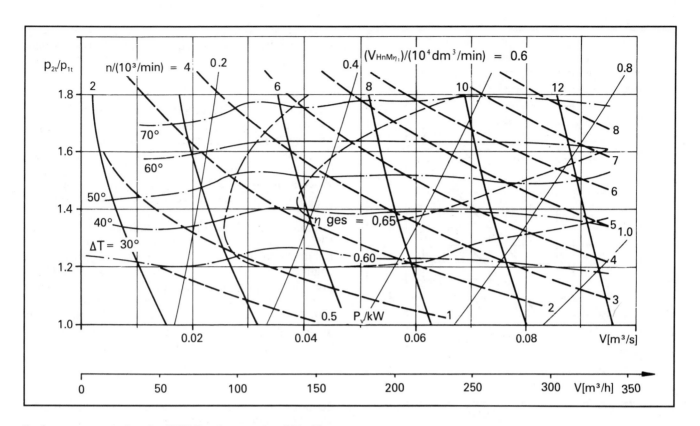

Performance map for the KKK Ro-charger size R20. The designations used in the diagram refer to the following:
[KKK]

Ro-charger:

p_{2t}/p_{1t} = total pressure ratio

ΔT = temperature differential

V = volume flowrate

η_{ges} = overall efficiency

P_v = power absorbed

n = charger speed

$n/(10^3/min)$ = lines of constant speed

Internal combustion engine:

V_H = swept volume

n_M = engine speed

η_1 = volumetric efficiency

$(V_H n_M \eta_1)/(10^4 dm^3/min)$ = engine running lines constant speed

Sprintex Lysholm spiral compressor as examples of the type of information which is needed in order to make a correct supercharger selection.

Even more different are the performance characteristics for the 'Comprex' pressure wave supercharger. It is difficult to directly compare these with either turbocharger maps or positive displacement supercharger performance curves as they can only be fully plotted for a specific engine installation. Nevertheless, an example is given for an engine with a CX93 charger which uses volume flow and pressure ratio as the main axes of the

Supercharger performance data for the Sprintex S102 Lysholm type spiral compressor. This diagram shows the relationship between engine speed, pressure ratio and volumetric efficiency ... *[Fleming Thermodynamics]* **9p10**

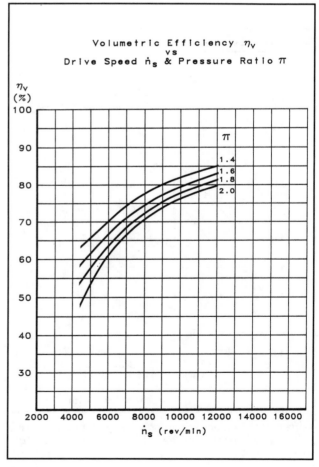

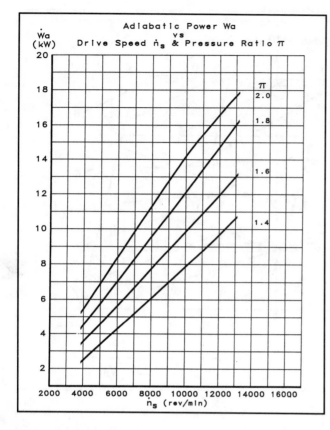

map. Curves are plotted on this graph for constant overall efficiency and various engine speeds, and the idle and full load boundaries are defined.

Another illustration was obtained from a CX85 Comprex installation on a Volkswagen 1.6-litre engine, which shows how the brake mean effective pressure and engine speed are related to different pressure ratios and adiabatic compression efficiency. At present, the interpretation of performance characteristics for the Comprex pressure wave supercharger is still an art which is known to few outside Asea-Brown Boveri and the engine manufacturers who have already installed Comprex units. However, this art is likely to need to become more widespread in the future amongst the after-market installers of supercharging systems, alongside their already extensive knowledge of turbochargers and mechanically driven superchargers.

Performance maps for a CX85 Comprex supercharger used on a Volkswagen 1.6-litre engine. [ABB]

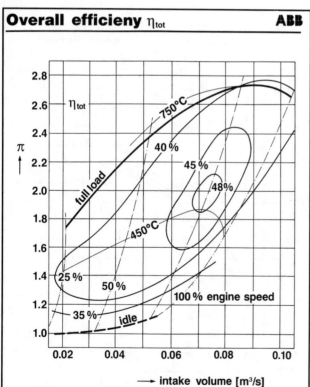

Apparent performance map for a Comprex pressure wave supercharger, plotted in the conventional manner. [ABB]

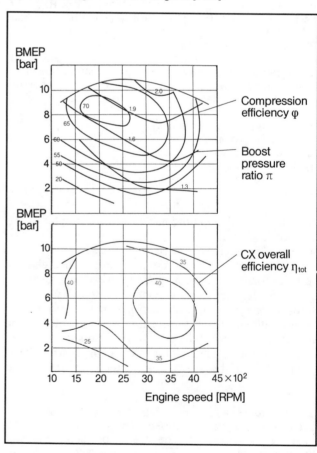

10

Turbocharger Design

The design trend in the passenger car industry is for lower and shorter hoods to reduce aerodynamic drag, with more equipment being crowded into the remaining space. The use of catalytic converters on gasoline engines and particulate traps on diesel engines all make additional demands on space. To a slightly lesser extent, the same squeeze on space also applies to truck engine compartments. One attraction of the turbocharger as a means of obtaining forced induction is its small size for a given mass flow; it has a large 'gulp' capacity.

Average performance turbomachines can be built with nothing more than just good basic mechanical engineering sense, but to build the high-performance machines of high 'gulp' capacity and small dimensions demanded by the automotive industry requires a lot of aerodynamic work of an analytical and experimental nature, supported by powerful digital computers. Modern turbochargers are very compact packages of high precision engineering components. It is easy to

forget that the internal power of a turbocharger can be likely 20% of the engine output, and potentially it could be as much as 100%.

A variety of different structural configurations have been used over the years for combining the compressor and turbine into one assembly. Early machines used the straddle bearing layout which was usual for steam turbines, and this is still used today for some large turbochargers. The bearings are well away from the compressor and turbine wheels, allowing ample axial space for seals for oil, air and gas. The stubshaft diameters can be made small because they do not influence the critical speed of vibration, giving low bearing peripheral speeds and losses. The bearings are commonly water-

Alternative bearing configurations for turbochargers
(a) straddled
(b) single overhang
(c) double overhang

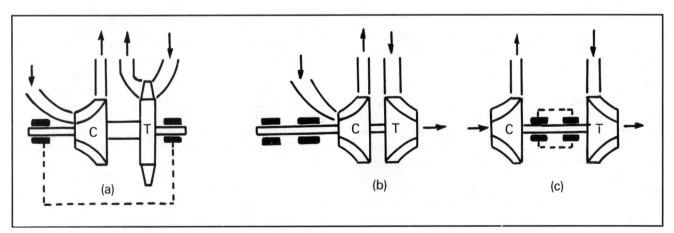

cooled. However, the structural connection between the bearings has to go through or around the air and hot gas flow passages which presents some difficulties.

The single overhung rotor, where the turbine and compressor wheels are back-to-back on one side of the bearing housings, is also used for large engines. This design can eliminate the disk friction in the gases, thus improving overall efficiency, although there are often problems of differential expansion between the compressor and turbine. The large overhang moment of the rotor assembly puts substantial bending stresses on the shaft. Air loss at the periphery of the compressor helps to cool the turbine wheel.

The centre bearing arrangement has been very widely adopted and is the most common configuration for small automotive turbochargers. Bearing sealing can present problems because of the limited space, but the air and gas housing ports can be easily adapted to many different engine layouts. The central housing can be readily designed to handle the temperature differential between turbine and compressor. This configuration is very suitable for lightweight, low-cost applications.

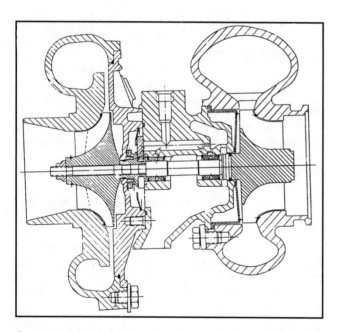

Cross-section of a typical small automobile turbocharger. The compressor is at the left and the turbine at the right. *[Garrett]*

Early turbocharger designs had ball or roller bearings with a separate lubricating oil pump, and the bearings were often water-cooled. As the size of the machines was reduced and the speed increased, it became increasingly difficult to get rolling bearings which could operate reliably at the high speeds. As a result, the majority of today's small-size turbochargers use sleeve bearings, lubricated and cooled by the main engine oil system.

The rotor will have hardened steel bearing surfaces

which run in simple sleeves fitted into recesses in the central housing. Aluminium has been used for these bearing bushes but the more common material is leaded bronze. Sometimes these bronze bearing sleeves have an added flashing of tin, lead or white metal.

Oil-lubricated sleeve bearings rely upon having a small clearance between shaft and sleeve into which the oil is dragged so that the shaft actually floats on a wedge of oil. This simple arrangement encounters problems as the speed of rotation increases. Every rotating object has a series of 'critical speeds' at which the object will start to vibrate like a tuning fork; the designer will try to make the rotor so stiff that the first critical speed is above the operating speed of the machine. Unfortunately, with the small high-speed turbocharger rotors this is not possible and shafts mounted in simple sleeve bearings started to 'whirl' at the critical speed. Because of the necessary clearance in the bearings, the centre of rotation of the shaft would start moving in the sleeves and the rotor could start violently rocking. The hydrodynamic forces on the oil film in the bearings tended to aggravate this situation.

A variety of different bearing sleeve designs were tried, including non-circular bores, together with many different oil grooves in the sleeves. The crucial development, now adopted in the majority of designs, was the introduction of the floating bearing sleeve. Not only does the sleeve have an internal clearance to the shaft, but it is also given an external clearance to the housing and is just located axially by circlips. In operation, not only is the shaft spinning in the bearing sleeve but the sleeve itself is also free to rotate in the housing at up to half the shaft speed. At the rotor critical speed, any forces which would start the shaft whirling are converted to sideways movements of the sleeve and are damped out by the action of the oil film between the sleeve and the housing.

In order to maintain the oil films there have to be ports in the housing and grooves and ports in the bearing sleeves. Pumping action on these can starve the bearings of oil, and recourse has had to be made to shaping the bush wall thickness and even shaping the housing wall to force oil to pump inwards.

Because the bearing sleeves rotate in the housing, the latter must be made of iron or steel to avoid wear. An alternative design which avoids this problem is the semi-floating bearing. The bearing sleeves still have a radial clearance in the housing but are located by pins so that they cannot rotate. Experiment showed that the damping effect of the floating sleeve bearing still applied, and a lower oil pressure could be used. As the sleeve has negligible movement relative to the housing, aluminium can be used for the housing without any wear problems. This can help to reduce the overall weight of the turbocharger.

The complete rotor assembly has to be located axially with some precision to minimise clearances around the turbine and compressor wheels. This is usually arranged by fitting a leaded bronze disk which forms

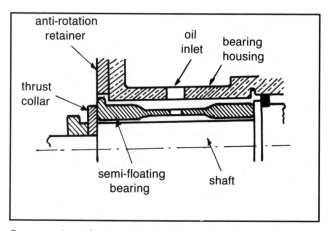

Cross-section of a semi-floating sleeve-bearing arrangement

a thrust bearing in conjunction with a shoulder on the rotor shaft. Despite this, due to the relatively large clearances which forced oil lubricated bearings must have, the clearance between the rotating wheels and their housing must be kept proportionately greater than that adopted on larger-size turbomachines; hence the peak efficiencies are lower due to leakage losses.

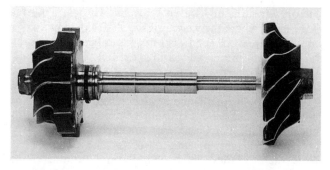

The turbine wheel, shaft and compressor wheel of a Garrett T2 turbocharger. The turbine is at the left. [Garrett]

The turbine wheel is usually much heavier than the compressor so the centre of gravity is closer to the turbine bearing. This complicates the stability of running, with any tendency to whirl occurring at the compressor end.

The turbine end bearing is exposed to extra heat conducted through the shaft and the housing and it is particularly important that the housing is designed to get rid of this heat as quickly as possible. During normal operation much of the heat will be carried away by the lubricating oil, but the serious problem comes when the engine is shut down. Heat from the exhaust system as well as the turbine wheel will continue to soak into the turbocharger, causing the bearing temperature to rise, possibly high enough to start decomposition of the residual oil film. If this happens, damage to the bearings can occur at the following cold start, as the turbine will usually start spinning before the lubricating oil

flow is fully re-established, and the build-up of layers of 'coke' can remove the needed running clearance.

To avoid this problem in high-performance, high-temperature engines it is common to use a water-cooled housing for the central part of the turbocharger. This is connected to the engine cooling circuit in such a position that even when the engine stops, the thermo-syphon effect will keep some coolant flowing. In addition, turbocharger manufacturers recommend the use of one of the synthetic engine lubricating oils, which are less likely to suffer breakdown at high temperatures.

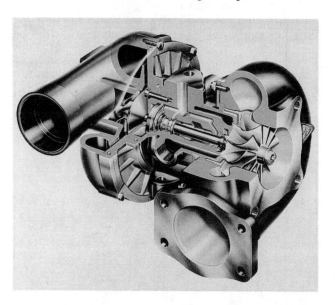

The KKK type K26 turbocharger with a water-cooled central housing. The cooling ducts close to the turbine bearing can be seen clearly at the right. [KKK]

The very high rotational speed of the rotor shaft, up to 200,000 rpm for some small turbochargers, causes the lubricating oil to be whipped up into a froth, which will then be mixed with any gas leakages from compressor and turbine. As a result, the oil drain-back to the main engine circuit has to be very large and free of any restrictions, to ensure that a smooth flow of this oil/gas mixture is maintained.

The central housing of the turbocharger contains a quantity of lubricating oil and the chambers at each end contain gases at varying pressures. It is therefore essential to provide some form of sealing to minimise leakage of oil outwards and air and exhaust gas inwards. Various types of non-contact labyrinth seals have been used over the years, but on small turbochargers the common solution now is to fit a piston ring into the housing just outboard of each bearing. The piston ring does not rotate; it is just designed to have a very small clearance on the shaft leaving only a thin leakage path.

At the turbine end the seal is nearly always subject to a positive pressure from the exhaust gases. The leakage past the piston ring will be entrained with the oil drain and usually released into the crankcase, to be taken away via the same route as the cylinder blow-by gases.

At the compressor end the problems are more complicated. Under high boost the situation is the same as at the turbine end, and high-pressure air which leaks past the piston ring seal will again be released via the oil drain. Although the compressor delivery or boost pressure at light engine load may be around atmospheric pressure, the pressure behind the compressor wheel can be much lower than this. Since there is a large quantity of oil in the centre housing, it follows that there is potentially a problem of this oil being sucked into the compressor housing. The piston ring reduces the flow but does not stop it completely; the piston ring is not an oil seal.

Some manufacturers use an oil deflector plate to separate the oil from the air. The tongue of the deflector plate must be well above the oil level in the centre

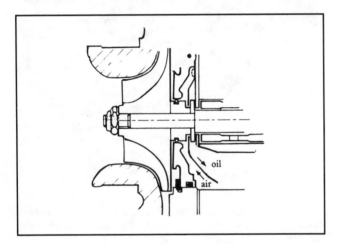

Example of an oil deflector plate fitted adjacent to the compressor bearing of a turbocharger in order to reduce the risk of oil being drawn past the piston ring seal. *[Garrett]*

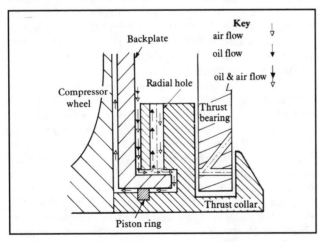

Arrangement of a dynamic oil seal. A mixture of gas and oil may get sucked towards the compressor wheel, but the perforated spinning seal plate centrifuges out the oil, allowing only the gas to reach the compressor. *[Garrett]*

housing to allow the air to pass underneath. The Garrett dynamic seal uses the thrust collar to separate air from the oil (see accompanying diagram). When the flow of oil and air reaches the radial holes in the thrust collar, the oil, being much more dense than the air, is centrifuged outwards and is separated from the air which continues to flow past the piston ring to the compressor housing.

For a diesel engine this design is quite satisfactory. However, the gasoline engine, using throttle control, can generate quite high vacuum conditions on over-run. Fuel injection systems can use a vacuum relief valve between throttle and compressor intake, or position the throttle after the compressor. If a suck-through carburettor is used, there is no alternative but to accept the high vacuum condition, and to deal with this requires some form of positive rubbing seal at the compressor end bearing.

Turbocharger speeds are much too high for the use of traditional synthetic rubber oil seals. The only effective contact seal has been a spring-loaded carbon disk rubbing against a shoulder on the shaft. This works well but it causes a significant loss of mechanical efficiency.

The floating bearing bushes do not rotate at low turbine speeds so the bearing losses increase. A number of experiments have been made in attempts to find satisfactory low-loss, high-speed bearings. Air bearings have been tried, where the weight of the shaft floats in a layer of compressed air, and also magnetic bearings, but so far the large size of the bearings required has closed off these developments.

More recently, high-speed ball bearings have been developed which are now widely used on video tape recorders and other consumer products. For turbochargers they are currently more expensive than sleeve bearings because of the need for heat resistance. Nevertheless, they have many benefits and some turbochargers are now in production using ball bearings.

Not only do they have low friction losses at all speeds, but the shape of the ball race eliminates the need for separate thrust bearings. Shaft movement is reduced, allowing smaller radial and axial clearances which give higher aerodynamic efficiencies. They still need some oil lubrication, but this is by a low-volume spray so that the leakage problems are reduced. The problem of heat soak-back is more serious and the turbine end bearing has to be water-cooled. Research work is leading towards the possibility of using a ceramic material for the ball which will ease the heat limitation problems.

Direct comparison of two turbochargers which differed only in the bearing type gave a bearing loss of 800 watts for the sleeve bearing version compared to 200 watts for the ball bearing version. The shaft movement maximum at 150,000 rpm was 0.025 mm compared with 0.13 to 0.25 mm for the sleeve bearings. As might be expected, the greatest efficiency improvement appeared at low speeds. With the ball bearings the turbocharger had a faster idle speed and this helped to improve acceleration response.

11

Supercharger manufacture

As with the discussion on supercharger performance in Chapter 9, this chapter deals first with the manufacturing issues for the most common supercharging device, the exhaust gas driven turbocharger. Features which are specific to the other types of supercharger on the market are covered at the end of the chapter.

In the turbocharger, the design of the compressor impeller has to be a compromise between aerodynamic

Alternate blades on this compressor impeller are shorter than their neighbours. This reduces the restriction at the central inducer point. *[Garrett]*

requirements, mechanical strength considerations and foundry capabilities. To achieve higher mass flow and compressor efficiency, very thin and sharp impeller blades are desirable, but to keep the levels of steady state and vibratory stresses low, a robust thick-at-the-root blade is needed. The tip thickness is dictated by considerations of casting techniques and blade stiffness. It is common practice to use splitter blades that extend from part way through the inducer up to the impeller tip to aid flow control while minimising blockage at the eye.

A straight-bladed impeller is easy to make using die casting or similar techniques, but it has a relatively low efficiency due to shock losses at the inlet. Curvature of the blades at the inducer is required so that air entering the impeller will be at exactly the same angle as the blade. Combined with the tip shaping this makes it difficult to manufacture.

Compressor impellers are normally manufactured in a high-strength aluminium alloy which can be cast at a relatively low temperature. The most commonly used manufacturing technique is the 'lost wax/plaster' process. A wax replica of the impeller is placed in a container which is filled with plaster. When the plaster is hard, the wax is melted out leaving a cavity corresponding to the desired impeller shape, which is then filled with molten alloy under pressure. When the casting is cold, the plaster mould is broken away to reveal the complete impeller. This process can give a very high surface finish. A recent development of the process uses a rubber pattern instead of the wax one.

The compressor housing will also be cast in an aluminium alloy. By carefully choosing the shape of the openings for the impeller wheel and the air intake and outlet, it is possible to get a compromise housing design which can be produced by pressure die casting. The surfaces of the impeller and housing must be kept as smooth as possible to avoid eddy current losses in the air flow.

In early turbochargers, the turbine wheel would be built up from a series of separate blade segments, but today's small automotive turbines usually have the wheel cast in one piece. The material is normally a high-temperature austenitic nickel steel alloy, such as Inconel 713, which can work up to temperatures of 1,100°C. Alloys of this type are generally used in jet aircraft turbines and the material is readily available[49].

Early designs had the turbine wheel attached to the rotor shaft by bolting but this was soon replaced by more secure techniques. Brazing in an inert gas, electric resistance welding and electron welding have all been used at some time. Now the majority of turbine wheel/shaft joins are made using inertia friction welding. In this process the turbine wheel is held in a chuck on a heavy flywheel which can be spun up to a high speed. At the appropriate speed, the drive power to the flywheel is cut off and the end of the turbine shaft is brought into contact with the spinning wheel under pressure. The frictional heat generated melts the metal of wheel and shaft and they weld together under the axial pressure. The stored energy in the spinning flywheel is adjusted so that just the correct amount of heat is generated to obtain consistent welds.

A completed inertia weld of a turbine wheel to its shaft. This process gives a more consistent and stronger weld than any other current method. *[Garrett]*

New designs of bearings, particularly ball bearings, have reduced the importance of having hardened bearing surfaces on the shaft. In conjunction with improved foundry techniques this has given the possibility of using a single casting combining turbine wheel and shaft in one piece.

The geometrical layout of the vaneless turbine housing is designed to feed the exhaust gas into the rotor as if there is a vortex with its centre at the rotor centre, the aim being to give the gas a constant inlet angle and velocity around the periphery of the turbine rotor. This gives a characteristic spiral shape to the turbine housing.

Turbine casings are commonly cast in spheroidal graphite (SG) iron which is satisfactory for working up to about 700°C, a typical temperature for diesel applications. Above that temperature the regular temperature cycling can cause the metal to start scaling. For the hotter exhausts of gasoline engines, a high-silicon-content SG iron can be used for temperatures up to about 850-900°C, but above this temperature a high nickel content cast iron would be used. This can resist scaling at temperatures above 1,000°C, is less prone to

INERTIA WELDING

Today the turbine wheel is usually secured to the turbocharger shaft by inertia welding. Both shaft and wheel have a hole at the centre. The wheel is spun at high speed and then the shaft is forced against it with considerable pressure. The frictional heating as the two parts come together causes the metal around the holes to melt and weld together. *[Garrett]*

Compressor wheel balance being checked. This machine includes an automatic grinding facility to correct any balance errors at the same work station. *[Garrett]*

cracking from thermal cycling, but is more expensive. The high nickel alloys are likely to be used for marine applications even on lower-temperature diesel engines because of the 'higher corrosion risk in the salty atmosphere.

The compressor impeller will sometimes be attached to the end of the rotor shaft by shrink fitting, but the most common technique is to roll a thread on the end of the shaft and hold the impeller on with a self-locking nut. The impeller would also retain on the shaft the thrust bearing ring as well as any oil flinger sleeve and spacers. If the turbocharger has a right-hand rotation there could be a tendency for a normal right-hand-threaded nut to loosen, so a left-hand thread may be used.

A crucial stage in the manufacture of turbochargers is the balancing of the rotor components. At one time, only the complete compressor/turbine rotor assembly was balanced, but this could still give out-of-balance forces within the assembly and it also presented problems if any maintenance had to be done. Current practice is to balance each component separately, the compressor impellers and the welded turbine/shaft combinations, and then check the overall balance after assembly.

The thread for securing the compressor wheel on to the turbine shaft is rolled rather than cut to optimise the overall strength. *[Garrett]*

The component to be tested is spun in a special machine where sensitive electromagnetic detectors measure vibrations and display them on an electronic display which identifies the locations for the removal of small amounts of metal. A suitable cutting tool or grinding wheel is usually incorporated in the machine so that the trimming can be done automatically. The balance is then rechecked and the process repeated if necessary until the out-of-balance is within design tolerances.

It is normal practice with modern small automotive turbochargers to assemble the turbine wheel and shaft, bearings, seals, and compressor impeller with the central housing into a complete 'cartridge' which is commonly the maintenance replacement assembly. When this unit is complete it will be placed into a test rig which provides lubrication to the bearings and uses compressed air to spin the assembly up to its design speed. A final check on vibrations will be made at this point.

The complete central assembly of the Garrett T2 turbocharger with the turbine wheel at the left, an air-cooled central housing, and the compressor impeller at the right. This would be the normal maintenance replacement unit. [Garrett]

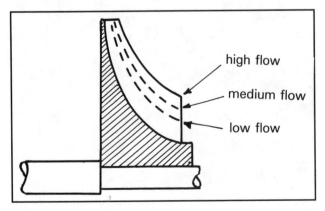

An illustration of different 'trim' sizes to produce a family of turbine wheels from the same basic casting.

Compressor and turbine housings are attached to the central assembly by clamps which allow the housings to be rotated relative to the central unit to any angle required by the engine manufacturer. For one particular size of central unit there will be a number of different compressor and turbine housings to meet the required mass flow conditions. To match this, the standard impellers are machined for the different flow rates.

The Garrett T2 range shows how these manufacturing ideas are applied in practice. The standard and high-flow versions of the T2 cover gasoline (diesel) engine displacements from about 1.2 to 2.5 litres (1.4 to 3.0 litres)[45].

A 'family' of turbochargers which are suitable for diesel and gasoline engines in a power range of 20 to 350 kw per turbocharger. [KKK]

For maximum applicability to a range of engine types, the standard T2 turbocharger is offered in three compressor wheel trims. Trim is defined as the ratio $(D_i/D_t)^2$, where D_i and D_t are respectively the inducer and tip diameters of the compressor wheel. It has also five different turbine housing sizes, as measured by five values of the turbine housing parameter A/R, where A is the cross-sectional area of the turbine housing at the wheel inlet and R is the radius of the centroid of the housing at this point. The turbine housing size is selected to match the engine flow and back-pressure (power extraction) requirements of a given application.

The compressor impeller has backward-curved blades which help achieve the wide flow range required for passenger car turbochargers; it has 12 blades, six full and six splitters. The T2 has a radial inflow turbine 47 mm in diameter with 11 blades and a 0.57 trim. The five A/R values cover an approximate two-fold range in turbine flow rate.

The complete Garrett T25 turbocharger with integral wastegate, servo motor and water-cooled bearing housing. This compact unit is standard equipment on many smaller automobiles. *[Garrett]*

Mounting is by the turbine inlet flange. The turbocharger centre line is installed within ± 10° of the horizontal to ensure adequate oil drainage from the centre housing. To accommodate different installations, the angle between the turbine housing and the compressor housing may be varied over a range of 290°. The maximum operating speed is 190,000 rpm.

As turbochargers have been applied to ever smaller engines a number of problems have been encountered which are associated with the reduction in size. The minimum working clearances, the surface roughness of the components and the bearing frictional losses all remain the same, so the efficiency of the unit inevitably drops. The developments which have taken place in an attempt to address these problems also coincide with the need to improve the transient response of turbochargers under the rapidly changing conditions of passenger car use. Attention has been focused on reducing the friction of the rotating group, reducing the moment of inertia of the rotating components, and changing the inlet geometry of the turbocharger.

At turbocharger speeds of less than 40,000 rpm, bearing friction is the major hindrance to good response. Friction losses occur in the bearings and the seals and, depending on bearing type, oil viscosity and oil pressure, in conventional turbochargers the losses are in the region of 0.2 to 0.3 horsepower at 40-50,000 rpm.

Over the main working range of the turbocharger the 'moment of inertia' of the rotor is the critical factor in how quickly the speed can change. The 'moment of inertia' is the measure of the resistance of a rotating mass to any change in speed. Any rotating mass, for example a turbine wheel, could be replaced by a very thin representative ring of the same mass (M) whose radius is known as the 'radius of gyration' (K). The moment of inertia (I) is then given by K^2M. To use the weight (W) instead of the mass, it is necessary to introduce the gravitational constant (g), so that $I = K^2(W/g)$.

For larger mass flow engines, a simple way of reducing the effective inertia to get better transient response is to use two smaller turbochargers instead of one large one, and this is common with V-6 or V-8 configuration engines.

The moment of inertia is proportional to the fourth power of the diameter, so reducing diameter seems to

The 'moment of inertia' of a rotating object is the measure of its resistance to any change of speed. Any rotating mass, for example a turbine wheel, can be replaced by a representative thin ring of the same mass (M) whose radius is known as the 'radius of gyration' (K).

The moment of inertia $I = K^2M = K^2W/g$, where W is the weight and g is the acceleration due to gravity.

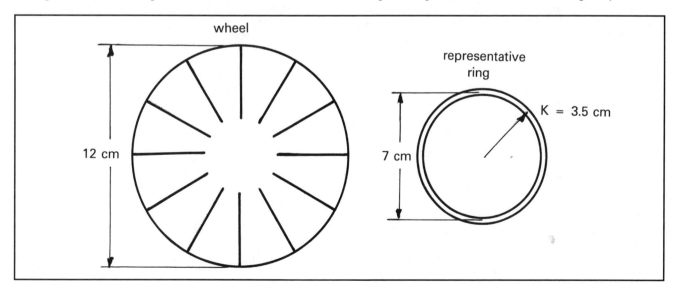

be one way to reduce the inertia. However, a smaller diameter means greater speed to maintain the necessary tip velocity, and the higher speed can result in greater mechanical stresses. The use of a turbine wheel in which the flow is much more axial instead of the more conventional radial wheel can also reduce the rotating inertia, as the turbine rotor accounts for about 85% of the moment of inertia.

Much development work has been done in introducing the use of ceramics for turbocharger rotors. The materials normally used have a much lower density than steel so that the rotating system potentially has a much lower moment of inertia and faster response to transients. In practice, due to the lower tensile strength of the ceramics, the rotor wheels must have thicker sections so that the net weight saving is not quite as great as might be expected. Ceramics are, however, cheaper than the exotic high-temperature metal alloys which are frequently needed[47].

A ceramic turbine wheel can survive much higher temperatures, which even for passenger cars can now exceed 1,000°C. Because of the lower density, the thermal energy stored is less than for the equivalent steel wheel, which all helps to improve the transient response.

The turbine and compressor housings always have to be thick enough to contain any fragments in the event of the rotor bursting due to overspeeding. The lower stored energy in the lighter ceramic rotor allows the wall thicknesses to be reduced a little.

The German company KKK have made and tested silicon carbide and silicon nitride one-piece injection-moulded turbine wheels with integral shafts, and have been obtaining rotor weights in the region of 0.05 kg compared with 0.19 kg for the previous metal rotor. The target for metal rotors is 1,080 to 1,100°C operating temperatures; the target values for the experimental ceramic rotors were set at 1,230°C temperature, and a peripheral speed of 500 metres/second.

The basic problems of ceramic rotors are brittleness, vulnerability to particle impact from exhaust manifold scaling, and the difficulty of maintaining consistency of production quality. Life expectancy in service needs to be greater than 90,000 km and tests have so far exceeded 150,000 km.

The Honda Formula 1 racing engine, which was used until the change of formula in 1989, used an IHI type RX6 turbocharger. This had a 62.9 mm diameter turbine and an 82.0 mm diameter compressor impeller, with a total weight for the unit of 4.1 kg. The maximum pressure ratio was 5.5, the maximum speed was 160,000 rpm, and the maximum exhaust gas temperature was 1,170°C. The turbine wheel was made from silicon nitride, and the complete rotor assembly ran in ball bearings using a special M50 metal with oil-jet cooling.

Nissan carried out a series of tests on four variations of a standard turbocharger[40]. They reduced the number of compressor blades from 11 to 9, but improved the aerodynamics. This reduced the moment of inertia by 25% and enhanced the boost pressure by 14%. The turbine rotor was reduced from 60 mm to 49.9 mm in diameter, which gave a 34% reduction in the moment of inertia compared with the equivalent metal rotor. They introduced a simple, single-flap vane, variable geometry turbine which gave effective A/R changes from 0.21 to 0.77. They also changed the sleeve bearings to ball bearings which were of 8 mm inside diameter and 22 mm outside diameter, and finally they changed from a metal to a ceramic turbine rotor. The comparative performances for these different variations obtained under test conditions are listed in the following table:

	Time to 40kPa boost press (sec)	Improvement in response %
Standard	5.3	100	base
Small diameter	3.8	72	28
Small dia/variable geometry	2.7	51	29
Small dia/var geom/ball bearings	2.1	28	45
Small dia/var geom/bb/ceramic rotor	1.6	21	24

If the use of ceramics allows the turbine rotor to operate at a much higher temperature, it is likely that the limiting factor may become the turbine housing. In an attempt to ease this problem and reduce the need for expensive high-temperature casting alloys, experiments have been made on depositing a ceramic layer on the inside of the turbine housing. One aspect of permitting increased turbine inlet temperatures is the need for better jointing techniques between exhaust manifold and turbocharger. Conical profile joints mounted with a non-positive connection are being used so that the joint will be completely free of tensile stress.

Another change in manufacturing methods which is beginning to appear derives from experience with high-performance aircraft. The inside of the compressor casing is treated to give a very fine controlled roughness which can delay the onset of air flow stall.

Other types of superchargers

The detail manufacturing processes for the various types of mechanically driven superchargers all differ, but they have a number of principles in common. They make considerable use of high-strength light alloys for the rotating elements and for the housings in order to minimise the total weight and to reduce the inertia of the rotor. Although high-inertia rotors do not directly affect the pressure/speed relationship, they place great loads on the drive system during rapid engine speed changes.

Use is made of low-friction plastic coatings and strips for un-lubricated sealing of air leakage paths. Synchronising gears between the various rotating elements will generally be helically cut to achieve quiet running and will run in a lubricant which is kept in a separate chamber from the main air flow; a connection to the engine lubricating oil system is not normally needed.

Because of the low running speeds compared with turbochargers, it is possible to safely use rolling bearings. At least one bearing on each shaft will be a caged ball type which is able to accept the axial thrust which comes from the helical gears as well as any aerodynamic forces.

Because the compression principle of the device usually defines where the inlet and outlet ports have to be relative to each other, there is not a great deal of flexibility in the pipe connection options. The engine manufacturers will therefore usually have to make some form of adaptor to match the supercharger mounting to the engine manifolds; these are commonly formed in die-cast light alloy.

Use of a toothed or grooved belt to drive the supercharger from the engine crankshaft is still the favoured method. These belts are today very reliable and can transmit quite large amounts of power. Care has to be taken, however, to ensure that the bends in the belt around the pulleys are not too sharp, that sufficient contact area is given to avoid any risk of slip, and that adequate arrangements are made for tensioning the belt. Spring-loaded tensioners are sometimes used to help to absorb the inertia load peaks during rapid engine speed changes.

Opel have proposed an installation arrangement which mounts the alternator on the back of a mechanically driven supercharger, with the two shafts coupled

together. This simplifies the belt drive arrangements which, with drives for cooling pumps, hydraulic pumps and air conditioners, can become very complex on modern automobile engines.

Let us now look at how these general principles have been applied in some specific examples, starting with the 'Sprintex' spiral compressor.

The two spirally-vaned rotors are made from Teflon-coated aluminium, mounted on manganese-molybdenum alloy steel shafts, and they are machined to allow the smallest possible clearance between them as they mesh – less than 0.002 mm. The male rotor has four lobes and the female rotor has six flutes, and they are designed to have great stiffness to avoid any resonances with crankshaft vibrations. The rotors are mounted in an anodised cast aluminium casing which is also machined to the same very fine tolerances and which is externally finned to assist cooling.

Drive for the rotor shafts is via a set of helical, precision-ground timing gears. These gears are in their own separate chamber, running in an oil bath; a breather vent allows for any leakage past the rolling bearings. A toothed belt drive is used.

The KKK rotating piston Ro-lader has the inner and outer rotors coupled together by 3:2 ratio concentric gears which maintain the synchronisation between the elements. The outer gear, attached to the 'cylinder' rotor, has the teeth on the inside, and these engage with the teeth on the central gear mounted on the 'piston' rotor.

The concentric shafts are mounted in ball bearings, and the bearings and gears are grease-lubricated, needing no lubricating oil supply from the engine. The working principle allows for a very compact unit to be built relative to the air volume which is handled. The rotors and housing are all made of light alloy so that the over-

A design for the combination of generator and mechanically driven supercharger with a single belt drive. *[Opel]*

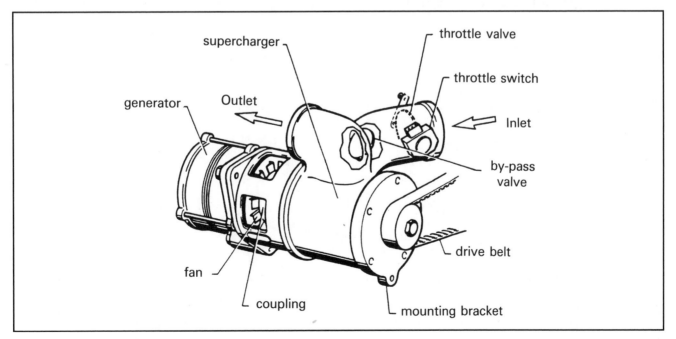

all weight is also kept down. A ribbed vee-belt is used for the drive from the engine crankshaft. No contact seal system is possible with this configuration and pressure losses are minimised by accurate machining of the components to leave only small leakage paths between the various elements.

The Volkswagen G-lader exhibits some interesting constructional features as a result of its unusual semi-rotating movements. The housing, including the fixed spirals, is aluminium, pressure die-cast in two halves. The displacer spiral itself is made of magnesium and is assembled between the two halves of the outer casing.

Because the drive shaft is only slightly eccentric, even at high engine speeds only low relative speeds occur between the displacer spiral and the housing. This makes it possible to use simple, unlubricated sealing elements of a PTFE/bronze compound to minimise gap losses. The seals, which are fitted to the edges of the fixed spirals, also act to locate the moving spirals axially. The low inertia of the driven elements also minimises the stresses on the drive from the engine.

The auxiliary shaft which guides the blower spiral is driven via a toothed belt from the main shaft, at the opposite end from the main drive. To compensate for dimensional deviations because of machining tolerances and expansion due to heating, the eccentric bearing of this shaft is mounted in a rubber element with coordinated spring characteristics. The main drive shaft bearings are directly connected to the engine oil circulation; the auxiliary shaft runs in maintenance-free roller bearings. An internally ribbed belt is used to take the main drive from the engine crankshaft.

The importance of this design to the development of mechanical supercharging is that, unlike most of the other designs on the market, it does not depend upon high-precision machined components for its effectiveness, and the few components lend themselves to the type of mass-production operations which are cheap to carry out. This should ensure that the G-lader is competitive with the simple turbocharger when applied to engines up to 2 litres.

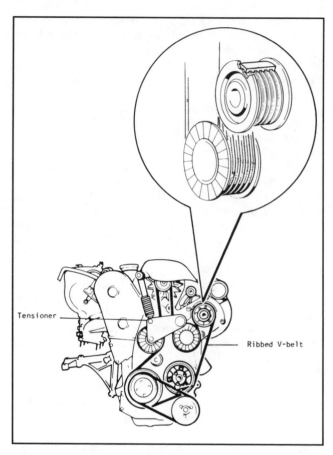

The belt drive system for the G-lader supercharger on the Volkswagen 1.8-litre Golf engine. *[Volkswagen]*

12

Exhaust systems

In an earlier chapter it was shown how there was energy available in the engine exhaust gases which could potentially be made available for driving a turbocharger. Let us now look at these exhaust processes in more detail.

Illustrated is an ideal four-stroke pressure/volume diagram for a turbocharged engine. P_1 is the supercharging pressure, P_7 is the exhaust manifold back pressure, and P_a is the ambient pressure. During the induction stroke (12-1), a fresh charge at the compressor delivery pressure enters the cylinder. This is followed by compression, combustion and expansion (1-2-3-4-5). When the exhaust valve first opens (point 5), some of the gas in the cylinder escapes to the exhaust manifold, expanding along the line 5-7, and the pressure of the remaining gas in the cylinder falls down the line 5-13.

During the exhaust stroke (13-11), the cylinder contents are displaced through the exhaust valve into the exhaust pipe against the back pressure P_7. At the end of this stroke the cylinder retains a volume (V_{cl}) of residual combustion products, which for simplicity can be assumed to remain there. The maximum possible energy that could be extracted during the exhaust stroke will be represented by the area 7-8-10-11, where 7-8 represents expansion down to the ambient pressure.

There are two distinct areas representing energy available from the exhaust gas – the blow-down energy (area 5-8-9) and the work done by the piston (area 13-9-10-11). The maximum possible energy available to drive the turbine will clearly be the sum of these two areas. However, it is difficult to devise a system that could harness all this energy. To achieve that, the turbine inlet pressure must rise instantaneously to P_5 when the exhaust valve opens, followed by expansion of the exhaust gas through P_7 to the ambient pressure ($P_8 = P_a$). During the displacement part of the exhaust

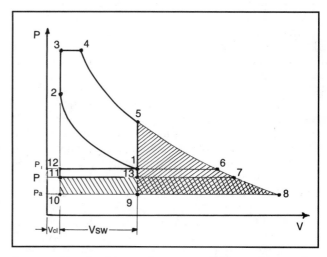

An example of a four-stroke pressure/volume diagram for a turbocharged engine showing the available exhaust energy. The exhaust portion of the cycle has been exaggerated to emphasise the different areas.

process, the expulsion stroke, the turbine inlet pressure must be held at P_7. Such a sequence of processes is clearly impracticable.

Consider a simple arrangement in which a large chamber is fitted between the engine and the turbine inlet, in order to damp down the pulsating exhaust gas flow[42]. By forming a restriction to flow, the turbine may maintain its inlet pressure at P_7 for the whole cycle. The available work at the turbine will then be given by the area 7-8-10-11. This is the ideal 'constant pressure' system. Next consider an alternative system, in which a turbine wheel is placed directly downstream of the exhaust valve. If there were no losses in the port, the gas would expand directly out through the turbine along line 5-6-7-8. If the turbine area were sufficiently large, both cylinder and turbine inlet pressures would drop to P_9 ($= P_a$) before the piston had moved significantly up the bore. Hence the available energy at the turbine would be given by area 5-8-9. This can be considered the ideal 'pulse' system.

These two alternatives, the constant pressure and pulse systems, represent two distinct, mutually exclusive design approaches for turbocharger exhaust systems, each having its own preferred application area.

In a constant pressure system the volume of the exhaust manifold should be sufficient to damp pressure pulsations down to a low level. It depends on engine type, number of cylinders, etc, but is likely to be in the range of 1.4 to 6 times the total swept volume of the engine. If the volume is not large enough, the 'blow-down' pulse from a cylinder will raise the general pressure in the manifold. If the engine has more than three cylinders it is inevitable that this will coincide with another cylinder nearing the end of its exhaust process, and impede that process. In this system the turbine will run in its most efficient state because of the relatively constant working pressure. Any heat lost from the exhaust manifold will result in reduced energy available at the turbine, so it is sensible to insulate the manifold. The manifold is usually simple to construct even if it is bulky, and this can be a great benefit on large engines.

In a pulse exhaust system, at the moment the exhaust valve starts to open, the pressure in the cylinder will be many times the pressure in the exhaust manifold. As a result the pressure drop across the valve is above the critical choking pressure ratio, and the flow in the valve throat will be sonic (Mach number = 1). At this point, throttling losses at the valve are high. As the pressure in the manifold rises the velocity becomes sub-sonic. The speed at which the valve opens to its full area and the size of the exhaust manifold become important factors so far as energy utilisation is concerned. A small exhaust manifold causes a rapid fall of manifold pressure towards the end of the exhaust process, improving scavenging and reducing pumping work in a four-stroke engine. Some of the pumping loss in clearing out the cylinder is compensated by the motoring effect from the incoming high-pressure air.

Because the initial gas velocity at the exhaust valve opening is sonic, a pressure wave is generated which travels along the pipe at high velocity, carrying a substantial amount of energy. A large proportion of this energy is pressure, and only a small portion is the kinetic energy of gas movement which is affected by any pipe friction. Thus, small diameter pipes from port to turbine are highly desirable. The optimum will be a compromise, but the cross-sectional area should not be significantly greater than the geometric valve area at full lift. These connections should be kept short and free of sharp bends.

The actual gas flow through a pulse exhaust system

is, of course, very unsteady and is affected by pulse reflections from the turbine and closed exhaust valves. Consider, for simplicity, a single cylinder engine connected through a narrow exhaust pipe to a turbine. During the first part of the exhaust process, the pressure rises in the pipe at the valve and is transmitted along the pipe in the form of a pressure wave. This wave, arriving at the turbine, will be partially reflected by the small throat area of the turbine. The reflected pressure wave will return along the pipe and may impede flow at the exhaust valve, dependent on the time at which it arrives there.

The reflection time is a function of the exhaust pipe length and, to a lesser extent, temperature, since the velocity of sound is a function of temperature. The effect of the reflected wave on the pressure at the exhaust valve is shown in the accompanying diagram with four different pipe lengths. In case 1, the pipe is long and the reflected wave arrives after the exhaust valve has closed, having no effect. For a shorter pipe (case 2) the reflected wave arrives in the middle of the scavenge period, preventing a two-stroke engine from running at all and impairing the performance of a four-stroke engine. In case 3, a still shorter pipe results in a partial addition of pressure waves creating a second pressure peak in the middle of the exhaust process. This secondary pressure peak raises the available energy in the manifold, but since it occurs during the second part of the exhaust process, after blow-down, when the piston is displacing the exhaust gas, this gain will be at the expense of increased piston pumping work. If the exhaust pipe is very short (case 4) the pressure waves will be virtually superimposed, increasing the available energy during the important blow-down period.

The pressure pulse arising from the exhaust of a cylinder travels along the manifold until it reaches a junction. At the junction it divides into two pulses, one travelling down each pipe, and each of smaller magnitude due to the effective area increase. One pulse will travel towards the turbine, the other will arrive at the exhaust valve of another cylinder. This type of interference, due to the direct action of a pressure wave from another cylinder, is quite separate from the action of a pressure pulse reflected from the turbine.

The overall pressure wave system that occurs in such a manifold will be very complex, with pulses propagating from each cylinder, pulse division at each junction, total or partial reflection at an exhaust valve (depending on whether it is closed or not), and reflection from the turbine. Fortunately, pulse division at junctions weakens the pulses and hence the system of pressure waves is weakened at each point and each reflection, so it is usually only the direct pulses and first reflections that are important.

On a multi-cylinder engine, narrow pipes from several cylinders can be connected through a single branched manifold to one turbine. A four-stroke engine which can have its cylinders grouped in threes is particularly attractive. Due to the phase angle between the

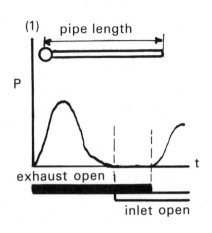

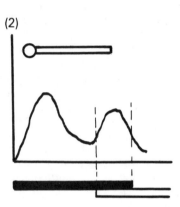

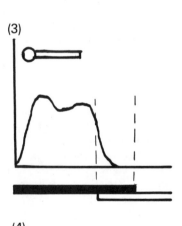

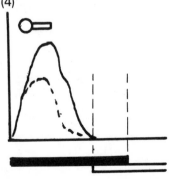

Changes of exhaust pulse reflections with pipe length
(1)   Long pipe – the reflected pulse arrives after the exhaust valve has closed.
(2)   Shorter pipe – the reflected pulse arrives during the scavenge period, causing impairment in engine performance.
(3)   Even shorter pipe – partial addition of the pressure pulses but at the expense of increased piston pumping work.
(4)   Very short pipe – pressure waves are superimposed, increasing available energy.

cranks of the three cylinders, the opening periods of the exhaust valves follow successively every 240° with very little overlap between them. Thus a sequence of pressure pulses arrives at the turbine which virtually eliminates long periods of windmilling, although the average turbine efficiency will remain lower than that obtained with a correctly matched constant pressure system. However, even for engines whose number of cylinders is not a multiple of three, the loss in turbine efficiency due to unsteady flow is usually more than offset by the additional energy available at the turbine, hence the pulse system is used far more widely than the constant pressure system.

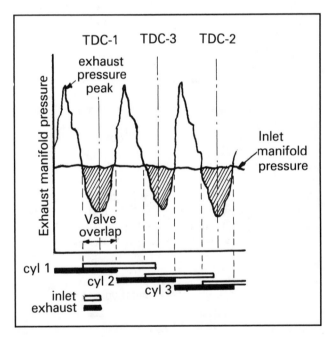

Exhaust pressure pulsations in a three-cylinder manifold branch of a six-cylinder engine.

Other attractive features of the pulse system are that it is possible to arrange for the pressure just downstream of the exhaust valve to fall substantially below the cylinder and inlet manifold pressure during any valve overlap period, giving good scavenging even at low engine load when boost pressure is low; in addition, better acceleration response is obtained because the small-volume exhaust gives rapid energy transfer by pressure waves to the turbine. In one particular test, pulse turbocharging gave a 24% improvement in transient response.

A disadvantage is that a turbocharger correctly matched to an engine operating with the pulse system may need a larger turbine than would be fitted for a constant pressure system, as the turbine must be sized to accept the higher instantaneous flow rates.

Large-volume, constant pressure exhaust manifolds are best applied to large engines operating for long periods at constant speed and medium to high loads, for example power generation and marine propulsion. The small-volume pulse manifolds are most appropriate for engines with rapidly varying load and speed, and have therefore been generally adopted for automotive applications. An exception to this is the Comprex pressure wave supercharger which has to operate with a near constant manifold pressure for best effect.

Three-cylinder engines are not very common, but six-cylinder ones are, and the use of twin turbochargers on such engines allows a very efficient pulse exhaust system to be designed. Where the engine is not large enough to justify twin turbochargers, a split inlet turbine may be adopted. This is a common arrangement for diesel engines but, as was noted in an earlier chapter, the dividing wall becomes a likely source of failure at the higher exhaust temperatures applicable with a gasoline engine. Two cylinders feeding one turbine (or turbine inlet) is not a very attractive option due to the amount of idling time in the cycle when the turbine rotor will just be 'windmilling'. Four cylinders is the more common grouping, and careful manifold design can obtain a substantial pulse effect without too much reflection loss.

A technique which has been adopted to link simple pulse system manifolds into a single turbine entry is the use of 'pulse converters'. A pulse converter is a specially designed pipe junction which includes geometrical arrangements to introduce relatively large pressure losses in certain directions so that the useful pressure pulses are propagated with minimum loss while undesired reflections are reduced. The detailed analysis of such

junctions is quite complex; an asymmetrical junction layout needs 12 different loss coefficients to be evaluated.

In 1946, R. Birmann patented the first 'pulse converter' system[42]. His objective was to design a device that preserved the unsteady flow of gases from the cylinders while maintaining a steady flow at the turbine. To achieve good scavenging Birmann proposed a 'jet-pump' system, using a high-velocity jet of gas, issuing from a central nozzle, to reduce the pressure in short pipes connected to the exhaust valves. A by-pass tube was used to provide the jet for the first cylinder and to maintain an almost constant pressure at the jet nozzles.

This work was never really successful but it led to many other ideas. Brown Boveri and Sulzer started a test programme with pulse converters on a four-stroke diesel, and in 1964 Petak reported on this. Rather than apply a complex 'ejector-junction-diffuser' arrangement at each cylinder as Birmann had done, pairs of cylinders were joined in the conventional arrangement of a pulse system. The pulse converter was used only to join groups of cylinders that would normally be kept separate.

Most pulse converters in use today are based on the concept of minimum energy loss, even if this means not only a loss of suction effect, but some pressure wave interference. To avoid high mixing losses at the junction, the area reduction in the inlet nozzles is usually small (junction area > 50% of pipe area) while the mixing length and plenum chamber used by Petak, and often the diffuser as well, are omitted completely. These simple pulse converters have the added advantage of adding little overall length to the exhaust system, and can frequently be incorporated into a single manifold casting.

The design of pulse converters need not be restricted to two inlet branches and a single exit. The logical step is to try to connect all the cylinders of an engine to a single turbine entry. The objective is to minimise pulse interference by a combination of area reduction at the inlet nozzles, the connecting of a large number of cylinders together so that the effect of one exhaust pulse on the others is reduced, and the connecting of a large number of cylinders to a single turbine whose inlet area is very large compared with the cross-sectional area of each exhaust pipe. Pulse converters have been produced which match eight cylinders to one turbine. Such a multi-entry pulse converter system ranks between the

The 12 different pulse loss functions which can be measured for a simple exhaust pipe junction.

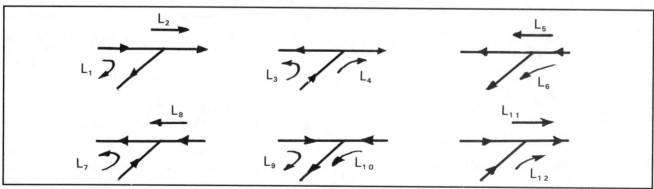

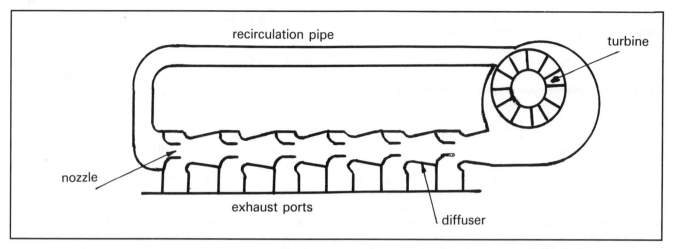

Schematic of Birmann's patented 'pulse converter' exhaust system. The high-velocity jet of gas emerging from each exhaust port combined to reduce the pressure at subsequent ports and enhance the energy available at the turbine. The by-pass tube provided the jet for the first cylinder.

Petak's version of a pulse converter system, using matched junction pipes, a mixing length and plenum chambers. Shown here being used on an eight-cylinder engine, four pairs of cylinders are grouped through two pulse converters to a dual-entry turbine.

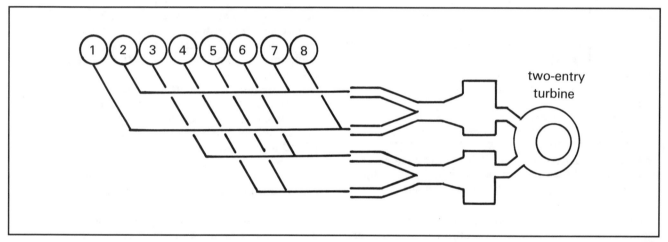

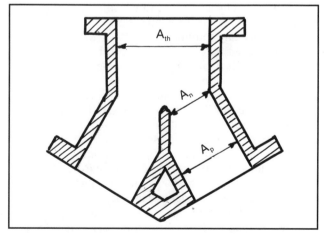

Design principle for a simple pulse converter.
Area ratio (nozzles) = A_n/A_p (0.65 – 0.85)
Area ratio (throat) = $A_{th}/2A_p$ (0.5 – 1.0)

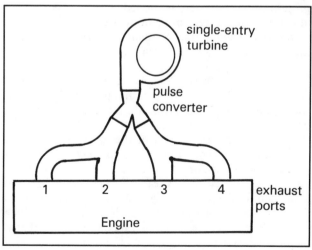

A simple pulse converter used on a four-cylinder exhaust manifold.

simple pulse converter and constant pressure systems as far as turbine admission conditions and general performance are concerned.

A refined version of the original Birmann concept is that referred to as a 'modular pulse converter'. The initial nozzle, fitted at each exhaust port, accelerates the flow, reducing pressure. The cross-sectional area of the main pipe is kept relatively small to maintain a high velocity but low pressure. Thus, the exhaust manifold pressure is low relative to the boost pressure, ensuring good scavenging and reducing piston pumping work. A diffuser connects the narrow main pipe to the turbine inlet. Such a design has the big advantage of simplicity of exhaust manifold construction for large multi-cylinder engines, where the usual pulse exhaust system can need complex piping which is prone to failure.

The design of efficient exhaust systems is still very much an art, based on empirical test results which are

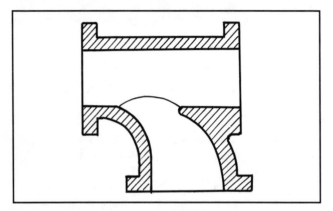

The 'modular pulse converter'. Units of this type can be fitted at the exhaust ports of each cylinder to build up a complete manifold for a multi-cylindered engine.

usually the proprietary knowledge of a particular manufacturer. Numerous complex computer programmes have been developed in recent years in an attempt to turn it into more of an accurate science, but as noted earlier for the calculation of junction losses, the number of factors which need to be taken into account are legion.

The critical feature of any add-on turbocharging system is the exhaust manifold, and priority when positioning the turbocharger should be given to the turbine position. A prime consideration for the manifold is its strength to carry the weight of the turbocharger when working at high temperatures, up to 1,000°C. The frequent rapid expansion and contraction can cause internal scaling and corrosion leading to cracking. A large area manifold is not usually a good thing as it slows down the exhaust gases unnecessarily. A typical turbine with a 76 mm diameter wheel running at 120,000 rpm has a tip speed of about 500 metres per second, with a typical housing gas velocity of about 600 metres per second. For short exhaust manifolds, the reduction of heat losses and the maximum use of pressure pulses is

more important than a uniform exhaust gas flow to the turbine.

Exhaust manifold gaskets on turbocharged engines are subject to arduous duty and a gasket material reinforced with stainless steel wire or incorporating stainless steel eyelets at the port apertures may be needed. Some cars do not have gaskets on exhaust manifolds and this can give problems with leakage due to higher pressures if a turbocharger is added.

Where a wastegate is fitted to control boost pressure, difficulty can arise if a twin-entry turbine is used. General opinion at one time was that this type of housing could not be used in conjunction with a single wastegate because of the unbalanced flow and heating. Some recent tests, however, indicate that this may not be a real problem, as no significant difference could be measured on a test engine using a single or dual wastegate.

Due to mismatches in blade and gas speed, the gas flow from the turbine exit is usually swirling in a helical manner and this needs to be quickly changed to a laminar flow. To achieve this requires the fitting of a diffuser with a sharp angle at the turbine housing exit before the catalysts, mufflers and tail pipe.

At one time it was common practice to use restrictors in exhaust and inlet as a means of controlling the maximum boost pressure from a turbocharger, but this is now very rare.

There are some theoretical benefits in insulating the exhaust manifold and pipes to minimise energy loss. However, this can give a risk of burning through at the highest temperature points and has been usually restricted to small marine diesel engines. For automobiles, the exhaust manifold and hottest parts of the exhaust pipe are provided with metal heat shields to protect neighbouring components from radiant heat. With the introduction of catalytic converters, insulated exhaust systems are starting to appear on automobiles to ensure quick heating of the catalyst.

If twin turbochargers are fitted, some manufacturers will fit a pressure balance pipe between the turbines, although this can complicate the pipework even more. It can be argued that if a pulse system is used the effectiveness of such a pipe is questionable.

With the continual tightening of emissions control regulations it is more likely that exhaust particulate traps will have to be fitted to diesel engines, particularly truck engines. The most difficult problem involved in operating a particulate trap is the assurance of sufficiently frequent regeneration. Since this is essentially a function of the exhaust gas temperature, it would be wrong to locate the trap downstream of the turbine in the expanded and hence colder exhaust gas; the trap belongs as close to the engine as possible. Particulate traps require a certain pressure drop in order to function correctly and during operation this drop increases and can reach as high as 1 bar. With turbochargers, the use of the pulse energy is not practicable if a particulate trap is needed.

13

Induction systems

In the earliest attempts at forced induction, the carburettor inlet was simply exposed to the air flow created by the vehicle movement. This use of the 'ram' effect has continued throughout automotive history and has been particularly important for high-speed competition vehicles. It is easy to obtain and involves no mechanisms which can go wrong, but obviously has little relevance to low-speed torque!

Another technique which became part of the competition car designer's art was the tuning of the induction pipes to get additional charge into the cylinders. In the last century, Helmholtz carried out a great deal of research into the resonance of gases within tubes. His work has been extensively applied to musical instruments, but is also relevant to engine intake systems. Many normally aspirated engines today make use of some form of Helmholtz tuned induction system and it can also be combined with forced chargers, either mechanically driven superchargers or turbochargers[35].

A typical system includes a damping reservoir volume following the compressor which feeds resonance chambers connected by tuning pipes to the inlet ports. The sudden opening of an inlet valve causes a pressure wave which triggers pulsations within the inlet pipe and resonance chamber. As with pulse exhaust systems, inlets are combined into groups which have no overlapping inlet valve operations. At the tuned speed the resonance pulsations build up so that the charge is boosted to a pressure higher than the delivery pressure of the compressor. This can be used to enhance the brake mean effective pressure and torque over the lower engine speed range where turbocharging has little more than marginal effects on performance. High boost and peak loads over the upper engine speed range are avoided by deliberate frustration of the pulsations, achieved by

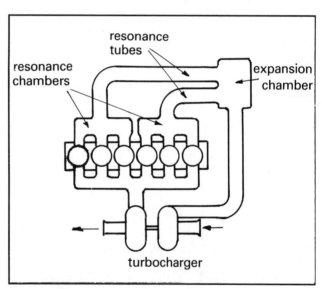

Helmholtz resonance tuned inlet manifold system. The pressure waves caused by the opening of the inlet valves build up a resonance in the tuning tubes and chambers, enhancing the boost pressure.

arranging that the pressure waves are out of phase with the inlet valve openings. Resonant induction systems can give as much as an extra 3% on maximum torque, but in carburetted gasoline engines the long fuel-wetted pipes can give transient response problems, so the system is more popular on fuel-injected engines[50].

MAN in Germany produced a turbocharged six-cylinder diesel engine which used the resonance tuning system with a charge air cooler between the compressor and the resonance chambers. This gave a characteristic with almost constant power output, and the

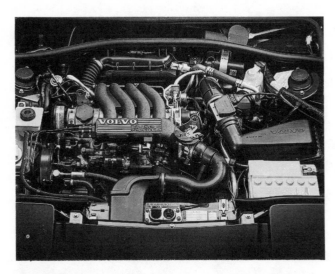

Engine compartment of the Volvo 480 Turbo automobile, showing tuned induction pipes. *[Volvo]*

associated rising torque, over a speed range of several hundred revolutions per minute below the rated speed, and then a constant torque over the rest of the useful speed range (see diagram).

Performance characteristics for the MAN turbocharged diesel truck engine with resonance tuned induction system. *[Ansdale[35]]*

The disadvantage of the tuned induction system is having to choose one speed for the resonant action to take place. Cser has researched the logical solution to this problem and has produced a double resonance system[68]. In addition to the normal resonance cham-

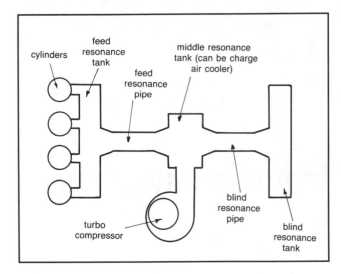

Cser's double resonance induction manifold system. The dummy blind resonance tank is formed as part of the inlet manifold casting. On a four-cylinder gasoline engine with a rated speed of 6,000 rpm, this system gave one resonance peak at 1,500 rpm and another at 2,000 rpm.

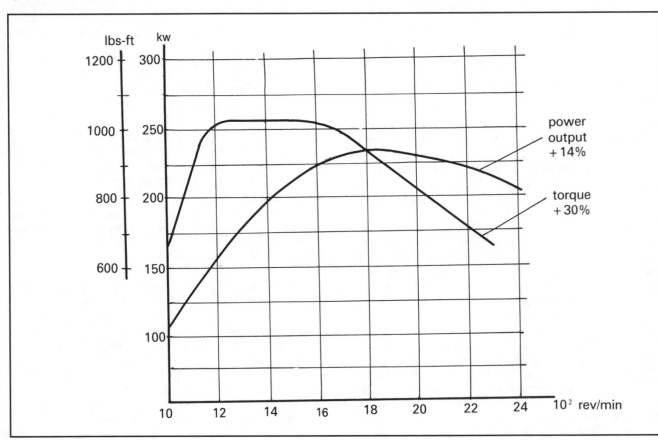

bers and pipes he provides a dummy blind resonance tank which gives the system two resonance points. On a gasoline engine with a rated speed of 6,000 rpm, the first resonance occurs at 1,500 rpm followed by the second at 2,000 rpm. The blind resonance chamber is formed by an additional tube parallel to the main inlet manifold chamber and incorporated into the same casting so that the additional space requirement is small. The use of this type of resonant system has been shown to give substantial improvements in particulate and NOx emissions.

Inlet piping and manifold design is greatly simplified for diesel and port-injected gasoline engines where air flow is the only consideration. For gasoline carburettor engines the handling of the fuel/air mixture after the

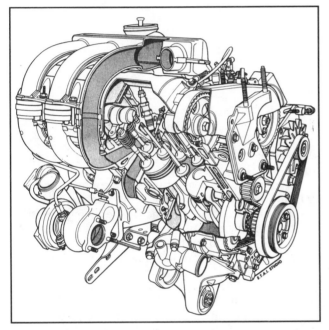

Tuned induction manifold on a 2-litre automobile diesel engine. *[Peugeot]*

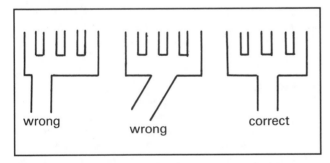

On a gasoline engine, the feed to the inlet manifold must be connected in the centre and at right-angles to the plenum chamber, otherwise the distribution of the droplets of fuel can be uneven between the cylinders.

carburettor presents additional problems. It is important that this mixture should enter a manifold cross tube at the centre at right-angles. The fuel droplets tend to carry straight on and if coming at an angle may give excess fuel to some cylinders. One or two quite sharp bends in the piping can, however, be helpful in breaking up laminar flow and ensuring good mixing of fuel and air[26].

The compressor discharge diffuser pipe should be designed with a gradually increasing cross-sectional area from the compressor connection point to the inlet manifold. The longitudinal manifold rail should have an inside diameter at least equivalent to the carburettor choke area.

The positioning of a turbocharger is usually determined by exhaust manifold and piping considerations. This means that the air delivery ducting can be quite long where exhaust and inlet are on opposite sides of the engine. Away from the heat of the exhaust and before any resonance chambers, the air delivery will typically be via smooth flexible silicone rubber or metal ducting.

Where a charge air cooler is fitted, pipes are obviously required from the compressor outlet to the heat exchanger inlet, and then from the cooler outlet to the inlet manifold. If the cooler is carefully positioned, the extra duct length involved in its connection may not be all that much more than the direct route from compressor to manifold.

Allowance must be made, when specifying the intake air filter requirement, for the additional volume of air used by a pressure charged engine compared with a normally aspirated one, typically 40-100% more. Air filters also act as noise mufflers on the engine intake. The greatest volume of the intake noise is generated by the pressure waves resulting from the abrupt valve opening action.

It will be found that any supercharging compressor will provide almost complete acoustic separation between the intake and the engine, substantially attenuating the noise. The compressor itself may of course generate its own noise, but it is likely to be at a much higher frequency (greater than 500Hz) and therefore more easily suppressed. Standard production air filters are designed for effective sound absorption at low frequencies, so a different type is needed when a supercharger is added.

The same is true on the exhaust side when a turbocharger is fitted. The engine noise which comes down the exhaust pipe is quite well suppressed and it is often possible to simplify the exhaust mufflers fitted. Because of the high-frequency nature of the noise, the straight-through absorption type of muffler is particularly attractive. The low back pressure associated with such mufflers enhances the performance of the turbocharger/engine combination.

14

Cooling systems

A higher charge density will allow a greater mass of oxygen to pass into an engine, which in turn allows more fuel to be burned and a greater output to be obtained – this is the basic principle of all forms of supercharging. It was shown earlier that the gas laws require that any compression will be accompanied by a rise in temperature which will in turn reduce the density again, reducing the effectiveness of any compressor.

If T_1 and P_1 are the absolute temperature and pressure at the inlet of a supercharging compressor, and T_2 and P_2 are the outlet values, then $T_2 = T_1$ x $(P_2/P_1)^{0.286}$. If the inlet air temperature is 20°C (absolute temperature 293°K) and the inlet pressure is 1 bar absolute, then for a boost pressure of 1.1 bar (absolute pressure 2.1 bar) the theoretical outlet temperature will be:

$$T_2 = 293 \times (2.1/1)^{0286} = 293 \times 1.236 = 362°K$$
(89°C)

This temperature rise of 69°C is the theoretical value in an ideal compressor working with air, and for a practical adiabatic efficiency of 70% the actual temperature rise through the compressor would be 69°/0.7 = 98°C.

If this compressed air is passed through a heat exchanger it will be cooled back down towards the temperature of the coolant. Any practical heat exchanger cannot of course get the temperature of the charge air down to the same temperature as the coolant, and a measure of the effectiveness of any given cooler will be the ratio of (actual temperature drop)/(maximum possible temperature drop).

Let us assume for the example that an air-to-air heat exchanger is fitted, with an effectiveness of 70%. For the compressor exit temperature of 118°C (20 + 98) and ambient air temperature of 20°C, this would give a temperature reduction in the heat exchanger of

(118 – 20) x 0.7 = 69°C (approx)

so that the temperature of the air entering the engine would be (118 – 69) = 49°C.

If our example engine without cooling produces 200 bhp with the full 1.1 bar of boost pressure, and there is a pressure drop through the heat exchanger of 0.07 bar, then the increase in density as a result of using the cooler will be given by the ratio of the cooler inlet to outlet absolute temperatures multiplied by the ratio of the cooler outlet to inlet absolute pressures:

[(118 + 273)/(49 + 273)] x (1.03 + 1)/(1.1 + 1)] = (391/322) x (2.03/2.1) = 1.17

The engine will be able to put out 17% more power at the same speed with 0.07 bar less manifold pressure, that is 234 bhp. There will be a resulting drop in the exhaust temperature and pressure which, for turbocharging, will slow down the turbine, further reducing the inlet pressure, so a smaller turbine housing may be needed to get back to the same boost pressure.

The use of a heat exchanger in this manner to reduce the temperature of the air entering an engine is given different names – aftercooling, intercooling, and charge air cooling. Intercooling is widely used, but can be confused with the cooling used between the compressors when two stage supercharging is used. Aftercooling is more correct, but is not popular. In this book we are using the generally acceptable and explicit phrase – charge air cooling.

Experiment has shown that any reduction of the inlet temperature is reflected through into the exhaust temperature. As a simple rule of thumb for gasoline engines, every degree of reduction in inlet manifold temperature is accompanied by a 1° drop in exhaust temperature. Reducing the charge air temperature also affects favourably the onset of pre-ignition and detonation in gasoline engines. Charge air cooling enables substantial power increases to be achieved without significantly increasing the engine thermal loading.

The advantages of charge cooling are clear, but it does have some disadvantages:

- Air flow through the cooler results in a pressure loss offsetting some of the density increase from cooling.
- A cooling source must be provided.
- Mounting space for the cooler must be provided.
- Excess cooling can cause condensation in the inlet manifold.
- Extra cost.

There is always a pressure drop across any heat exchanger, and it is generally of little value to use a charge air cooler until the amount of boost exceeds 0.4 bar as the drop across the cooler will offset the benefits at lower boost levels. Mounting space limitations for the cooler can mean that the volume between the compressor outlet and the cylinders is large, adversely affecting transient response.

Alternative configurations for charge air cooling systems
(a) air-to-air heat exchanger mounted in front of the main engine coolant radiator and transferring heat to the ambient air
(b) air-to-water heat exchanger with circulation of water from the engine cooling jacket
(c) air-to-water heat exchanger with separate pumped water circuit to another water-to-air radiator mounted in front of, or adjacent to, the main engine coolant radiator.

Charge air cooling moves the operating regime of a turbo compressor away from the surge line and the constant engine speed operating lines are more parallel with the surge line. A wider air-flow characteristic is needed, though.

The lower adiabatic efficiency of many mechanically driven superchargers will make the provision of a charge air cooler a more likely need.

Various cooling media have been used for charge air coolers – ambient air, engine jacket water, a separate cooled water circuit, ice water, and sea water.

Jacket water cooling is not usually practical unless the compressor exit air temperature is at least 170°C. The use of ice water, acetone or alcohol with dry ice is restricted to sprint competition cars where a high degree of cooling over a short period is needed; it can cause freezing in the heat exchanger on a humid day. Marine engines have the luxury of a readily available cooling medium from the water in which the vessel floats.

The most common form of charge air cooling for automotive application uses an air-to-air heat exchanger which is mounted in the air stream at the front of the vehicle. It may be positioned in front of, alongside, or behind the main engine coolant radiator, and will be connected to the compressor outlet and the inlet manifold by smooth bore plastic or rubber tubing. It is not usually necessary to provide a fan for the air cooler as it is not required to function except when the engine is under load and there will presumably be ade-

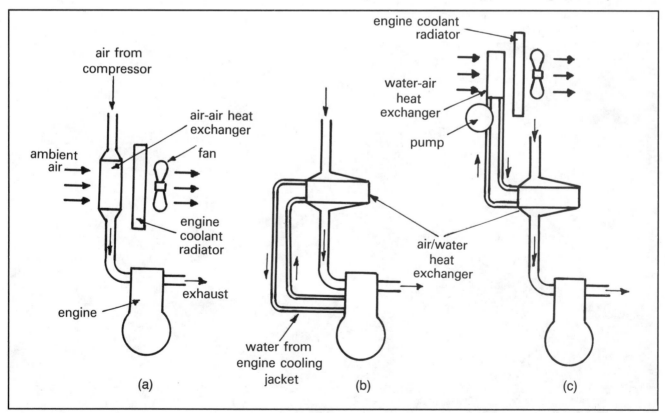

(a)   (b)   (c)

The charge air cooler installation on the Citroen CX25 car. [*Citroen*]

quate ram effect from the vehicle slipstream.

For vehicles with rear or mid-mounted engines, getting an adequate air flow through a charge air cooler presents more of a problem. One approach, which has been used by Lotus, is to use an air-to-water heat

Air-to-water charge air cooler on the Lotus Esprit Turbo SE. This heat exchanger is fitted to the rear-mounted engine with its own water-to-air radiator at the front of the car, and a separate water circuit with pump. [*Lotus*]

exchanger mounted on the engine, fed from a separate water circuit with its own pump and radiator. The small water radiator needed can then be accommodated at the front of the vehicle or elsewhere in the slipstream.

Another alternative is to use the conventional air-to-air heat exchanger and give it a ducted fan so that air can be drawn in from some suitable high-pressure zone near the rear of the vehicle. The fan can be electrically driven, but units have been made in which the fan is driven as a turbine by directing a stream of compressed air onto its blade tips. This air supply can be obtained as a bleed from the charge air ducting.

The traditional materials used for automotive heat

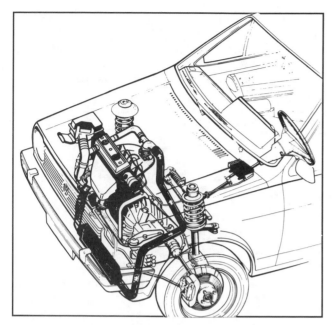

The charge air cooler installation on the Volkswagen G40 Polo. [*Volkswagen*]

exchangers were brass or copper, with the parts soldered together. More recently, reliable techniques of vacuum brazing have made the use of aluminium the preferred material. Copper and brass are still used for some truck radiators, but the weight savings associated with aluminium mean that it is almost universal for auto-mobile charge air coolers and radiators.

One type of mass-produced unit is built up from strips of aluminium which are machine folded to make zig-zag pieces. These are interleaved with plain strips to form a series of small ducts at right-angles to each other (see diagram) which build up to give the total cooling area needed. End plates are fastened to this core assem-

bly and then the complete heat exchanger is passed through a vacuum brazing furnace to form a homogeneous unit.

When the core is complete, header tanks are attached to the two ends of it. For liquid cooling and for large air-to-air heat exchangers, the headers will be fabricated or cast in metal and attached to the core by brazing or edge rolling. For the smaller air-to-air exchangers, the use of plastic mouldings for the headers is now very common, reducing the cost and weight even further.

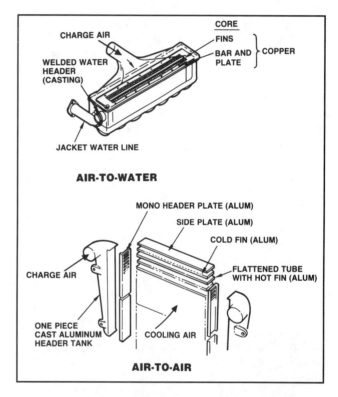

Alternative construction methods using flattened aluminium tubes for air-to-air coolers, and copper fins and plates for air-to-water coolers. [*Garrett*]

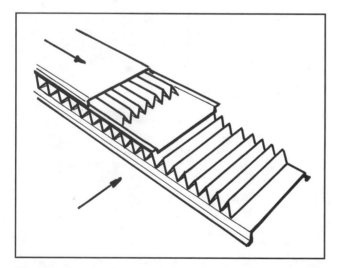

Diagram showing how an air-to-air heat exchanger can be built up from sets of zig-zag strips.

A combined engine coolant radiator and charge air cooler for a truck. [*Llanelli Radiator*]

Standard off-the-shelf units can be purchased for use by the individual or the small-volume manufacturer. For the large-volume vehicle manufacturer, the charge air cooler construction is designed to use standard components, but it will be arranged to optimise the installation in the vehicle. For truck use, it is common to find the charge air cooler combined in the same assembly as the engine jacket cooling radiator.

Oil cooling

The higher power available with supercharging for a given engine volume means a greater heat density. A substantial proportion of the engine heat losses are transferred to the lubricating oil and must be dissipated to the atmosphere to avoid overheating of the oil. For automobiles, the main means of achieving this has traditionally been from the surface of the crankcase sump. However, refinements in vehicle aerodynamics have made it more difficult to achieve adequate cooling by this means, and the engine compartment temperatures have continued to rise. When turbochargers are added, where the lubricating oil has to keep the turbine bearings cool, additional specific oil coolers may need to be provided.

The oil cooler may handle all the oil flow for the whole vehicle or may just be piped specifically for the turbocharger flow. There may also be a circuit to give extra cooling for the oil feed to an automatic transmission system.

Oil cooler construction will be very similar to that discussed above for charge air coolers, but obviously the oil circuit must be sealed and tested to withstand the high pressures associated with engine lubrication. It is usually desirable to install a thermostat so that flow through the cooler only takes place when the oil is above the preferred working temperature.

It is now quite common in highly rated supercharged engines to find that lubricating oil is used as a coolant for the piston crowns. Occasionally this will

be by providing oilways through the connecting rods to transfer oil from the big-end bearings via the little-end bearings to the piston. The more common arrangement now is some form of spray feed via special pipes in the crankcase which are aimed up into the pistons.

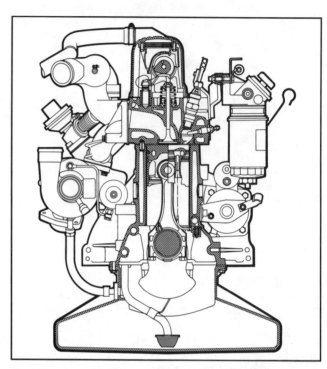

Cross-section of a turbocharged diesel engine showing the piston cooling system. Fixed oil jets spray up into passages in the piston crowns. [*Opel*]

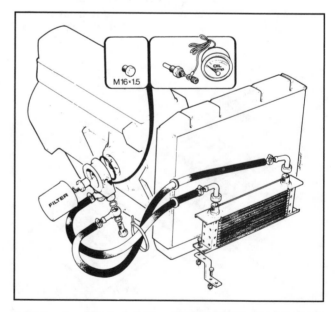

Add-on oil cooler installation. The connection block which fits between the engine and the oil filter includes a thermostat. [*Setrab*]

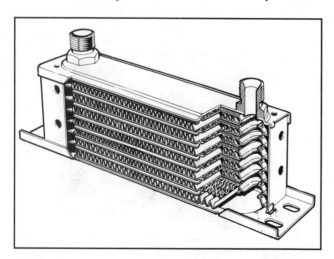

Sectional view of oil cooler construction. [*Setrab*]

Water injection

Reference has already been made to the benefits of charge air cooling in reducing cylinder temperature and thereby delaying the onset of detonation in gasoline engines. Detonation can also be avoided by enriching the fuel/air mixture and by retarding the ignition timing. Nevertheless, the onset of detonation is one of the limiting factors in determining how far a given engine can be supercharged. One technique for reducing combustion chamber peak temperatures and avoiding detonation is the injection of water, either combined with the fuel or as a separate system.

The first recorded use of water injection was in about 1900 by a Hungarian engineer named Benki. In 1913 Professor Hopkinson in England carried out some tests with large industrial gas engines. In 1920 Hobson undertook more work on the idea of injecting water into the combustion chamber of an engine to keep down the cylinder head temperature, and a number of farm tractor semi-diesel engines with hot-bulb ignition used this. In the early 1930s Ricardo carried out extensive tests which led to patents being obtained in 1936 for the use of anti-detonant injections[6]. Water injection was employed in the high-performance supercharged aircraft engines used for altitude and speed records in the '30s, and later became standard practice in fighter aircraft during the Second World War, allowing very high power peaks to be obtained for short periods.

Practical anti-detonant injection systems no longer use pure water. The usual is a water/methanol mixture, up to a 50/50 ratio. The methyl alcohol gives better evaporation, provides some additional fuel, and also avoids any risk of the liquid freezing. It also helps to keep the inside of the combustion chamber very clean, and has some effect on reducing polluting exhaust emissions because of the lower peak temperature. A corrosion inhibitor would normally also be added to the injection mixture[26].

The water can be mixed with the fuel or injected into the fuel/air mixture after the carburettor. With fuel injection systems the water is normally injected into the inlet manifold at a point of high air velocity. The boost pressure can be used to pressurise the water tank, but then the injection must be into the compressor inlet, giving the evaporation in the compressor rather than in the engine cylinder. The better system uses an electrically driven separate water injection pump which is usually controlled by the boost pressure.

Methanol – methyl alcohol (CH_3OH) – has less than half the energy per volume of gasoline, and this must be compensated for in the fuel/air mixture settings of the main fuel supply. When water/methanol injection is used, it is also likely that more ignition advance will be needed – up to an additional 15°. Nitrous oxide (N_2O) was also used in Second World War aircraft to achieve an extra power boost, and nowadays it is widely used in drag racing. It is not a fuel, but liberates extra oxygen which helps to burn more fuel. Because of the high latent heat of evaporation, it also helps to keep down the charge temperature.

Schematic of a typical water injection system. The electronic control unit responds to rising boost pressure by increasing the amount of water injected. The sensor in the tank triggers an alarm condition if the tank empties or freezes.

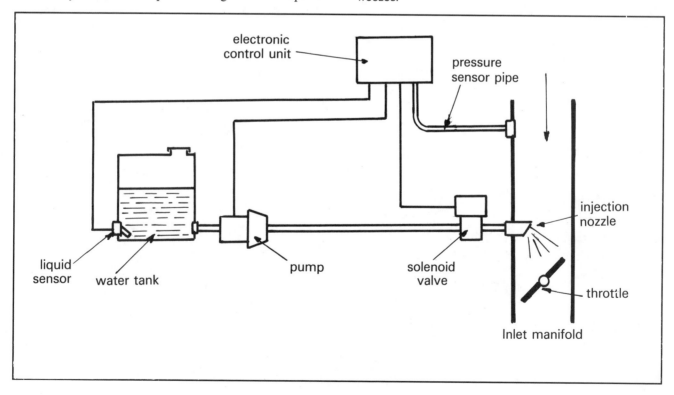

The first production turbocharged car, the Oldsmobile Turbo Rocket, in 1962, was based on a standard non-supercharged engine and had a 10.25:1 compression ratio. To avoid detonation it was provided with a system which injected a mixture of ethyl alcohol, distilled water and corrosion inhibitor, which was sold as 'rocket fluid'!

Water injection has become common practice for racing and rally cars, and for other applications which require high peak cylinder temperatures and pressures, but its adoption for normal road use has not been popular because of the cost and the need to keep replenishing the injection fluid tank as well as the fuel tank.

Complete add-on kits are now available which provide the necessary electric pump, filter, injection nozzle, interconnecting pipes and electronic control unit. The latter may be preset or may allow the driver to vary the injection rate while in motion. The latest control systems provide for boost pressure and speed sensing so that the amount of water injection is automatically adjusted to maintain optimum conditions. If the pump should fail, the water tank run dry, or the water freeze, an alarm will sound, and in some systems the boost pressure will be automatically limited to a safe level.

15

Boost control

Boost control systems are provided for three reasons. First, to limit the compressor outlet pressure to keep it from destroying the engine; second, to limit the speed of a turbocharger to keep it from destroying itself; and third, to match the characteristics of the charging system to the desired engine behaviour. This chapter looks at how such boost controls can be achieved; a later chapter considers how overall engine controls are integrated with these specific boost control devices.

It is in principle possible to choose the supercharger to so closely match the engine needs that it can never generate too much boost or overstress itself. If only a small amount of boost is needed, this can be an acceptable approach for a mechanically driven supercharger installation, but would usually give an unacceptable characteristic for a turbocharged engine. Here, matching is made much more difficult because of the different behaviour of the volume machine – the reciprocating engine, and the speed machine – the turbocharger. Other important factors which manufacturers must take into consideration are the difference between the performance of a development engine and the version which can be reliably produced in quantity, and the deterioration which takes place during the lifetime of a vehicle.

The mechanically driven, positive displacement supercharger offers little choice in methods of control. The speed ratio chosen for the drive from the engine will determine how the boost pressure will change with engine speed and the maximum pressure achieved. To achieve a satisfactory boost at low engine speed will frequently mean that the pressure at top speed will exceed the safe value. Unless a complex variable speed drive system is to be used, the only practical control is a pressure relief valve to vent excess air at high speed. The valve may have some form of servo control which allows

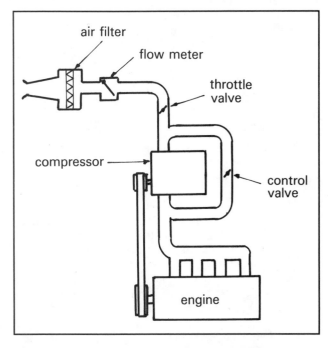

Use of an air by-pass valve to control the boost pressure from a mechanically driven positive displacement supercharger.

an engine management system to match the boost curve more accurately to the desired engine characteristic than can be achieved with a simple blow-off valve.

There are many more options available when a turbocharger is to be used. The 'free-running' turbocharger is selected so that the combination of compressor and turbine maps gives an acceptable compromise over the normal working engine range. This arrangement was widely used in early turbocharging applications and is still common for truck and industrial diesel engines whose operating range is restricted and predictable.

In early automotive applications, restrictions were used in either or both inlet and exhaust ducting. Selection or adjustment of these restrictor orifices allowed the basic free-running behaviour to be modified to some extent to prevent over-boosting and over-speeding while still leaving an acceptable boost effect at lower speeds. The great attraction of this technique is the absence of any mechanisms with moving parts to go wrong; the big disadvantages are the limited control ability, the difficulty of choosing the correct size orifice, the lack of any direct linkage to the engine behaviour, and the loss of efficiency.

A simple spring-loaded pressure relief valve at the compressor outlet can be used for a mechanically driven supercharger, but if used alone with a turbocharger it does not directly affect the turbine speed, and over-speeding can still result. A valve of this type can have a tendency to flutter and would usually now only be used as an ultimate protection for the engine in high-boost competitive applications. Using an air pressure relief valve after the compressor causes a drop in efficiency as the work expended on compressing the excess air is thrown away.

Another possible control point is at the compressor inlet where some form of boost-pressure-regulated throttle valve will limit the delivery pressure. This arrangement avoids the wasted energy in compressing air only to vent it again, and a compact in-line unit was produced by IMPCO for this type of application. Like the blow-off valve, throttling the compressor inlet does little to control turbine speed in a turbocharger set-up, and it can also aggravate oil-sealing problems in the compressor.

Valves may be installed in the air system which are only part of an overall and more complex control system. There may be a compressor automatic by-pass valve which allows the engine to run naturally aspirated until the compressor pressure builds up. This may be necessary for a positive displacement supercharger; the obstruction caused by a turbo-compressor is less of a problem. Simple reed flap valves have been used for this job.

In the Porsche 911 engines a mechanically actuated pressure relief valve was used when they were first turbocharged, to drop the manifold pressure immediately that the throttle was closed. In later models this was changed to respond to the intake manifold pressure. A spring normally keeps the valve shut, but when the throttle is closed on over-run, the vacuum generated in the manifold opens the valve to dump all the compressor pressure even though the turbine is still spinning very fast. The braking and throttle response was greatly improved by this addition, and compressor surging was avoided.

A point worth noting about this installation, which

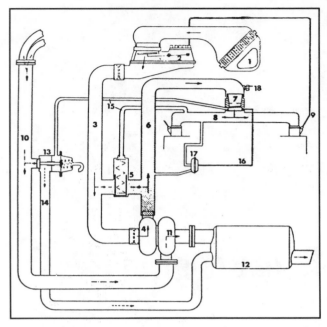

Use of a pressure relief valve in the inlet system of a Porsche 911 engine. [*Porsche*]

1 air cleaner
2 air flow metering and fuel injection control unit
3 low-pressure air hose
4 turbocharger compressor
5 boost pressure relief valve
6 high-pressure air hose
7 throttle valve housing
8 inlet manifold
9 fuel injection line
10 exhaust gas collecting pipes
11 turbocharger turbine
12 muffler
13 boost pressure control wastegate
14 by-pass pipe
15 control lines
16 control line to auxiliary air valve for over-run
17 vacuum control valve for over-run
18 safety switch for boost pressure

may apply to any compressor dumping valve, is that the air volume has already been metered once before entering the compressor, so the air by-pass must stay within the closed circuit and not vent to atmosphere in order that the fuel/air mixture control remains correct.

On the other side of the turbocharger, a simple exhaust pressure relief valve responding to exhaust manifold pressure can protect the turbine from over-speeding. As for the air blow-off valve, such an exhaust valve may suffer from flutter and will still only control the desired turbine and compressor parameters indirectly.

The most widely used method of turbocharger boost control is generally known as a 'wastegate'. This is a spring-loaded valve, usually a poppet type, fitted immediately before the turbine. It is not operated,

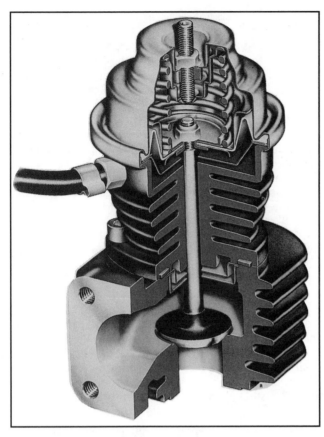

An exhaust by-pass valve ('wastegate') for separate mounting in a supercharging system. A poppet valve, similar to a standard exhaust valve, is used, operated by a pneumatic servo motor. The whole assembly is heavily finned to avoid overheating. [*KKK*]

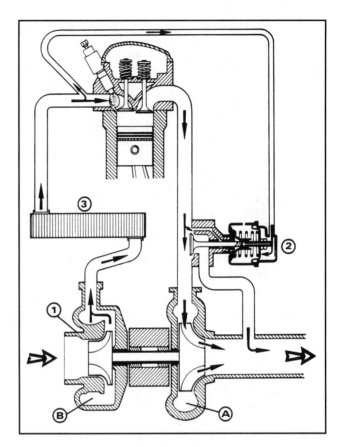

Schematic of complete turbocharger circuit using a 'wastegate' for pressure control. [*Citroen*]

(A) turbine
(B) compressor

(1) inlet from air filter
(2) pressure control wastegate
(3) charge air cooler

however, by the exhaust pressure but in response to some function of the compressor delivery pressure. When the valve opens it passes a portion of the exhaust gases through a by-pass around the turbine direct to the exhaust outlet. The valve may be a completely separate device, but for many small automobile turbochargers it is incorporated into the turbine housing so that there are no external high-temperature exhaust pipe joints to give trouble.

Use of a wastegate obviously reduces the potential overall fuel efficiency slightly because no use is made of the energy released, but the benefits which are derived from the control capability outweigh this. There is no need to provide inlet or outlet restrictions and, using a wastegate with a simple pressure controller, the sum of the tolerances influencing the compressed air pres-

A turbocharger with an integral exhaust by-pass 'wastegate' valve. The swinging-arm-type valve can be seen at the top right, adjacent to the turbine wheel. It is operated by a pneumatic servo motor, visible at the rear, which is actuated by a pressure feed taken from the air delivery pipe. [*Garrett*]

sure of the supercharged engine in an as-new condition and over the vehicle's life can be corrected.

The simplest application of a wastegate control will take a boost pressure feed and apply it to a diaphragm which is opposed by a spring. When the boost pressure is high enough it will overcome the spring pressure and the valve will start to open. The spring pressure may be adjustable by a screw, and some manufacturers colour-code the springs to indicate their strength. Increasingly, though, mass-produced small turbochargers have their control units completely sealed after adjustment on the production line.

The point where the wastegate control pressure is taken can have a considerable influence on the engine speed versus boost pressure curve. The optimum position is usually on the compressor housing outlet or near to it. A recent, patented, technique uses two pressure-tapping points on the compressor housing, one at the maximum pressure point and the other at a smaller radius where the detected pressure is lower. A simple electrically operated valve then allows the driver to switch between these two values on the road to give a low/high boost option.

Many wastegate valves look just like standard engine exhaust valves with an axial movement. The valve spindle should preferably pass through the exit passage so that the spindle seal is subject to a lower pressure and is exposed to hot gases only when the wastegate is open. Some compact units have the valve head mounted on a swinging arm so that the hot seal is to a slightly rotating shaft rather than to the sliding valve stem. It is important that the wall shape adjacent to the valve

head and the operating servo behaviour are designed so that there is no tendency for the valve to flutter as it opens, as this can produce pressure surging.

The other major control option which is chosen is the use of some form of variable geometry turbine. This can give an effective change of A/R over quite a wide range under some form of servo control related to the desired boost pressure. The higher efficiency of vaned turbines has meant that they are used frequently on large diesel engines; the additional complexity of providing an adjustment mechanism for the vanes can be accepted in such applications. Transferring these benefits to the smaller, cheaper automotive turbochargers has presented difficulties in getting the costs down and the reliability up. Nevertheless, a number of designs are now in volume production and their application is becoming more widespread. Five different approaches to achieving the variable geometry effect are illustrated here[63].

The 'variable entry' design has a housing scroll divided into two chambers by a wall similar to a conventional twin entry housing. A selector valve at the turbine inlet controls the entry of exhaust gases to one chamber. The control method is simplified because only two modes, open and closed, are used. In the closed position, exhaust gas flows through only one passage. There is a reduction in turbine efficiency due to increased surface friction on the extra wall, wake loss

Diagram of a 'variable entry' turbine with a swinging selector valve. The gas inlet volute is divided and the valve closes off the secondary portion until the extra area is required.

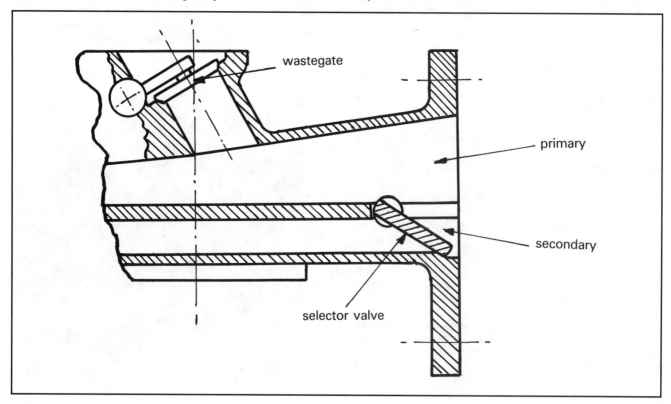

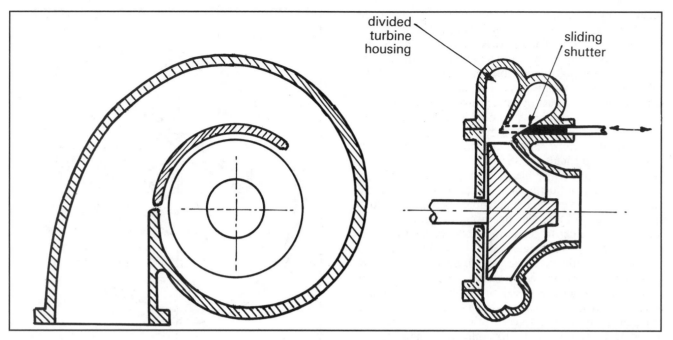

Diagram of a 'variable entry' turbine with a horizontally sliding gate which closes off part of the volute at slow speed.

at the dividing wall and at the abrupt contraction of the flow at the entry valve, and the thin dividing wall is vulnerable in the high-temperature operating regime of a gasoline engine. A variation on this design uses a horizontally sliding blade to isolate part of one of the flow passages instead of the swinging gate.

The 'variable nozzle' design has a single movable vane located at the turbine inlet which controls the gas velocity approaching the turbine wheel by changing the apparent throat area; continuous capacity control is possible by swinging the vane. It has a potential high reliability due to the small number of moving parts, and has a wide turbine flow capacity. Efficiency, however, is lowered due to the leakage loss from the side vane clearance, the wake loss after the flap valve, and the non-uniform velocity distribution caused by the unmatched scroll area distribution.

The classic 'variable geometry' design has multiple nozzle vanes, usually more than eight, around the periphery of the turbine housing. These vanes are linked

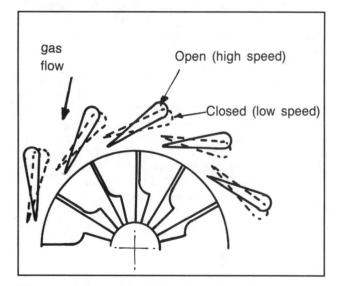

Schematic diagram of a 'variable nozzle' turbine. A single movable vane is located at the turbine inlet, which controls the exhaust gas velocity entering the turbine wheel.

Diagram of the action of the classic 'variable geometry' turbine. The series of vanes arranged around the turbine wheel periphery can be rotated by a linked mechanism to vary the aperture between them. This controls the speed of the turbine.

together by a mechanism so that they can be rotated simultaneously to vary the gap between them and thus vary the inlet area. The capacity range from the minimum to maximum flow is broad and good efficiency is obtained. The multiple components give complexity, a substantial cost penalty, and a reduction in reliability. A bigger turbine housing is needed to accommodate the vanes, and there can be significant leakage at the clearance between the vanes and housing wall. The reaction forces on the vanes makes the control system servo design more difficult.

An example variable geometry design gives 5% more torque low down compared with a conventional vaneless design. Despite the potential for improving low-speed torque and the wide operating range, it has been found that in order to get a satisfactory match to vehicle requirements, a wastegate valve is likely to be still required. This adds to an already complicated construction and installation requirement.

A variant on the vaned turbine arrangement was experimented with by ABB. In this model the vanes were not adjustable relative to each other but were made as a ring which could slide horizontally in the housing just outside the periphery of the turbine wheel. A regulation range of 1:4 was achieved with a simple construction and operation at 1,000°C was faultless. It was found that it had a higher efficiency at the outer limits of its range compared with the conventional moving-vane-type, but a lower efficiency in the partially open states.

Mitsubishi has developed a 'variable inlet' design which has two vanes located in the turbine housing volute. The pivot pin of each vane is located on the ideal area distribution line to give constant acceleration of the exhaust gas through the turbine housing. Control is achieved by the vanes being operated simultaneously so that a continuously variable throat area is available. It has few moving parts so reliability is high, and a good efficiency is obtained from low- to high-flow conditions. There is no increase in diameter when compared to a conventional, fixed geometry turbine housing, making it easily adaptable to existing installation arrangements.

This variable inlet design also still needs a wastegate to cover the total engine speed range for passenger car application. When tested on a 2-litre gasoline engine, the variable inlet turbocharger made full boost available at a 13% lower engine speed than a conventional turbocharger. The vanes are closed up to 1,750 rpm when they start to gradually open until the full open position is reached at 2,400 rpm. Above this speed, when the vanes are fully open, the wastegate starts to open. The engine torque at an engine speed of 1,750 rpm is 25% higher with

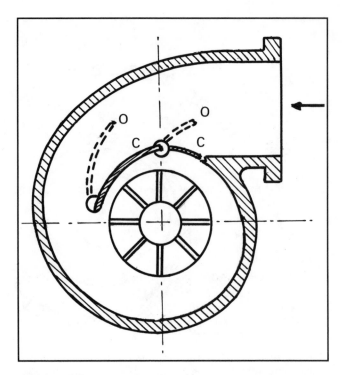

Schematic diagram of a 'variable inlet' turbine. Two vanes are mounted in the turbine housing volute, with the pivot pin of each vane located on the ideal area distribution line.

O = vane open position
C = vane closed position

the variable inlet design when compared to a conventional turbine. Above 2,500 rpm the engine output is equivalent to the fixed geometry turbocharger. There is a 40% improvement in the time required to meet full boost.

Although the variable inlet turbine system was intended to have continuous variation of vane position, it has been found that simple on-off controls work quite well. The control parameters used are boost pressure, engine speed, wastegate valve status, and the variable inlet vanes' status.

The early applications of the Comprex pressure wave charger used a conventional wastegate control. Later developments introduced additional exhaust gas pockets to achieve a wider performance range; they were fed by grooves from the adjacent main exhaust ports. It was discovered that if these gas pockets were given their own separate feed with a controlling valve, a boost pressure ratio variable between 1.7 and 2.8 in the same machine could be obtained at higher efficiency, and the wastegate could be eliminated.

16

Effect of boost control

Each of the different methods of boost control described in the previous chapter has its own characteristic curves for torque and power relative to engine speed. In the accompanying graph, torque curves for similar engines

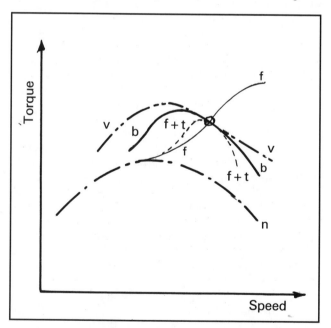

Shape of boost pressure curves for different types of control.

n naturally aspirated engine
o target torque/speed
f free floating turbocharger
f + t turbo with addition of throttling
b wastegate control
v variable nozzle control

have been plotted, scaled so that they all pass through the same target torque/speed point. The reference curve is that obtained for a naturally aspirated version of the engine; the other curves relate to various turbocharger control systems[26].

If a turbocharger is just left free-floating with no control mechanism at all, it can be seen that the required torque comes low down on the potential torque curve, with the higher values only available at much higher engine speeds. Adding inlet and exhaust restrictions changes the shape to a much more usable curve, with the target torque near the peak of the curve but with a narrow spread. Providing wastegate control gives a torque/speed curve with a more usable spread of the high torque region and higher values at lower speed; this is nearer to the shape for a naturally aspirated engine of similar output. Finally, the curve for a variable nozzle turbine control system has been plotted and the further improvement can be seen.

These curves all apply for steady-state running, but the response to transient changes of torque needs is critical for any automotive application. The next graph plots the relationship of the amount of combustion air available, and hence the possible torque, following the sudden opening of the throttle. There is always a basic amount of air available consistent with natural aspiration; then an additional amount of air is needed from the compressor to give the maximum torque required. If a free-floating turbocharger is used it will be seen that there is a virtually instantaneous availability of the naturally aspirated combustion air, which is then followed by a gradual rise in the volume as the turbocharger increases speed. The matching for such an installation would usually result in an overshoot of speed for the turbocharger, giving an excess of charge air pressure.

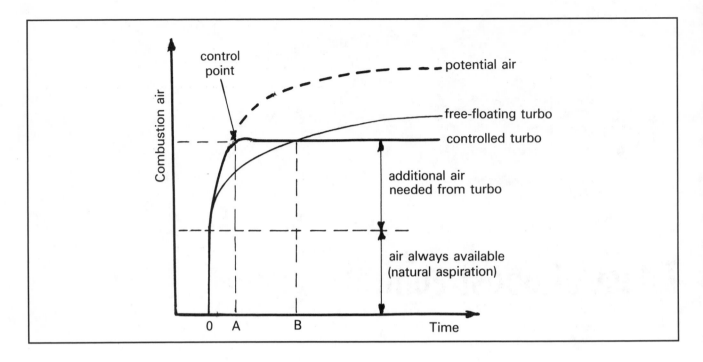

The transient air availability after sudden throttle opening, for free-floating and wastegate-controlled turbochargers.

If a wastegate is fitted, the turbocharger characteristics can be chosen to give a very much faster rise in charge air volume, but with the accompanying much higher potential over-boost value. As the inlet boost pressure reaches the value which gives the required amount of combustion air, the 'control point', the wastegate will start to open and will then hold the inlet supply at approximately constant volume with only a slight over-run. The difference between response times for the uncontrolled and controlled versions is quite clear.

It is possible to adjust the turbocharger variability mechanism, either wastegate or variable geometry, by purely manual means or by some simple mechanical linkage to, for example, the accelerator pedal. Apart from some specialist competition vehicles this is a technique which is not acceptable for the modern production automotive application, and some form of automatic servo-control system is needed. These can be very complex, and the integration of turbocharger controls into full engine management systems is discussed later; let us here consider the simplest of direct servo systems applied to wastegate control.

Earlier, a brief description was given of a wastegate actuator which took a pressure air feed from the compressor outlet. This is the simplest form, which has been adopted for large numbers of small turbocharged automobiles. There are, however, a number of variations on this simple device which are worth examining to show the flexibility available for different applications, and these are illustrated in the accompanying diagram.

In the first case, the two sides of the diaphragm inside the wastegate actuator are connected to the inlet and outlet pressures of the compressor (P_{c1} and P_{c2}). The actuator will then respond to the differential pressure rise across the compressor ($P_{c2} - P_{c1}$). In practical applications it is assumed that the compressor inlet pressure (P_{c1}) is very close to the ambient pressure and one side of the diaphragm is vented to atmosphere, thereby avoiding a second pressure connection having to be made.

In the second case, the delivery pressure (P_{c2}) is balanced by a sealed bellows with a very high vacuum inside it. In this case the actuator responds to the absolute delivery pressure; as with the first type, a biassing spring is also fitted to the actuator.

If a diaphragm is fitted as well as the high vacuum capsule, and the spring is omitted, the valve movement will depend upon the pressure ratio between inlet and outlet (P_{c2}/P_{c1}).

The final, more complex, version replaces the high vacuum capsule with one filled with a dry nitrogen charge at a known pressure. The sensor then needs to be placed in such a position that not only is it exposed to the delivery pressure (P_{c2}) but also to the temperature of the exit air flow from the compressor (T_{c2}). The actuator will then respond to changes in air density.

Why should any of these other versions be used in preference to the simple pressure differential type? If compressor outlet pressure (P_{c2}) is plotted against outlet temperature (T_{c2}), the different temperature behaviours can be seen. The actuator which responds to absolute pressure will attempt to hold P_{c2} constant and will plot as a horizontal line with changing temperature. The constant density sensor will give a sloping straight line following P_{c2}/T_{c2} = constant, while a pressure differential controller will give a line following the

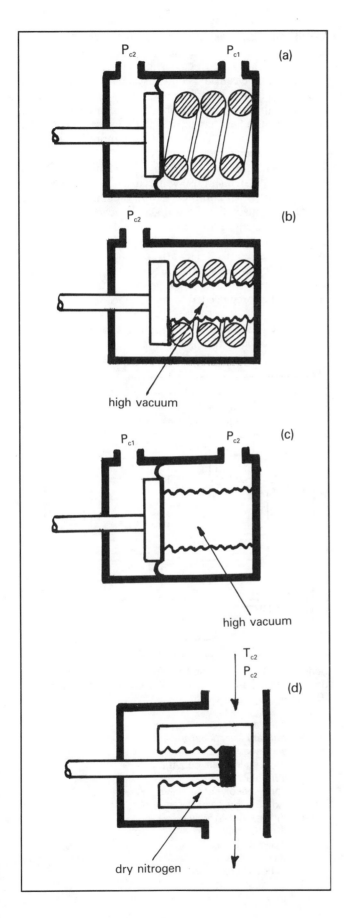

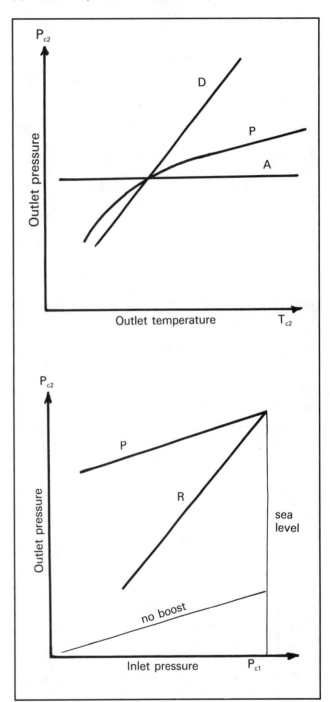

Different operating principles for simple wastegate actuators.
(a) differential pressure (c) pressure ratio
(b) absolute pressure (d) density

Comparison of the effects of the different actuator operating principles.

D   constant density P_{c2}/T_{c2} = constant
P   constant pressure differential $P_{c2}/\sqrt{T_{c2}}$ = constant
    $P_{c2} - P_{c1}$ = constant
A   constant absolute pressure P_{c2} = constant
R   constant pressure ratio P_{c2}/P_{c1} = constant

curve $P_{c2}/\sqrt{T_{c2}}$ = constant. The objective of supercharging of any form is to get a greater density of air in the charge so that the constant density controller has an attraction despite its extra complexity. There may be a reason which sets an explicit limit on the maximum inlet pressure to the engine, and here the constant absolute pressure controller would meet that need. The simple pressure differential controller may give an acceptable compromise.

If absolute compressor outlet pressure (P_{c2}) is plotted against absolute inlet pressure (P_{c1}), another interesting set of lines is obtained. The basic reference is a no boost line where $P_{c2} = P_{c1}$, and the vertical line at the right represents the ambient pressure at sea level. With increasing altitude, the inlet pressure (P_{c1}) will drop, and the different characteristics of the pressure differential and pressure ratio controllers can be seen. These differences are obviously relevant to the turbocharging of aircraft engines, but are equally important when designing vehicles which have to spend a significant proportion of their life in mountainous country, particularly trucks.

Modern high-accuracy fuel injection systems usually incorporate some form of measurement of the actual air mass flow into the engine. When this is incorporated into a full electronic engine management system it has now become possible to control the behaviour of a turbocharger so that it delivers the desired mass flow, instead of working with some indirect parameter such as delivery pressure.

The simple wastegate control servo not only uses the compressor outlet pressure to sense the action to be taken, but also uses that pressure to move the valve. If there is no air pressure, there will be no need to open the valve; it has an attractive simplicity. So much so that even when an electronic control system is used, the compressor pressure is still generally used for the servo power, with an electrically operated valve being inserted in the pressure feed line to modulate the wastegate movements by adjusting the amount of compressor pressure allowed to reach the servo actuator.

Larger, more complex engine installations may have other servo systems in use which draw their power from specially provided compressed air, vacuum or hydraulic systems. If this is the situation, that power may also be used for wastegate or turbine vane actuation as well, although it would not normally be introduced just for turbocharger control. The attraction of such sources of servo power is the strong force readily available. This can be relevant if a variable geometry turbine is being used, as the force needed to move the vanes can be considerable.

Porsche used a number of the control techniques which have been discussed when they developed the

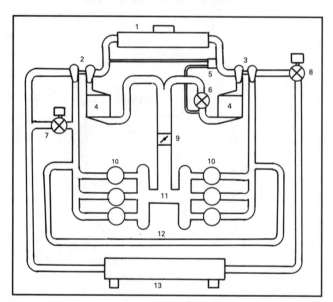

Schematic diagram of the two-stage turbocharging system used on the 2.9-litre Porsche 959 Group B sports saloon. [*Porsche*]

1   inlet air filter
2   primary turbocharger
3   secondary turbocharger
4   twin charge air coolers
5   vent valve
6   compressor cut-in valve
7   exhaust by-pass valve (wastegate)
8   turbine cut-in valve
9   throttle valve
10   cylinder banks
11   inlet manifold
12   exhaust cross-over pipe
13   exhaust muffler

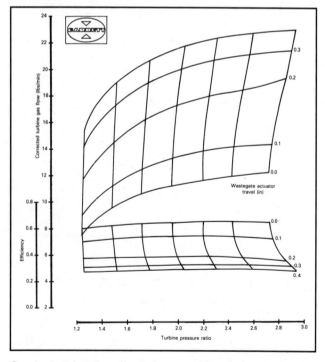

Graph showing the effect of wastegate opening on the gas flow and efficiency of a Garrett T025 turbine. [*Garrett*]

turbocharged 2.85-litre engine for the 959 Group B sports car, and they introduced an interesting sequential system using twin turbochargers[51]. This has three distinct operating phases:

At full load and low engine speed all the available exhaust gas is directed to the left-hand turbocharger. The right-hand turbocharger is isolated by a special cut-in valve which constructionally is similar to a separate wastegate and which is closed during this phase. The compressor of the right-hand turbocharger is also isolated from the compressed charge air system by a cut-in valve of the IMPCO in-line type. The wastegate is also closed during this phase.

As the engine speed increases and the required boost pressure is reached, excess exhaust gas has to be dumped. This is achieved by the turbine cut-in valve being part opened by the control system. This speeds up the right-hand turbocharger without it supplying any air to the engine. A vent valve prevents the right-hand turbocharger from pumping.

When the cut-in speed is reached, the turbine cut-in valve opens fully and the air vent valve is closed. The compressor cut-in valve then opens as boost pressure builds up from the right-hand compressor. This has now brought the right-hand turbocharger into full action. As the speed continues to rise, the boost pressure is regulated by blowing off excess exhaust gas through the wastegate.

An overboost safety switch is fitted to cut off the fuel supply should the wastegate fail to open and the pressure exceed about 1.1 to 1.4 bar.

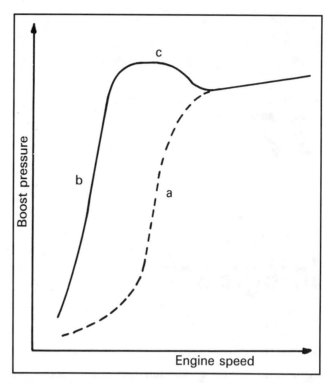

The effect of the Porsche two-stage system on boost pressure build-up.

(a) conventional dual turbocharging
(b) single turbocharger stage of two-stage system
(c) full two-stage supercharging

17

Integration

A mechanically driven supercharger or a turbocharger cannot just be added to an engine without considering the overall implications of the addition. The combination of engine, supercharging device, fuel system and, for gasoline engines, the ignition system, must all be treated as one total system rather than individual elements. The ultimate expression of this overall view comes with modern electronic engine management systems, and these are considered later. First, we will look at the detail changes needed for fuel and ignition systems and for valve timing.

The fuel requirement characteristics of a supercharged engine can change significantly from those of the equivalent naturally aspirated engine. Up to 12% reduction in specific fuel consumption is not uncommon, a 1.3-litre turbocharged engine being equivalent to a 2-litre naturally aspirated one.

Any fuel system must provide a number of basic features:

- mixture enrichment for cold starting;
- correct mixture control at idle speed;
- main fuel supply for normal cruising;
- a power system to deliver maximum power and acceleration;
- some form of transient control to handle acceleration requests.

Supercharging has tended to be associated with high performance vehicles, and for today's gasoline-powered passenger vehicles this usually means that a fuel injection system is used. However, as was discussed earlier in this book, supercharging is now adopted for other reasons than high power, notably emissions control. This has meant the use of mechanical superchargers or turbochargers on small, cost-sensitive engines where traditional carburation is still the norm. In addition, the

do-it-yourself after-market is often interested in turbocharging older engines fitted with carburettors.

Carburettors were developed long before superchargers became common, and some adaptation is needed to meet the changed situation. Most types of carburettors can be adapted to give good results with supercharging, although some are easier than others. There are two basic alternatives when installing a supercharging compressor – either after or before the carburettor.

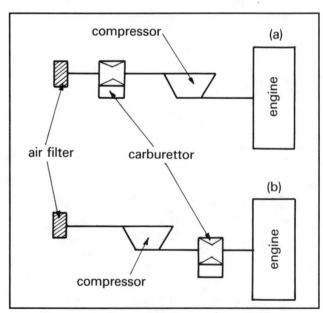

Different possible arrangements of carburettor and supercharger

(a) suck-through   (b) blow-through

These are generally referred to as 'suck-through' and 'blow-through', and each has its advantages and disadvantages, the choice usually being determined by the particular engine layout and planned usage.

If a suck-through installation is chosen it has the advantage that the carburettor will be working with the normal, relatively constant air pressure and temperature[17]. No special modifications are needed to the carburettor other than jet changes to match the new fuel requirements. The action of the compressor, particularly the high-speed impeller of a turbocharger, will help to break up any fuel droplets and give a more uniform fuel/air mixture. The evaporation of the fuel will give latent heat cooling of the compressor, resulting in a reduced delivery temperature to the engine.

With a suck-through carburettor on a turbocharged engine, when the throttle is closed during gear shifting, the air flow through the compressor will drop instantly, even though the turbine is still being accelerated by the exhaust gases. As soon as the gear shift is complete and the throttle is opened again, an extra boost is available immediately.

The prime disadvantage of a suck-through installation is that closing the throttle on engine over-run causes a high vacuum to be generated at the compressor inlet. This tends to suck oil through the compressor bearing seal, and a special type of turbocharger must be used which has a seal suitable for this duty. This will be associated with higher friction losses in the turbocharger and poorer transient response.

The carburettor must also be moved away from the preferred position adjacent to the inlet manifold in order to get it in front of the compressor. For a turbocharger this will usually be adjacent to the exhaust of the engine where the charger is normally mounted. Turbocharged gasoline engines often suffer from high engine compartment temperatures due to large, very hot exhaust surfaces. Having to move the carburettor nearer to the hottest regions can also give fuel boiling problems. The carburettor may be now also a relatively long way from the cylinders, and this can adversely affect transient response and polluting emissions due to the amount of fuel/air mixture held in the delivery duct.

Some carburettors incorporate correction jets to counteract low speed enrichment under heavily pulsating air flow. In a supercharged engine with a suck-through carburettor positioning, the compressor and ducting may damp out these pulsations, requiring a modified jet balance. The compressor inlet pressure will always be below the ambient pressure due to the necessary pressure drop through the carburettor. This may require the choice of a larger size of compressor to achieve the correct matching.

Because the compressor is handling a mixture of air and fuel, care must be taken to ensure that no liquid fuel can gather in the compressor housing. An air dump valve at the compressor exit is not generally an acceptable method of pressure control as it would require its outlet to be connected back to the compressor inlet to ensure that no fuel was lost. It is also not usually sensible to attempt to fit a charge air cooler after the compressor. With the carburettor mounted in front of the compressor, some heating of the manifolding may be needed to get good slow running, particularly when starting from cold with the air temperature below 10°C.

The blow-through carburettor configuration has the advantage that the compressor inlet is always at the ambient pressure so that the maximum capacity is available from the compressor. There is also no need to move the carburettor from its optimum position. A charge air cooler, with its associated long ducts, can be fitted without any problems, and the benefit of the fuel evaporation cooling is felt directly in the combustion chambers.

The biggest disadvantages with the blow-through arrangement result from the carburettor having to work under the boost pressure. It has to be completely sealed from the normal atmospheric pressure and the usual hollow control floats have to be replaced by ones which can resist the boost pressure. The fuel feed pump must also operate at a higher pressure which is adjustable to compensate for the varying boost.

The simple venturi which is used in the majority

The pressurised fuel feed system needed for use with a blow-through carburettor layout.

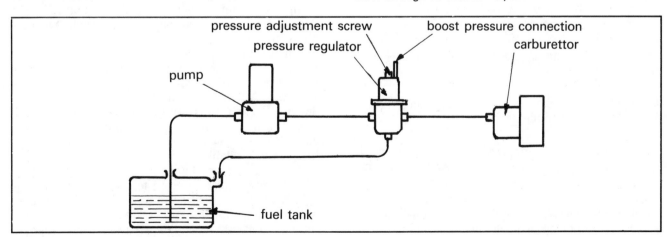

pressure adjustment screw   boost pressure connection

pressure regulator   carburettor

pump

fuel tank

of carburettors for flow metering is sensitive to air density changes. In the absence of any proper density compensation, the use of a carburettor placed after the compressor becomes less attractive the higher the boost pressure. In addition, the operating temperature of the carburettor will change due to the varying exit temperature from the compressor; low temperature at low boost, higher at high boost. With a turbocharger installation there is also the possibility of compressor surge on over-run with the throttle closed.

Modern engines with emissions control systems often vent the crankcase blow-by gases and the fuel tank evaporation connections into the carburettor. With a blow-through supercharging arrangement these connections are likely to need to be changed, possibly by adding check valves. Brake and other servo systems commonly draw their vacuum power from a carburettor connection. With a blow-through system this may give an intermittent supply and also require a check valve to be fitted.

These various advantages and disadvantages are summarised in the accompanying table[26]

Feature	Blow-through	Suck-through
Carb location & linkage	no change	must be moved
Fuel pump	extra pump or compensate for higher variable pressure	no change
Positive crankcase ventilation	move to compressor inlet	no change
Fuel evaporation system	needs check valve to stop pressure on fuel tank	no change
Carb leakage	all holes must be sealed or boxed	no change
Distance carb to cylinder	no change	much longer
Carb float	may need strengthening	no change
Turbo oil seal	nothing special	must have positive seal on compressor
Compressor surge	can be problem on deceleration	not usually a problem
Compressor size	inlet always ambient press so max capacity available	inlet below ambient needs slightly larger
Carb inlet temp	low temp at low load high temp at high load	constant temp for any load
Vacuum source for brakes, etc	sporadic, requires check valve and reservoir	no change

Many modern carburettors are already quite well sealed for use up to about 0.5 bar boost. The most vulnerable points are the throttle shaft and the float chamber lid. A non-sealed carburettor can often be modified by drilling a pressurising hole which connects the throttle shaft bearing to a point above the venturi throat which will always be at a slightly higher pressure. This will ensure no atmospheric pressure leakage at this point. The float chamber lid can be sealed by a good gasket if one is not already fitted. The traditional float made from thin metal is liable to collapse under boost pressure and needs to be replaced by a stronger plastic one. It is now possible to buy carburettors which are designed to operate under pressure and have all these matters already dealt with.

The standard fuel pump fitted on a naturally aspirated engine will only give enough pressure to overcome filter resistance and deliver the fuel to the carburettor float chamber. For a pressurised carburettor application a higher-pressure pump must be provided and this is usually a separate electrically driven one. This must have a high enough delivery pressure to overcome the maximum boost pressure which may be reached. Unfortunately, at low boost pressure the fuel pressure may force the float chamber valve open and flood the carburettor, so a pressure regulator is also needed. Weber supply one which can accept a control feed of boost pressure to it, returning any excess fuel back before the pump. This regulator will always ensure that the delivery pressure is at a fixed (but screw adjustable) amount above the boost pressure.

In suck-through installations it may be necessary to change the connection which gives pressure sensing for full power to a point downstream of the compressor. This will depend on the individual carburettor design. Where a progressive multi-barrel carburettor is used its action should be changed so that the secondary barrel is only brought into action when the supercharger pressure is available.

Side-draught carburettors, such as the SU and Weber types, are usually easier to adapt to a supercharging configuration than down-draught types. If a tuned manifold is used, care must be taken with any modifications, as even minor piping changes can change the efficacy of the additional resonance charging.

Combining a supercharger with a fuel injection system can be much simpler. However, if the injection system is one of the new simplified single injection point types, used on some small cars, many of the positioning arguments apply just as for carburettors. With the port injection systems used on higher-performance/more expensive vehicles, there are no positioning issues at all; the compressor will always be before the fuel entry point. The only requirement will be to change the mapping of the fuel control system to provide the necessary engine fuel requirements appropriate to the higher density charge of air.

The ideal, or stoichiometric, air/fuel ratio for a naturally aspirated gasoline engine would be 14:1. With a supercharged engine the higher density charge and the need to minimise detonation require that a slightly enriched mixture at full load is to be preferred, in the range 12.5-13.0:1. This would apply only to simple carburettor systems. The very high accuracy of combustion conditions needed to conform to the latest emissions control regulations requires a more refined 'closed loop' control system which is dealt with elsewhere in this book.

The essential changes needed to the fuel system of a diesel engine when it is supercharged are more straightforward. The pressure charging will enable more fuel to be burned and this obviously has to be reflected in the setting of the fuel injection pump and the injection nozzle selection. There will be an increase in the cylinder pressure existing when injection starts, and also an increase in peak pressure, and this may require an increase in the delivery pressure of the injection pump to maintain adequate atomisation of the fuel.

Where the boost pressure is obtained from a turbocharger there will always be a lag between opening the throttle and the boost pressure building up. Ways of minimising this lag by turbocharger design and control system design have been discussed elsewhere, but there will always be the inherent limitation that the energy to increase the speed of the turbocharger can only come from first burning some more fuel.

A supercharged diesel engine is normally running with an excess of air, so that a sudden opening of the throttle, producing an immediate increase in fuel supply, will initially just reduce the amount of this excess but still give acceptable combustion conditions. If, however, a full throttle request is made at a low speed point, when the amount of boost and the corresponding excess air is small, the resulting mixture, although still burnable, can produce an unacceptable level of smoke and other pollutants until the turbocharger builds up speed and restores the air/fuel ratio. Developments have taken place in diesel fuel injection pumps to try to avoid this problem.

In 1985 Opel introduced on their turbocharged diesel engines a version of the combined distributor/injection pump which was fitted with a control sensitive to the charging pressure, and this is shown in the

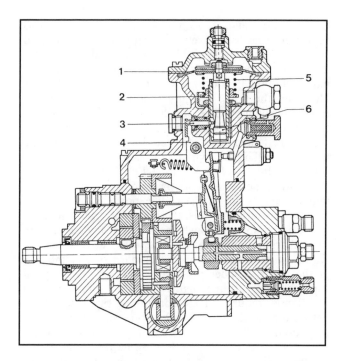

A diesel fuel injection pump with boost pressure control to avoid smoke on sudden throttle transients.

1 boost pressure sensing diaphragm
2 pressure setting adjustment
3 control sensing pin
4 pump stroke limiting lever
5 pressure balancing spring
6 limit control plunger [Opel]

accompanying diagram. The pump is provided with an adjustable stop (4) which can limit the maximum amount of fuel delivered when the boost pressure is low. As long as no pressure is generated by the turbocharger, the diaphragm (1), which is pushed upwards by the spring (5), remains at rest. The guide pin (3) is pushed outward by the adjusting plunger (6) and limits the quantity injected by means of the stop lever (4). As soon as the diaphragm is pushed downwards by the pressure in the intake manifold, the guide pin slips inwards along the conical adjusting plunger and releases the full load quantity by allowing the stop lever to withdraw.

BMW have gone even further and have developed in conjunction with Bosch a diesel fuel pump which can be integrated into a full digital electronic engine management system. The fuel injection pump has been fitted with a rotary electromagnetic actuator which can set any desired injection volume under the control of the microcomputer master controller. This allows a diesel-engined vehicle to obtain all the advantages of the electronic control systems developed for spark ignition engines.

Ignition

In gasoline engines, part throttle working has traditionally been accompanied by a lean air/fuel mixture, and

117

the ignition point is advanced well before top dead centre in order to ensure that combustion is completed correctly. When an engine is supercharged this combination would be likely to lead to the early onset of detonation, and the ignition spark point needs to be retarded. However, the boost pressure produces a denser, more rapidly burning mixture, which naturally needs less ignition advance. Reducing the amount of advance will reduce the tendency of the fuel air mixture to detonate by reducing the peak cylinder pressure and temperature. This can be effective up to 9-12°, but with further retardation there can be an increasing tendency to pre-ignition and a fall in the engine power.

In opposition to this, the reduction in the geometric compression ratio which is likely to accompany supercharging will require an increased advance of the ignition timing due to the slower burn rate of the fuel at the lower cylinder pressures. As a result, a typical supercharged gasoline engine with a compression ratio of 8:1 may require an ignition timing of up to 12-14° before top dead centre at idle, increasing rapidly to a maximum of 28-34° at 2,000 rpm approximately. Thereafter, as the boost takes effect, some retarding of the ignition will be needed, retard increasing in steps of 0.5-1.2° per 0.05 bar boost increase.

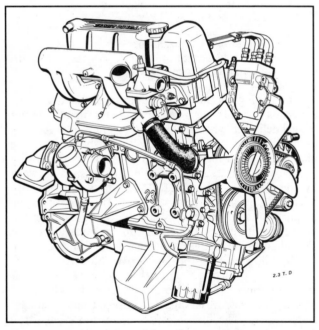

A turbocharged diesel engine showing the bearing oil feed and drain pipes for the turbocharger. [*Opel*]

The older-style distributors controlled by a centrifugal mechanism can be modified by reducing the movement of the bob weights to reduce the amount of advance. This can be done by reducing the length of the slot in the mechanism, putting a sleeve over the stop pegs, or moving the pegs. It is now possible to obtain double-acting pressure diaphragms which allow a boost

pressure feed as well as a vacuum feed to give an effective retardation with boost. Electronic ignition control systems will usually have some facility for changing the basic characteristic curve.

Because of the higher combustion chamber pressure and temperature which will result from supercharging, a change will need to be made in the spark plugs. One step cooler in heat range is desirable to cope with the higher temperature, and the plug gap should be reduced slightly to ensure that reliable sparking will still occur at the higher pressure.

Valve timing

In theory the valve timing of a naturally aspirated four-stroke engine should be arranged so that the exhaust valve closes at top dead centre after the exhaust expulsion stroke, at which point the inlet valve starts to open. In practice, because neither valve can move instantaneously from open to closed and vice versa, if such an arrangement was adopted there would be residual exhaust gases left in the cylinder and the new charge drawn in would not completely fill the cylinder. It is therefore normal to provide a degree of overlap between the exhaust and inlet valves, the inlet starting to open before top dead centre and the exhaust closing after it.

At low speed this overlap does not need to be great, but as the speed rises it becomes increasingly difficult to get an adequate charge into the cylinder. As a result, the design of the camshafts which operate the valves becomes a compromise between getting adequate exhaust scavenging and charge filling at high speed, and adequate torque and stable running at low speeds. The 'hot cams' beloved of competition drivers exaggerate the power at high revolutions by accepting a degree of rough running and absence of torque at low speeds. However, if the inlet starts to open too early there is a risk of exhaust gases getting back into the inlet manifold causing back-fire in gasoline engines.

When an engine is supercharged, this conventional approach to valve timing needs to be reviewed. If no change is made, the usual substantial overlap will allow the new charge which is forced into the cylinder by the boost pressure to completely scavenge any remaining exhaust gas and then start to follow out through the exhaust valve. For a diesel engine this is not a bad thing to happen as the cylinder is completely cleaned out with fresh air, and any excess spilling into the exhaust manifold can be used to keep down the peak temperature of an exhaust turbine. Some diesel engine designs have actually exaggerated the amount of overlap to take advantage of these benefits, as the boost pressure will stop any risk of exhaust gases getting back into the inlet, although the size of the cut-outs in the piston crowns will limit the possibilities.

For a gasoline spark ignition engine there will be a problem if excessive valve overlap is used with supercharging. It is unacceptable that any of the fuel/air mixture shall be allowed to escape through the exhaust port, and the degree of valve overlap has to be reduced to cater for the faster cylinder filling.

Most automobile engines which are turbocharged have available a potential excess boost which is relieved by a wastegate, a result of designing to minimise the dreaded turbocharger lag with sudden throttle opening. This potential excess boost can be put to good use by compensating for a delay in opening the inlet valves. It now becomes possible to design the cam shape to give the best torque characteristic at low speed, when the engine is effectively naturally aspirated, and rely on the supercharger to give adequate filling of the cylinders at high speeds.

In 1957, Miller published details of a new system he had introduced for giving variable valve timing on large diesel engines in order to avoid these design compromises[9]. In the Miller system the camshaft operated the inlet valve through a cam follower and pushrod. An eccentric on a control shaft was coupled to the cam follower so that rotation of the control shaft moved the contact point of the cam follower on the cam surface, thereby effectively moving the timing point for the valve opening.

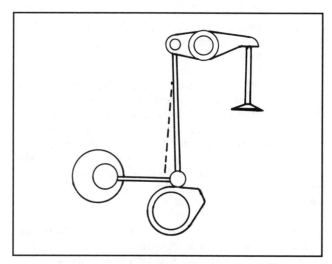

The principle of the Miller variable valve timing system. Rotation of the control eccentric varies the contact point of the cam follower and thus the instant of inlet valve opening.

More recently Alfa Romeo adapted this variable inlet valve timing idea to an automobile gasoline engine. A simple hydraulically operated mechanism allows the drive sprocket of the inlet camshaft to be rotated relative to the cams by a fixed amount, 16°. On the Alfetta Gold Cloverleaf model this gives a change from 0° to 32° before dead centre.

An annular piston with helical splines is fitted on the camshaft inside the sprocket. Oil under pressure forces the piston to move against spring pressure, thereby giving the desired rotation. The engine lubricating oil circuit is used to give the necessary hydraulic servo pressure and this is controlled by a solenoid valve

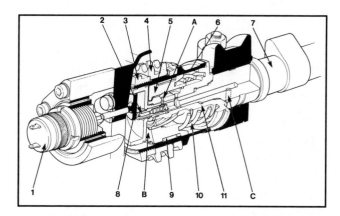

Layout of the Alfa Romeo variable inlet valve timing system. Operation of the solenoid causes lubricating oil pressure to force the piston to move against the control spring, resulting in the rotation of the drive sprocket relative to the camshaft. [Alfa Romeo]

1 solenoid	8 actuator
2 oil drain port	9 helical pinion
3 lockring	10 spring
4 timing chain sprocket	A oil port from engine
5 straight-tooth piston	B actuating chamber
6 sleeve	C oil port
7 camshaft	

from the Bosch Motronic engine management system. This system has been shown to give a 28% improvement in urban cycle fuel consumption.

Subsequently Ferrari, Fiat, Mercedes-Benz, Nissan and Toyota have all followed the initiative of Alfa Romeo by introducing variable valve timing systems.

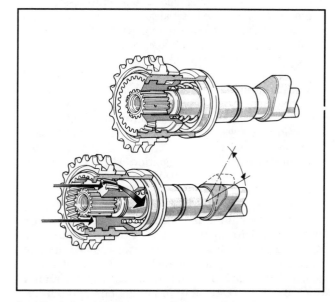

Detail of the Alfa Romeo variable timing operation. The actuating piston has straight splines on the inside and helical splines on the outside. As the oil pressure forces it inwards, the helical teeth will cause the drive sprocket to be rotated relative to the camshaft. [Alfa Romeo]

119

18

Engine control systems

Early automobiles had very simple engine controls. Levers mounted at the steering wheel allowed the driver to vary the throttle opening, the fuel mixture strength and the ignition timing. Very quickly, simple automatic features were developed to ease the burden on the driver. Carburettors were refined so that only a 'choke' was needed for cold starting and a speed sensitive mechanism was added to the ignition system to adjust spark timing. With the addition of a manifold pressure adjustment for ignition timing and a temperature-sensitive automatic choke, these basic ideas remained as the main control elements for gasoline engines for decades, and are still used on simple, cheaper vehicles.

Increasing competition between manufacturers put pressure on the need to improve fuel economy and engine smoothness, and this led to continual improvements in carburettor and ignition system design. Fuel injection systems began to be used for competition cars, then gradually began to appear in expensive luxury cars. Simple electronic controls were introduced for some functions, in particular for ignition where the unreliability of the mechanical contact breaker could be eliminated.

Since the early 1980s the pressure to reduce atmospheric pollution has focused engineers' attention on ways of improving the accuracy of engine control systems, and the introduction of emissions control laws in many countries has accelerated the resulting developments. The ready availability of electronic circuitry which could work reliably in automobile applications has helped to remove the inherent weaknesses of many of the traditional mechanisms.

A designer can work out from test results the optimum fuel and ignition conditions to accompany all the load/speed situations likely to be encountered by the vehicle in which an engine is to be fitted. This complex set of requirements, the preferred engine 'map', will then have to be approximated by the mechanisms available for actual fuel and ignition control. Inevitably, this set of approximations, in order to avoid dangerous operation at any point, will be sub-optimal at many points.

This design now has to be transferred to the realities of the production line, where every component has a tolerance. Again, in order to ensure that the limiting conditions are not breached, the operational points will become even more sub-optimal. The problems do not end there; any engine can be expected to deteriorate during its operating life and allowance must be made for this in the initial set-up. The net result of all this is that the engineers knew that they could build an engine which would satisfy the forthcoming legislation, but they had no chance of getting a practicable production version which would pass. A new approach was needed.

All the early mechanisms provided what is known as 'open loop' control. Some measurement, such as engine speed, would be obtained and used to adjust an item, such as ignition timing, in accordance with a rule built into the control mechanism design. No notice was taken of whether it actually achieved the desired result.

Any truly effective control must operate in a 'closed loop' system, where the resulting change in the output is fed back to adjust the control so that the correct result is obtained. Automobiles have always had one overriding closed loop control system – it is called the driver! A request for more speed is made by depressing the accelerator pedal, and the result is fed back to the driver's brain by looking at the speedometer. When the desired speed is approached, the foot is lifted a little to level off at that speed.

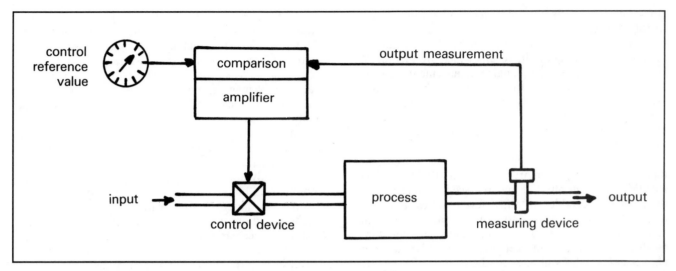

The principle of 'closed loop' control systems. A measurement is made of the output from a process which is then compared with a pre-set control reference value. The difference between them is amplified and used to control the input to the process.

As electronic controls were introduced for automobile engines it became feasible to introduce closed loop systems. Fuel injection systems could monitor all the different parameters of the engine, combine them to determine the probable amount and timing of fuel injection, then measure the resulting effect on speed, temperature and air mass flow to make any necessary adjustments. Ignition systems could also have some feedback built in, and we have already seen how turbocharger wastegate controls can be set up to obtain the necessary feedback of boost pressure.

The early electronic controls consisted of circuits built from standard components and designed to do one specific thing. Many of them operated in what is called 'analogue' mode; measurements were made of varying quantities, usually expressed as electrical voltages. However, the trend in electronics has been towards 'digital' mode working, where quantities are stored as numbers, and the high-volume cheap components supported this trend. Use of digital electronics allows more complex calculations to be performed, involving several parameters, and easier interpretation of the preferred mapping for an engine, but often requires analogue to digital converters to accept the input signals from sensors, and digital to analogue converters to drive the output devices. With the provision of these features, the special-purpose control units were becoming very complex.

A logical next step was to start using the digital micro-computers which have revolutionised data processing and industrial control systems. The initial cost of providing the computer, with its power supplies and input/output devices, was comparable to the cost of the complex special-purpose electronics. However, once the computer was available it could be used for any of the engine management functions and could be adapted to any application. Typical functions are the optimisation of fuel economy, control of engine power output and torque, and the limiting of exhaust emissions.

A simple turbocharger management electronic control unit. Instead of using a programmed computer, this system uses a series of independently adjustable pre-set control points which determine the response to the varying boost pressure. [ERP]

A micro-computer is a standard piece of 'hardware' which will obey any sequence of a set of instructions which it understands. Such a sequence of instructions is called a 'program' and is described as the 'software' of the computer. Programs can be written to carry out any desired job and are simply stored in the computer memory ready to be activated when required. To change the application of a computer it is only necessary to change the software; the hardware remains the same.

Just like the early mechanisms or the later stand-alone electronic units, the computer can be programmed to follow a specific set of rules. It also has the power to do more than this; the rules can be changed during operation depending on the results which are measured, leading to total closed loop engine management systems. To avoid having to completely reload all the programs every time the computer is applied to a new engine or the engine characteristics are to be changed, the desired engine 'maps' are held in the computer memory as sets of numeric tables.

These tables are held in what are called 'programmable, read only memory' chips, or PROMs. The PROM can be unplugged and replaced by one with a different set of tables within a few minutes, and this allows the manufacturers to use the same engine in several different vehicles with different characteristics. It also gives an after-market opportunity for the 'hot chip hackers' who will alter the behaviour of your car for a price!

Sensors

Once a computer system has been introduced, it is natural that it will be used to control as many functions around the engine as possible. In order that the correct decisions can be taken, the computer must know what is going on, and to this end a variety of 'sensors' are provided to give this input. Which sensors are provided depends upon the individual manufacturer's approach, but a number of the most common ones are described below.

In order to determine the basic request from the driver, a sensor measuring throttle position is needed. Some newer systems dispense with the mechanical linkage from accelerator pedal to throttle and sense the pedal position, relying upon the electronics to set the correct throttle position. The most common sensor will be based on a variable resistor, a potentiometer, which will need an analogue-digital converter at the computer. Some experimental work has used a special sensing device which gives directly a digital signal read-out of angular position. Frequently, micro-switches are fitted to sense the fully-open and idle throttle positions.

At the other end of the control loop, a measure of engine speed is needed. This will usually be a magnetic (Hall effect) or electro-optical detector which responds to a marker on the flywheel, or ignition distributor, giving a pulse every revolution. The pulses are then counted during a known time interval to give engine speed. For ignition timing the actual crank position relative to top dead centre is needed. This can be determined by calculation from the speed reference pulse, but additional pulse points may be provided to give greater accuracy. Some control systems may also include in their calculations the road speed of the vehicle, and a similar revolution detector would then be fitted at the output shaft of the gearbox. These pulse generators may already be fitted to actuate electronic speedometer and engine speed meters.

For correct fuel control, the computer will need to know the mass-flow of air entering the engine[65]. Many semi-electronic fuel injection systems use a shaped paddle or float suspended in a chamber through which the engine air is sucked. The shape of the float is such that its movement in the air flow is proportional to the mass-flow. This can be fitted with a potentiometer-type position detector to feed the computer, but a preferred option is to use one of the newer hot-wire flow detectors which can give a digital signal directly proportional to air mass-flow.

Not only does the weight of air being drawn in need to be known, but also its pressure and temperature. The sensors for these variables will be fitted in the inlet manifold and are usually based on materials whose electrical resistance varies with pressure or temperature. This variation can be interpreted by an analogue-to-digital converter into the desired numerical value. For a supercharged engine it may be necessary to provide additional sensors to measure these values before the compressor, but this is not likely unless a very complex control system is trying to optimise the working position of the compressor within its map, as well as the overall engine parameters.

One type of pressure sensor makes use of a piezo-resistive semiconductor crystal chip whose electrical resistance varies as it is subjected to bending. This crystal is formed so that a chamber exists between it and the base on which it is mounted. This chamber is evacuated so that when the chip is exposed to the manifold pressure the amount of bend, and thus the electrical resistance of the chip, is proportional to the absolute pressure.

A sensor is also needed for the cooling water jacket temperature, to ensure that there is no overheating and to handle cold starting correctly. The exhaust pipe gas temperature may need measuring if a catalytic converter or a particulate trap is fitted, to ensure that it operates at its effective temperature.

One of the limiting factors in the operation of a gasoline engine, particularly when pressure charging is used, is the onset of detonation. To ensure that it does not occur simply by controlling other parameters means that a lot of margin must be left. It is therefore common practice now for 'knock' sensors to be fitted, which are basically a form of robust microphone which respond to engine vibrations.

One type makes use of the magnetostricture effect. If a small core of a high nickel steel alloy is subject to mechanical pressure it will change its magnetism. A coil around the core can detect these changes, which appear as electrical voltages. These are amplified and then filtered to remove the background noise of normal engine running so that the peaks caused by detonation starting can be identified.

Another type makes use of a piezo-ceramic element which responds to mechanical deformation by producing an electrical signal. The version used by Volkswagen is sensitive to engine vibrations in the range of 7-12kHz.

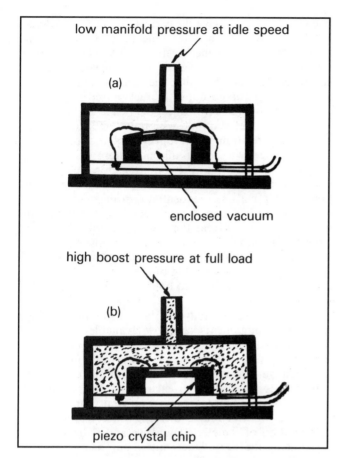

low manifold pressure at idle speed

(a)

enclosed vacuum

high boost pressure at full load

(b)

piezo crystal chip

Working principle of a pressure-sensing piezo crystal chip. The hollow chip is slightly curved (a) and is sealed to an insulating sub-strate with a vacuum enclosed within the hollow of the chip. The outer enclosure is connected to the boost pressure circuit. When the pressure rises (b), the crystal flattens and this bending causes an electrical signal to be generated at the electrodes connected to the chip.

To avoid confusion with the noise from auxiliary units on the engine, the signal from the detector is filtered so that only signals in the 12kHz region are recognised.

Optimum engine operation with simultaneous high efficiency under all operating conditions means that the control of the firing point should lie as close as possible to the knock limit. As an example, the Volkswagen 'Digifant' engine management system achieves this with the use of multiple knock sensors. If knocking occurs in one cylinder, this is detected cylinder-selectively and the control unit retards the firing point for the appropriate cylinder by 3.2°. If the knocking is eliminated, the firing point is advanced again in stages of 0.35° until the programmed map value is reached. If the knocking continues or reoccurs, the firing point for each cylinder can be retarded by up to 12.5°. If the sum of the ignition angle retards of all cylinders is more than 20° for a period of more than 8 seconds, the boost pressure is restricted.

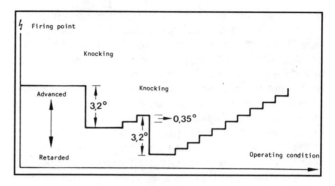

The control sequence for the Volkswagen system of detonation control. When knocking is sensed, ignition is immediately retarded by 3.2°. After a short pause the control system starts to advance the ignition again in 0.35° steps. If knocking again starts, a further 3.2° retard will be carried out, with a gradual advance taking place as conditions allow. [*Volkswagen*]

One of the most important sensors for modern engine management systems is the exhaust oxygen sensor, which is crucial for controlling the combustion conditions to minimise exhaust gas pollutants and thus maintain conformity with the regulations. The oxygen sensor is also commonly referred to as a lambda sensor as its purpose is to keep the fuel/air mixture correctly balanced so that a three-way catalyst can function correctly.

A typical lambda sensor uses a hollow ceramic probe the surfaces of which are coated with gas-permeable platinum electrodes. At temperatures above about 300°C, the probe ceramic element becomes conductive for oxygen ions. If the oxygen content is differ-

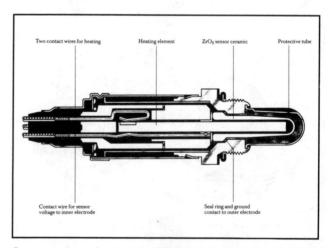

Cross-section of a pre-heated oxygen sensor, or lambda probe. The zircon dioxide ceramic tube sensor is connected to the atmosphere on the inside while its outside is exposed to the hot exhaust gases via openings in the protective sheath. Oxygen will permeate through the ceramic if the amount differs between the two sides, and this movement can be sensed at electrodes deposited on the ceramic. The heating element ensures that the probe reaches its working temperature (in excess of 300°C) very quickly. [*Bosch*]

ent on both sides, an electrical voltage is produced which can be amplified and used as a measure of the difference. The probe is mounted so that the inside of the element comes into contact with the ambient air, while the other side is contained in a protective shroud which protrudes into the exhaust gas stream. This shroud has apertures in it which allow the ceramic to contact the gas while protecting it against any contamination and overheating. A heating element is fitted which can bring the probe to its working temperature from cold within about 20-30 seconds. This gives greater freedom in choosing the mounting position for the lambda probe in the exhaust system as the probe warm-up time is independent of the engine temperature.

Actuators

With all this information about the engine behaviour, the computer can perform its calculations, using the stored rules and mapping tables, to determine the desired setting of the various controls. The controls which are available depend on the design of a particular engine and the control principles adopted by the manufacturer, but here are the most likely requirements.

The most important of the output controls is for the fuel supply. In general, the type of closed loop electronic engine management system being discussed here uses fuel injection, but an exception is the Ecotronic carburettor used by General Motors on the Opel Rekord. This is a two-barrel unit fitted with three throttles which are controllable by the electronic system through electro-

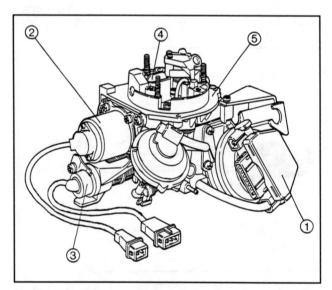

Ecotronic carburettor developed to operate with an electronic engine management system. [*Opel*]

1 throttle valve regulator with idle speed switch
2 pre-throttle adjuster
3 throttle valve potentiometer
4 pre-throttle
5 carburettor cover

pneumatic servos to give the correct mixture characteristics. The more commonly used fuel injection systems are fitted with electro-magnetic valves which allow fuel from a pressurised line to be injected under the control of the computer. The length of time the valve is held open will determine the total amount of fuel passed.

Some systems simply inject the fuel at regular intervals into the inlet manifold with no attempt to time the injection in relation to the opening of the inlet valve. Typically there will be two injections during a complete revolution cycle so that the conditions for the different cylinders are approximately the same. The more accurate (and more expensive!) sequential port injection systems will have the injection valve timed to match the opening of the inlet valve at the associated port. The electronic pulses applied to these magnetic valves are likely to be at two different current levels: a high peak current to get very fast opening of the injection valve, followed by a lower current to hold the valve open for the desired time.

The other major control is that for the spark timing. Electronic components are now available which can drive the high-voltage ignition coils direct with an amplified pulse from the computer. The traditional single high-voltage coil connected to a rotating distributor which feeds the voltage to each spark plug in turn is still the most common arrangement, but more vehicles are appearing which have 'direct ignition' features. The combination of the electronic drive and the possibility of reducing the size of the ignition coil has led to systems which eliminate all the problems associated with a mechanical distributor by providing one coil for each spark plug. These are likely to be mounted immediately adjacent to the plugs so that the risk of high-voltage leakage is minimised and all the energy is directed into the plug. The resolving of which plug to fire and when is carried out completely within the digital computer.

For the supercharged engines which are the subject of this book, the computer will operate an electro-magnetic valve which will control a usually pneumatic servo to actuate the wastegate, turbine vanes, compressor by-pass or other boost control mechanism which is provided. The rules for doing this, either as on-off functions or continuous variations, can be as complex as the computer programmer chooses to make them.

Many engines now have an exhaust gas recirculation facility to help minimise the generation of pollutants. This valve connects the exhaust manifold to the inlet manifold and is subject to severe thermal stresses. It will normally be operated by a compressed air or vacuum servo mechanism which is under the control of an electro-magnetic valve. This control valve will be activated by the computer as needed to maintain the correct oxygen level in the exhaust.

The air and fuel systems may be fitted with additional valves which are only activated during the engine warm-up phase or at idling speeds; these will also be electrically actuated as needed. The idle control valve may be involved in trimming the boost pressure when a mechanically operated supercharger is used. The main computer may also be given additional functions to look after such as anti-lock brake controls and air-conditioning equipment.

Computation systems

The fast rate at which road conditions change places very high demands on any control system. For an optimised example electronic engine management system, the computation time was 5 thousandths of a second (5 milliseconds), and the resulting throttle adjustment time was 150 milliseconds.

In addition, since the transient process associated with a power increase from an engine/supercharger system starts with an increase in the fuel quantity, and a turbocharger can only extract its energy from the exhaust gas when it becomes available one working cycle later, with supercharged engines transients are generally encumbered with a further dead time before the pressure starts to build up.

The emissions control function is also complicated by the dead time behaviour of the engine/supercharger combination. Starting from a steady state, if a distur-

bance is initiated by an increase in fuel injection rate, or a change in throttling, etc, a certain time will elapse before the lambda sensor recognizes the disturbance as a change in exhaust gas composition. This dead time is governed by the characteristics of the charge air duct, the exhaust gas duct and the engine itself. In addition, both the actuators and the lambda sensor itself exhibit their own behaviour.

A good computer program will have built into it a 'model' of the complete engine/supercharger characteristic which is expected so that it can help to minimise transient response by anticipating the behaviour of a turbocharger. A great deal of research work has been done on developing such models so that the fastest and most accurate control performance is obtained.

Most of the control issues which have been discussed in relation to spark ignition gasoline engines have an equal relevance to diesel engines, although obviously spark timing is not one of the controllable features. The application of full electronic engine management systems

Three-dimensional control map for the Volkswagen engine management system, relating engine speed, intake manifold pressure and ignition point. [*Volkswagen*]

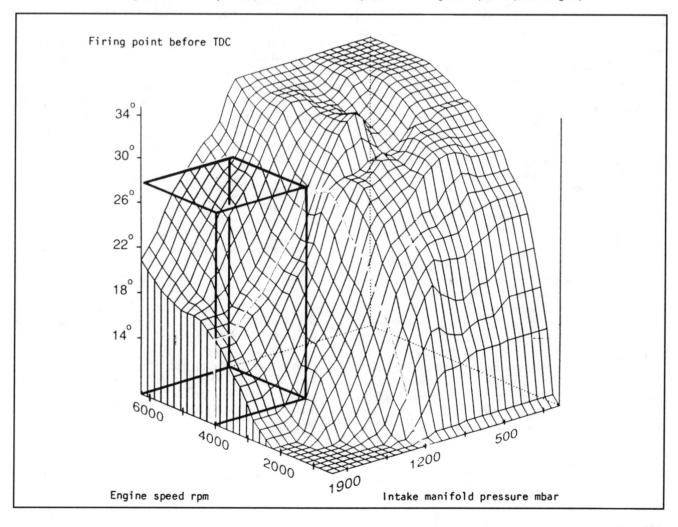

Firing point before TDC

Engine speed rpm

Intake manifold pressure mbar

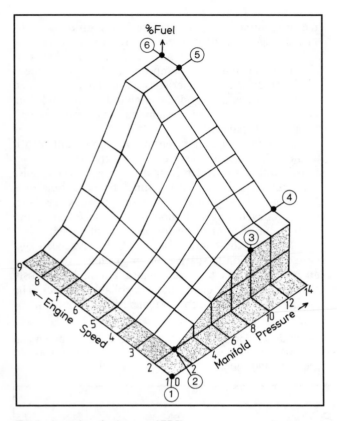

Typical engine fuel map. [ERP]

1 Start – engine at 1,000 rpm with no boost pressure, hence no fuel enrichment.

2 At 2,000 rpm the pressure threshold is reached and the fuel enrichment starts.

3 The system has arrived at the wastegate setting; the manifold pressure now stays constant and the fuel enrichment does not change.

4 At 3,000 rpm, the speed threshold is reached and additional fuel is now injected in proportion to the speed increase.

5 At 8,000 rpm the overall fuel enrichment has reached its maximum and no additional fuel is added.

6 Speed and pressure limit point.

to diesel engines has been slower, mainly due to the easier ability to meet the pollution regulations and the difficulty in producing satisfactory electronically controllable high-pressure injection pumps.

The greater use of diesel engines in automobiles and the further tightening of the pollution laws is, however, changing this. The introduction of the Bosch Digital Diesel Electronic (DDE) system by BMW in 1988 is an example of these recent developments. In the new injection pump a rotary electro-magnetic adjuster controls the injection volume and a separate electro-magnetic valve controls the instant at which injection starts. BMW

claim to have obtained a reduction in fuel consumption up to 4% when compared with a mechanical injection control system.

With a diesel engine the use of an exhaust oxygen sensor to control pollutants is complicated by the fact that the diesel normally runs with excess air conditions. The use of exhaust gas recycling under lambda sensor control thus becomes very difficult to apply when combined with a conventional turbocharger, where the changing pressure differentials between exhaust and inlet manifolds make control erratic.

The Comprex pressure wave charger gives a definite benefit in this situation. A simple throttle valve is fitted on the inlet and closing this will cause the rotor channels increasingly to fill with exhaust gas. Initially the throttling effect will cause the scavenging rate to be reduced, and only when it approaches zero does exhaust gas recycling start. From this point onwards, the exhaust gas is no longer diluted and its oxygen content can therefore be used as a reliable measure of the actual air-to-fuel ratio.

The bringing of all the engine controls together into one computer system carries with it increased risk in the event of component failure. Some products are built with total redundancy, with all circuits duplicated, but even without this extreme there will have been great attention paid to 'fail-safe' design. Any reasonably possible combination of faults is evaluated and the hardware circuits and software are set up so that the result will not be life- or equipment-threatening. One approach which is commonly adopted is to monitor the sensor and actuator signals to ensure that they remain within the normal bounds of safe working. For example, an indication of zero engine speed in conjunction with normal air flow measurements would suggest that the speed sensor had probably failed. If any such circumstance arises, the computer system will revert to simple open loop control using a pre-stored set of probably good values, while at the same time giving an alarm to the driver. This is often referred to as the 'limp home' mode.

Even with these fail-safe features built in, for very high power engines it is not uncommon to fit additional mechanical detectors which will shut down the engine if excess boost pressure, engine speed or temperature occur.

A natural result of having the computer power available is that statistics of engine and vehicle use can be maintained, leading to routine maintenance prompts. Also, any occurrences of control values outside the optimum ranges can be logged as possibly requiring attention. During vehicle maintenance the engine management computer can replay this stored data to the mechanic and also provide diagnostic aids for refining the tuning.

19

Vehicle characteristics

Having covered all the different aspects of supercharger and turbocharger design and the associated ancillary systems, this and the following chapter will look at how these ideas are applied in practice to provide a forced induction system for a vehicle.

The starting point for adding a supercharger to an engine must be to consider the vehicle characteristics which are needed. In this connection there is a lack of clarity, not only amongst the motoring public at large, but also among the experts. A number of terms which are regularly used have been derived from motor-racing and are wrongly applied to the performance of automobiles in the dense traffic of urban areas, with queues for traffic lights, as well as when driving on highways where positions are changing rapidly with overtaking. Obviously, if your application is the development of a competition car, notions such as the time to accelerate from 0 to 60 miles per hour and the flat out, steady-state top speed are very relevant, but they are quite unsuitable for the majority of passenger and commercial vehicle applications.

The 'elasticity' values which are given by the acceleration phases between two given speeds in various gears are an improvement, but they are difficult to consider in general terms in relation to driving behaviour. When optimising engine and transmission characteristics for a particular vehicle it is extremely helpful to be able to define 'vehicle performance' with a single parameter which can be described in objective terms and which takes into account the control loop formed by driver and vehicle.

One parameter which approaches this ideal is the notion of 'acceleration reserve' – the maximum spontaneously available engine mean effective pressure in excess of that required to maintain any particular steady vehicle and engine speed, on any gradient[37]. Here we recognize the decisive importance of the steady-state torque/speed characteristic of the engine, as well as that of the availability of torque with respect to time. The term 'spontaneous acceleration reserve' can be defined as the vehicle acceleration rate (m/sec^2) when utilising maximum acceleration reserve (bar) at a steady speed of 40 miles per hour in fourth gear on a level road (see the accompanying diagram).

However, it is essential to make sure that the following conditions are also covered over and beyond this main criterion: maintenance of the top speed on an uphill grade of up to 4%; starting with a load of twice the gross weight of the vehicle (eg a trailer) on grades up to 12%; and maintaining sufficient elasticity (torque characteristic and operating speed range) to ensure that overtaking is still possible.

Although the power required to propel a vehicle increases rapidly with speed, it is inappropriate to design an engine with this type of output. Consider the power and torque curves of two different hypothetical engines (see the accompanying diagram). One has a power curve which increases steeply with speed, together with a torque curve which also rises with speed. The second engine has a flatter power curve and its torque drops off with increasing speed.

If two identical vehicles fitted with these engines are running along a flat road at the same speed they will have the same engine torque output. When they come to a small hill the engine load will increase and, since both are at maximum torque available at that speed, the speed must fall. As the speed falls, engine 'b' will produce more torque to meet the load applied and the vehicle will continue up the hill at a lower speed. In contrast, engine 'a' will produce less torque as its speed

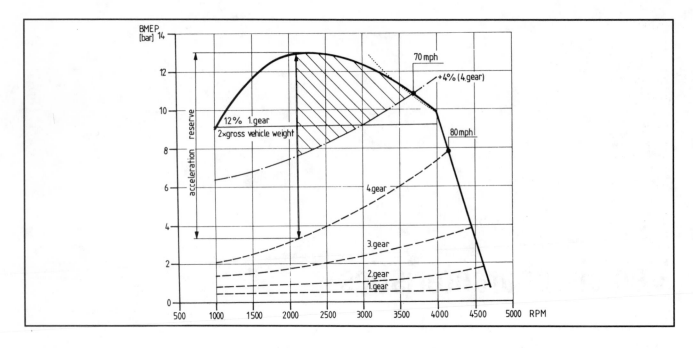

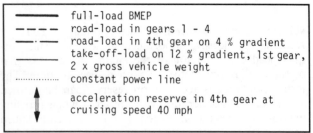

————	full-load BMEP
– – – –	road-load in gears 1 - 4
–·–·–	road-load in 4th gear on 4 % gradient
————	take-off-load on 12 % gradient, 1st gear, 2 x gross vehicle weight
··········	constant power line
↕	acceleration reserve in 4th gear at cruising speed 40 mph

Vehicle performance graph showing the principle of the acceleration reserve. [ABB]

The effect of different shape power and torque curves on a vehicle's hill climbing abilities. At point 'x' both vehicles are in equilibrium at the same speed. If a gradient is encountered they will both slow, but the torque of engine 'b' will rise and a new stable running point will be reached. For engine 'a', however, the torque will drop and the vehicle will slow even more, forcing a gear change.

drops, compounding the deceleration and forcing a gear change.

A torque curve that rises as speed falls is said to have good 'torque back-up'. With good torque back-up, the vehicle will benefit from high torque at low speeds to provide a margin for acceleration and to allow the vehicle to lug up very steep hills with a limited number of gearbox ratios. The next diagram shows the ability to climb hills if constant power were to be available over the whole speed range. The curves appropriate to the use of a five-speed gearbox with a more typical engine are superimposed. The shaded portions represent running conditions falling below the maximum power output but not achievable in practice because of insufficient torque at that speed[42].

An inherent problem which has always complicated vehicle design is that if an engine alone is to develop an adequate characteristic speed-torque output over the whole vehicle performance range, the torque ratio of the engine would have to be equal to the normal bottom

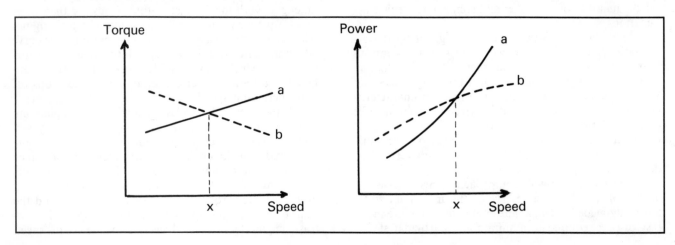

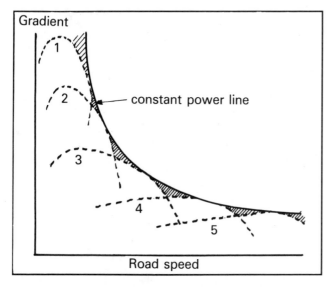

Relationship of gradient to road speed for a vehicle with a five-speed gearbox. The ratios are chosen to approximate the constant power line, but the shaded areas indicate parts of the engine performance which cannot be used.

gear ratio of the vehicle; that is, between 3 and 5 to 1 for automobiles and anything from 8 to 1 upwards for commercial vehicles, trucks and buses. Unfortunately, such high torque ratios could only be produced by unacceptably high mean effective and maximum cylinder pressures, especially in diesel cycle engines. As a result, all production vehicles are fitted with some form of gearbox or torque converter.

An additional complicating factor is that a turbocharged engine has a relatively low starting torque. Until the turbine builds up speed the available torque is that appropriate to a naturally aspirated version of the engine. For a highly pressurised engine this gives a very large spread between the minimum and maximum torque values, which has to be reflected in the gearbox ratios which are selected. This why twenty-speed gearboxes in large trucks are not uncommon, the problem being compounded by the narrow speed range of typical direct injection diesel engines. For the passenger automobile the problem is not so serious, but it is necessary to remember that the engine will be operating with little or no boost for much of its operating life.

The fuel consumption characteristic for an engine also has to be taken into account when determining the desired operating points. The minimum fuel consumption should be related to the power/speed conditions which are expected to dominate the vehicle use, and this is usually quite some way away from the maximum power point. A first great step in improving performance and fuel consumption is possible when the displacement of the engine is reduced ('downsizing') by the ratio of the supercharging rate. High-torque-rise engines allow furthermore the possibility of shifting the mean operating point along the constant power line, closer to the optimum fuel consumption point ('gearmatching').

The following demands are then imposed on the torque characteristic of the supercharged engine:
• The smaller the engine displacement, ie the smaller the power/weight ratio, the more important the increase in torque becomes to ensure a given acceleration reserve. A 30% increase in torque is regarded as necessary. This increase, compared with the values that were formerly common, results in vehicles actually being driven using lower engine speeds. A further increase in torque backup is not recommended, since during speed increase there must also be a discernible increase in power, otherwise the engine feels flat.
• The ratio of the maximum torque to the torque at the lowest full load speed should not exceed 50%, a good figure being 30%.
• The elasticity, characterised by the formula (maximum torque x nominal engine speed)/(nominal torque x engine speed at maximum torque) ought to attain a figure greater than 2.0.
• The maximum torque starting from zero load at any speed should be reached within about 0.5 second. Only then can it be regarded as 'available torque' for critical driving situations. This question of the availability of torque with respect to time is a key issue when matching any form of supercharger and its control system to an engine.

As well as increasing the available power of a given engine by supercharging, it has already been noted earlier in this book that using a smaller, supercharged engine instead of a relatively larger naturally aspirated one can have significant advantages. For example, in 1978 Buick used a 3.8-litre turbocharged V-6 instead of the 5.7-litre V-8 previously used in the same car. The same acceleration was obtained, there was a weight reduction of 40/50 kg, and a fuel consumption saving of 5%[27].

The following table gives a comparison of the advantages and disadvantages of using a supercharged engine instead of a naturally aspirated engine of equal maximum torque/power:

Advantages	Disadvantages
Reduced idle fuel consumption	Reduced compression ratio
Reduced frictional losses	Inferior transient throttle response
Reduced part load pumping	Inferior low speed torque
More compact combustion chamber	Increased thermal stresses
Reduced hydrocarbon emissions	Increased NOx emissions
Reduced engine mass	Improved lubricants needed
	Increased manufacturing costs
	Charge air cooler may be needed

20

Adding a turbocharger

We have already discussed the importance of being quite clear about the objectives for supercharging a vehicle, and this becomes quite specific when finally matching a chosen compression system to the engine. Are you looking at an out-and-out competition car or a general-use vehicle? A bus or truck engine must be matched so that the engine can live with the maximum boost when climbing up a long hill. A drag-racer only has to withstand full power for a few seconds, but the acceleration lag is very important.

Because of the predominance of turbocharging and the complexities of matching, this is the only type of supercharging considered explicitly here. Nevertheless, many of the topics covered are of equal relevance when some other form of forced induction is to be applied.

Having determined the engine operating characteristics that are required, the next stage in adding a turbocharger to an engine is to determine the size of unit to be fitted. Generally, the turbocharger turbine can operate efficiently over a wider mass flow range than its compressor. It follows, therefore, that for matching purposes it is more important to examine the engine air flow plotted on the compressor map than on the turbine map. Turbine selection is not generally a problem except for high-power racing conditions.

A detailed procedure for matching a turbocharger to an engine is given in Appendix B, but a summary of the steps which need to be taken to achieve a predetermined boost is given here.

The first step is to determine the engine speed to which the turbocharger is to be matched and the desired degree of boost at this point. Then, given the known swept volume of the engine, and allowing for a four-stroke engine the need for two revolutions per complete cycle, the theoretical volume flow rate of air can be cal-

culated. An estimate must be made for the volumetric efficiency of the engine's induction system to scale down the expected volume of air to be taken. It may be possible to actually measure the volumetric efficiency if the engine already exists, but an estimate is probably adequate. Given the target boost pressure, the compressor pressure ratio can also be determined. The air mass flow can now be calculated.

The compressor maps need to be obtained for possible suitable turbochargers on which the calculated working point of mass flow versus pressure ratio can be plotted and an appropriate selection made. The expected efficiency of the compressor can now be determined from the map and a calculation made of the air temperature rise after compression. This will reduce the density of the air which in turn will reduce the mass flow, causing the operating point to move on the map.

If wastegate control is to be used, limiting the maximum boost pressure, a further calculation should be made for maximum engine speed, assuming that this was not the chosen initial matching point. This should be towards the right-hand, high-flow side of the compressor map.

From the chosen working point on the compressor map, the desired turbocharger speed can be determined. The total exhaust mass flow is the sum of the inlet air mass flow and the fuel mass; the latter can be determined from the need to maintain a viable air/fuel ratio. The total gas flow through the turbine, taken in conjunction with the speed requirement from the compressor map, will determine the A/R housing and trim selection to be made from the range offered by the manufacturer for the particular model of turbocharger.

There are computer programs which can calculate the full range of operating points for a turbocharged

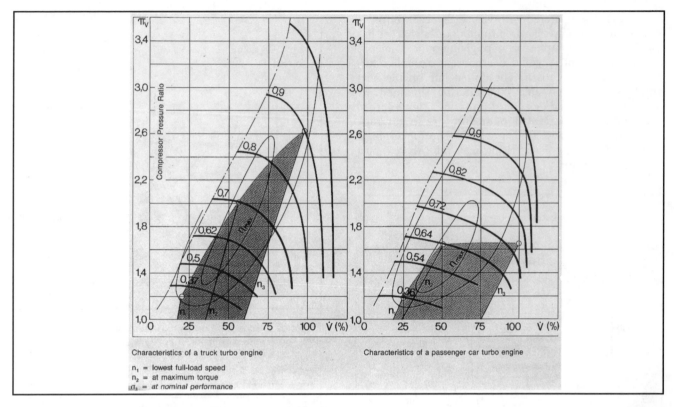

Characteristics of a truck turbo engine

Characteristics of a passenger car turbo engine

n₁ = lowest full-load speed
n₂ = at maximum torque
n₃ = at nominal performance

Typical compressor maps from turbochargers suitable for trucks and passenger cars. The completely different engine operating zones for the two applications can be seen. [KKK]

engine, but these are outside the scope of this book. Some examples are given, though, of the types of curve which have been obtained. The first diagram shows equivalent compressor maps for a truck and a passenger car engine. Three key operating points are plotted on

each – the nominal performance point (maximum power at the associated speed); the maximum torque point; and the lowest full-load speed. The operation of the compressor is likely to lie anywhere within the shaded area.

The next graph shows an example of the path followed by the engine operating point during extreme acceleration in one gear, when no control system is used. The following diagram then shows how this curve is modified when accelerating through the gears[26].

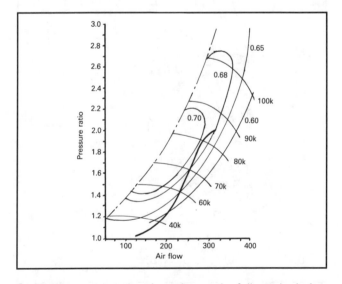

Compressor map showing the path followed during extreme engine acceleration. [McInnes]

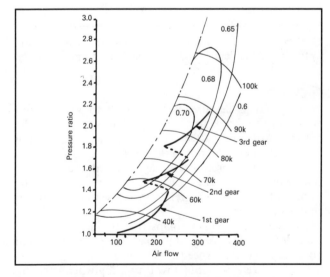

Compressor map showing acceleration through the gears. [McInnes]

An engine operated with very little carburettor or exhaust restriction with a free running turbocharger has one line on the compressor map, giving poor efficiency at mid-range, but it would overboost if a smaller turbine nozzle were chosen. The dotted line on the next graph shows a possible characteristic obtained by introducing inlet and/or exhaust throttling. This will then need a turbine nozzle A/R of smaller size to get back to the original boost pressure level. The higher back pressure caused by a restriction may raise the exhaust valve temperature.

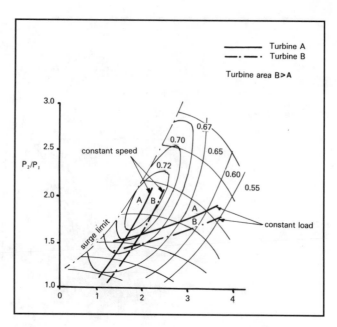

Effect of turbine area on the position of the engine running lines on the compressor map. [*Watson*]

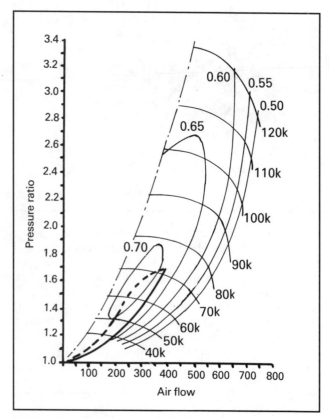

Compressor map showing the full-load engine operating line without any restriction, and with restriction control (dotted). [*McInnes*]

Reference has already been made above and elsewhere in this book to the way in which changing the turbine A/R ratio affects the turbocharger operating speed. The next diagram has been plotted to show two operating lines for constant engine speed and constant load when two different turbine areas are selected. The choice of a larger area tends to move the lines down and to the right.

Several compressor maps for specific engines are included which have the full-load line plotted on them for various engine speeds.

Here are some points worth noting when carrying out a turbocharger matching exercise. Many different makes and models can satisfy a particular application;

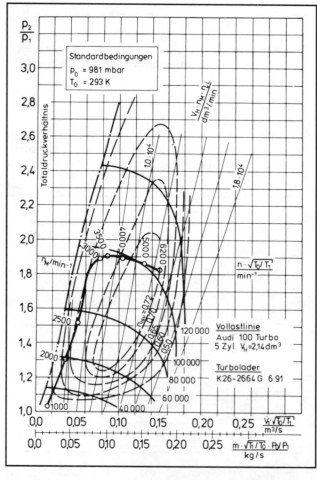

Example compressor map – five-cylinder Audi engine. [*KKK*]

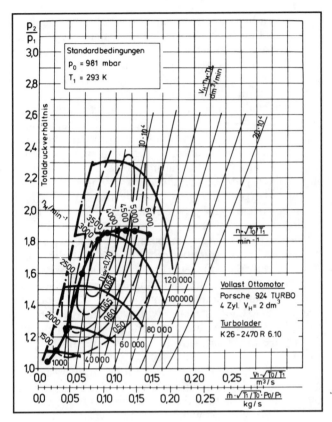

Example compressor map – Porsche 924 engine. [*KKK*]

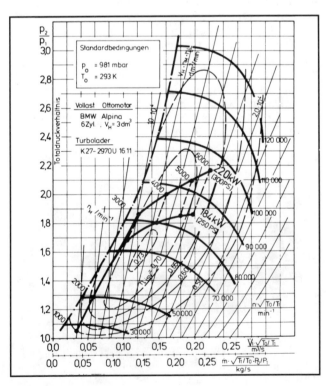

Example compressor map – BMW 3-litre, six-cylinder engine. [*KKK*]

your choice is likely to be influenced mainly by ready availability. Cam design will probably determine the best engine speed, and the turbocharger should match this. A turbocharged engine does not usually need as much valve overlap as a naturally aspirated one.

When selecting the operating points on a compressor map, try to avoid any points dropping below 65% compressor efficiency, avoid running into choke conditions at high mass flow, and most importantly give a healthy margin to the surge line.

Turbine speed increase merely increases the compressor pressure ratio rather than the mass flow. Speed can be changed by changing the turbine nozzle size, but if the compressor is not the correct size this change will not help.

It is difficult to compare add-on turbocharger systems directly with the original manufacturer's developments which are integrated into the engine design right from the beginning, but if care is taken good installations can be achieved. Some characteristics to aim for when doing an add-on are:
• to obtain a substantial power increase but to keep well within the thermal and mechanical design limits of the engine, with the smallest increase in overall fuel consumption;
• to obtain a torque increase over the widest speed range, yet to obtain this increase within the standard maximum rpm limit;
• to maintain or reduce overall noise levels;
• to maintain or reduce overall exhaust NOx and CO_2 emissions;
• not to affect starting or slow running ability under all conditions of town driving.

Use the lowest boost that will meet your needs, combined with the highest possible geometric compression ratio in order to obtain the maximum thermal efficiency at light load. When running with maximum boost the effective compression ratio for a gasoline engine generally should not be more than 10:1. A chart in Chapter 6 plots boost pressure against effective compression ratio for various geometric compression ratios.

Engines with a poor breathing ability in normally aspirated form will usually give a larger power increase for a given boost than those starting with a higher volumetric efficiency.

A maximum power increase of 25-35% and a similar torque increase is all that is necessary to give a substantial performance boost without impairing reliability or necessitating extensive internal engine modifications. For good all-round road performance, a broad, comparatively flat torque curve is far more important than a high maximum power output, and this can usually be achieved with a modest boost of from 0.3-0.5 bar.

For automobiles under normal road conditions, even when driven hard, the turbocharger will not be applying boost to the engine for more than 20% of the journey time, so that even with a power increase of up to 30%, the overall fuel consumption increase should be less than 10%.

Experiences from add-on turbocharging have shown that the performance is usually limited rather by over-heating than by mechanical difficulties. For super-charged gasoline engines, the maximum output is ultimately knock-limited, and difficulties with knock and thermal loading of the pistons, cylinder head and exhaust valves are likely to occur when uprating a normal production unit.

For production engines with the compression ratio in the 8.5-9.5:1 range, using 98 octane fuel, detonation may start at approximately 0.2-0.3 bar boost for the least efficient or highest compression ones. This can rise to over 0.8 bar boost for the most efficient or lowest compression examples. Even a small amount of detonation cannot be sustained for more than a short period without resulting in engine damage. The compression ratio can be reduced by fitting pistons with a lower crown, machining out the combustion chamber or, less desirably, by fitting a decompression plate.

Because of the small bearing clearances and high peripheral speeds in modern turbochargers, it is critically important to maintain a consistent supply of clean lubricating oil. A typical 60 mm diameter turbocharger needs up to 5 litres per minute. If there is any doubt about maintaining oil cleanliness, a supplementary fine oil filter should be fitted to the feed to the turbocharger bearings. It has been noted earlier that the oil gets churned up into a froth in its passage through the turbocharger. The increased volume of this mixture of air and oil must be allowed for in the design of the oil drain from turbocharger to engine sump. If the crank-case ventilation system is not adequate, the combination of the leakage gases from the turbocharger together with the normal piston blow-by gases can cause difficulty with the turbocharger bearing drainage.

A typical turbocharger will add about 5°C to the oil temperature passing through it; if the temperature goes above about 120°C it is necessary to add an oil cooler. Many higher boost applications will need the addition of an oil cooler, which should preferably be fitted with a thermostat. Synthetic lubricating oils can withstand higher operating temperatures and should be chosen for turbocharged engines. This is particularly important with air-cooled turbocharger bearing housings, where there is a risk of overheating from soak-back from the turbine when the engine is shut down and the oil flow stops.

Check if there is a need for increased water circulation through the cylinder head to avoid hot spots. Some four-cylinder engine designs tend to have overheating problems where the exhaust valves of the central two cylinders are adjacent. For high-boost applications, it may be necessary to consider the use of sodium-cooled exhaust valves to transfer heat away from the head as quickly as possible.

When making a turbocharger add-on, the easiest layout to work with is an in-line four- or six-cylinder engine, especially if the inlet and exhaust are on the same side. However, this is a fairly uncommon arrangement on modern high efficiency engines, which are commonly of a cross-flow type. With a vee type engine, if only one turbocharger is to be used there is a complication in providing the necessary cross-over piping. With the availability now of small turbochargers it is usually possible to obtain a match using twin turbochargers, one for each bank of cylinders; this not only simplifies the plumbing but will also usually reduce the response time-lag on acceleration because of the lower rotor inertia.

When adding a turbocharger to an engine which is coupled to an automatic transmission system, the matching problems are compounded by having to take into account the gear changing characteristics of the transmission system. Many detail changes may need to be made.

If turbocharging is to be applied to a two-stroke engine, there are a number of additional complications. Because there is no separate induction stroke, it is important to ensure that inlet and exhaust pressures are correctly balanced at all times to get a satisfactory charge and exhaust scavenge without losing fuel through the exhaust port. With a diesel engine this can be easier to achieve as excess scavenge air is generally a good thing.

If the traditional two-stroke lubrication system of a fuel/oil mixture is used, there will have to be a separate oil supply provided for the turbocharger. On larger two-stroke diesel engines which already have some form of mechanical scavenge blower, adding a turbocharger is much simpler. Do not forget that a two-stroke engine uses nearly twice the amount of air as a four-stroke with the same swept volume.

Matching turbochargers to marine engines is much simpler than for road vehicles. The engine speed is not directly linked to the hull speed – it is like having a built-in torque converter. The load and engine speed are linked together by a relationship which is known as the 'propeller law' which links the propeller pitch and shape to the thrust generated. To take advantage of the higher power available, it is usual to use a higher-pitched

Turbocharged 370L Sabre marine diesel engine 6.798-litre, 272 kw at 2,600 rpm. [*Sabre*]

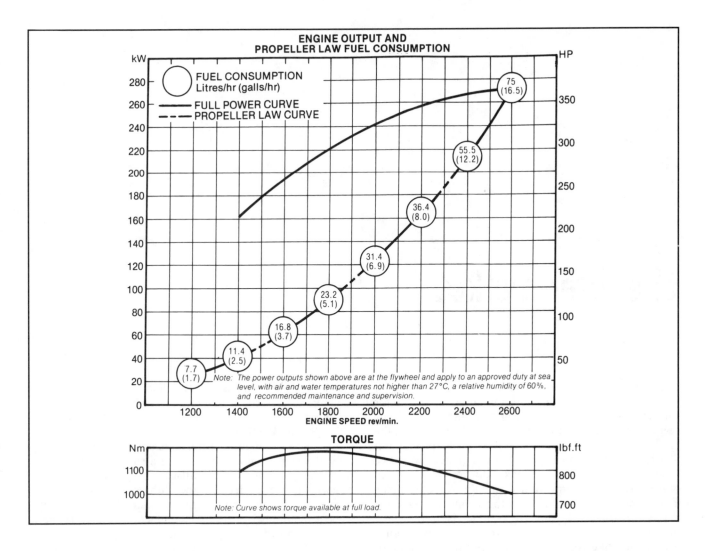

ENGINE OUTPUT AND
PROPELLER LAW FUEL CONSUMPTION

Legend:
- ○ FUEL CONSUMPTION Litres/hr (galls/hr)
- —— FULL POWER CURVE
- – – – PROPELLER LAW CURVE

Fuel consumption points:
- 7.7 (1.7)
- 11.4 (2.5)
- 16.8 (3.7)
- 23.2 (5.1)
- 31.4 (6.9)
- 36.4 (8.0)
- 55.5 (12.2)
- 75 (16.5)

Note: The power outputs shown above are at the flywheel and apply to an approved duty at sea level, with air and water temperatures not higher than 27°C, a relative humidity of 60%, and recommended maintenance and supervision.

ENGINE SPEED rev/min.

TORQUE

Note: Curve shows torque available at full load.

propeller on a turbocharged boat. If the engine is to be installed into a high-speed planing boat, the hull speed/power curve has a hump in it at the lower speed where the hull changes from a displacement type to lifting up on to the planing surfaces. The turbocharger matching must be done in such a way that there is sufficient low-down power to get over this hump.

The engine air requirements can be much better matched to the compressor map than with a car. For the car, the high-speed end of the power line extends into the low-efficiency area in order to give higher torque at the mid-range. In a marine application, it is possible to match the high-speed engine operation to the high-efficiency area. A much narrower compressor characteristic is acceptable, which tends to be accompanied by higher efficiency.

Obviously, in a marine application water cooling of both turbocharger bearing housings and charge air is very practicable. Water-jacketed exhaust pipes are also commonplace to minimise the risk of fire. Care must be taken to avoid high back pressure from exhaust pipes which are fitted with water traps and cooling water discharges.

Sabre 370L marine engine power and torque curves, with 'propeller law' curve and fuel consumption figures. [*Sabre*]

A KKK model 'K2' turbocharger with a water-cooled turbine housing suitable for use in installations with very limited space, such as power boats. [*KKK*]

21

The after-market

Ever since the automobile became of interest to the general public rather than the wealthy few, the major vehicle manufacturers have been surrounded by a large swarm of small companies catering for gaps in the market. The increasing efficiency of mass production which has made the car widely available at a low price has also been accompanied by a reduction in the choice of designs. The investment in setting up a plant to make a new model is so great that the manufacturer must make sure that the resulting product is sold to the maximum number of people with only minor variations. The buyers like the ready availability of the standard designs, but they do not like their sameness. It is so frustrating when your Chevvy or Nissan is the same as all the others in the street!

To try to satisfy this conflict between the manufacturing economics and the personal dreams of the customers, a multi-million dollar possibility has opened up. It is now generally referred to as the 'after-market' and the number of businesses working this market is in the tens of thousands world-wide. These firms vary from supplying simple accessories, such as pseudo-leopard-skin seat covers and steering wheel gloves, through serious performance modification kits, to specialist small-volume car manufacture, usually based on some production model.

The main manufacturers themselves have recognised this market need and have tried to meet it themselves. Nowadays, when a new vehicle is launched it will not just be one model. There will be a whole family based on the same manufacturing line but with a range of optional assemblies. Typically this will vary from the cheapest, simplest version (which probably nobody actually buys!), through the general family car and the estate car version, to the full high-luxury package, with a side salad of hot sports models and open coupes. The computer-controlled manufacturing systems in a modern factory allow relatively small batches of each variant to be produced profitably.

Where a manufacturer uses competition as a publicity means, there will often be a small manufacturing operation which specialises in producing high-performance models for the club competition market. This may be in the main manufacturer's name, or may be a well-known specialist manufacturer which has been bought by the major company.

It is fairly easy to see why there should be a style-oriented after-market. Every buyer will have their own idea of how they want their car to look, so the manufacturing and retailing opportunities become obvious. At the simplest this can be simply supplying 'go-faster stripes' and fancy fittings. The top end of the market, however, is represented by the specialists who help to produce the completely customised 'street machines' where it is difficult to identify the original vehicle which started the process.

The technical after-market requires a little more thought to realise why it exists and flourishes. The major manufacturers invest billions in their research and development operations and it seems that a new vehicle design should represent the best distillation of all this experience. Why, then, should a small ten-man business, for example, think that it can provide any modification to such a design which will make it better?

The answer lies in the fact that any production vehicle is necessarily a collection of design compromises aimed at specifically defined segments of the market. Vehicle suspension systems will almost always be a compromise between obtaining a soft, luxurious-feeling ride and the harsher needs of good road holding. Fuel economy will always be a trade-off with maximum power; space and weight compete; and so on. Every additional dollar, yen or mark spent on the manufacturing cost of a vehicle is reflected as a substantial multiple by the time the final selling price is reached. The after-market suppliers allow the individual owner drivers to make their own choices and modify their vehicles to get just the right combination that suits their needs and pocket.

The competition market is the biggest sector of the overall after-market. For the major manufacturers this is still much too small to be worth catering for directly, but they will support many of the after-market suppliers who will help to sell the unmodified base vehicles for customising. Competition modifications may be for local club rallying or track racing, or for national and international events. There are also the more specialist requirements of the sprint-oriented hill-climb and drag-racing events.

When we look at supercharging, the subject matter of this book, we find that the after-market is very important. If you desire the benefits of a mechanically driven supercharger on your vehicle, you currently have only a limited choice amongst the original vehicle manufacturers. You will either have to do it yourself or use the services of one of the many specialists in this business. Turbocharged vehicles are much more common, and so also are the after-market suppliers. In many cases it can be possible to buy the parts from the original manufacturer to uprate your standard 'cooking' car to something approaching the top-of-the-range sports model. A conversion kit developed in the after-market which proves to sell well may later be adopted by the original manufacturer for addition to the production line.

The most common reason for adding a supercharger or turbocharger to a car is to get more power or torque from the engine. This can be done fairly simply with a few bolt-on accessories, but the implications for the rest of the engine and the vehicle can be considerable. Some designs have sufficient safety margins for the extra power to be handled safely provided only a modest increase is called for, but others may already be operating close to the reliability limits. The latter are typically engine or vehicle designs which have been around for a long time and have been repeatedly stretched to keep them in production until a completely new design becomes available. Determining what is safe and what is not requires a great deal of detailed knowledge of the manufacturer's specifications, not only for the engine but also for the clutch, gearbox, transmission, brakes and suspension, all of which will be affected by an increase in engine power.

Manufacturers, wholesalers and retailers can supply a range of products to help in all of these fields, plus the superchargers or turbochargers themselves, exhaust and inlet manifolds, etc. Inevitably there are many inexperienced owners who tackle a modification project with inadequate knowledge and see their favourite automobile subside in a pool of oil and water after destroying itself. Even worse, there are many unscrupulous small firms who will do a cut-price job and then refuse to accept any responsibility when it all goes wrong.

The major reputable after-market suppliers, those who have support from the original equipment manufacturers, are very wary of supplying their conversion kits to individuals whose competence they do not know. They will usually insist on a conversion being done either by themselves or an approved dealer who has all the necessary special tools and facilities, including frequently an engine dynamometer and/or rolling-road test rig. If a modification is being made to a used vehicle, it is usual to insist on a complete overhaul being carried out prior to the upgrade, with any necessary remedial work being done to get back to the original designer's specifications.

The widespread adoption of digital computer engine management systems has added a new dimension to the tuning after-market. Computer programmers can alter the settings stored in the PROM chips of these electronic systems and completely change the characteristics of an engine. If these changes are part of a planned operation which recognises all the inter-relationships, this gives the tuner much more control. Unfortunately, the simplicity of such changes for a skilled computer 'hacker' has spawned a great leap in the number of unscrupulous operators. You can be offered a 'hot chip' for your motor which can be installed in the car park at the rear of your local bar. The immediate performance as you test it out is phenomenal, but when the engine blows up three days later there is no sign of the guy who had your money!

A recent study in the UK suggested that for every legitimate software tuner there are another two or three 'pirates'. Because it is still such a rarefied subject, tuning cars by electronic means is not nearly as well understood by the average driver as the more obvious mechanical changes. The majority of drivers understand little beyond the fact that they have paid out some money and in return have a car which behaves differently. Perhaps all that has been done is to lift the constraint on maximum boost pressure and delay the opening of the wastegate, removing the safety limits built in by the manufacturer for the benefit of the vehicle and your life. Another regular trick is to change the combustion conditions to achieve greater power but at the expense of taking the exhaust pollution levels well outside the legal limits, a problem which may not become apparent until the vehicle is failed on its next legal inspection.

If you, the reader, have already digested the information in the rest of this book, you should be aware of what needs to be done to add a turbocharger to a naturally aspirated engine, and how to relate this to your overall objective for your complete vehicle. To help you to check out your knowledge, the rest of this chapter gives some examples of how the professional after-market suppliers tackle the problem. It would have required another book, with much boring repetition, to cover all the vehicles for which forced induction kits are offered. Instead, only three popular engines for the extensive Ford range have been chosen. The way in which these are turbocharged by one of the leaders in the UK after-market, Turbo Technics, is examined in step-by-step detail. Hopefully this will remind you of those little changes which are necessary but easily overlooked.

1.6-litre Fiesta XR2

The Ford 1.596-litre CVH engine used in the XR2 and some other models came in two versions. After October 1986 a 'lean burn' version of the engine was used, and this is easier to turbocharge. The following description deals with this version as installed in the Fiesta XR2, but notes are given on the additional work involved if one of the earlier engines is being converted. The four-cylinder in-line engine is mounted transversely in the car and drives the front wheels. It is fitted as standard with a twin-choke carburetter and a high-energy electronic ignition system.

As for all of the Turbo Technics' conversions, the first stage is a complete check-out of the vehicle as supplied in order to ensure that it conforms to the basic manufacturer's specifications. Any remedial work which is needed will be quoted to the customer and carried out before the upgrade is commenced.

The Garrett Automotive type T25 low-inertia turbocharger is used, with integral wastegate and water-cooled central body to reduce bearing temperatures. The standard radiator and fan are retained in a slightly revised location, with the installation of a charge air cooler and a 'blow-through' feed to the carburetter. A new canister air filter with a foam element is incorporated. The fuel system is provided with an electric pump with no mechanical lift pump assistance. The carburetter and ignition settings have to be changed, and for the older engines a further modification is needed to the carburettor, and the compression ratio has to be changed.

A completely new exhaust manifold is used which has been designed to make maximum use of the pulse effect. The four individual cylinder pipes converge into a four-way pulse converter plenum chamber which has been shaped to minimise reflected pulses and maximise the pressure at the turbine. The manifold is cast in a high-nickel-content SG iron.

The earlier version engine must have its compression ratio reduced to 8.4:1 by machining the crown of the pistons. The cylinder head is then refitted using new bolts. The later lean burn engine is not changed from the standard compression ratio.

The existing exhaust manifold and down-pipe, and the air filter, are removed. The carburettor and distributor are removed for modification. The radiator and fan mountings are then cut and modified to allow the new mounting position to be achieved. The new larger air filter is fitted. The front panel is drilled ready for

Fiesta XR2 turbo system – exhaust components. [*Turbo Technics*]

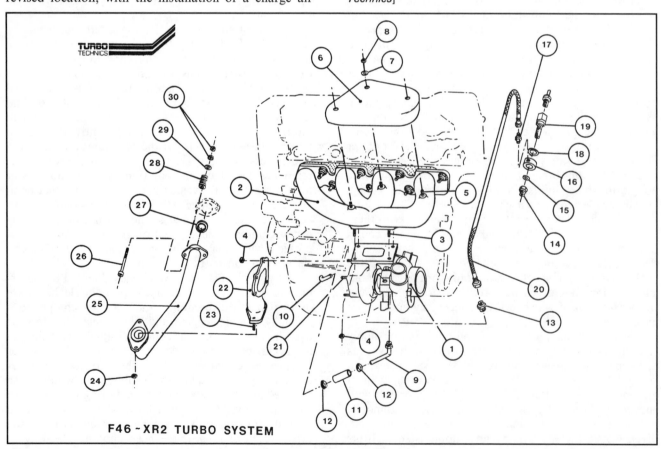

F46 – XR2 TURBO SYSTEM

138

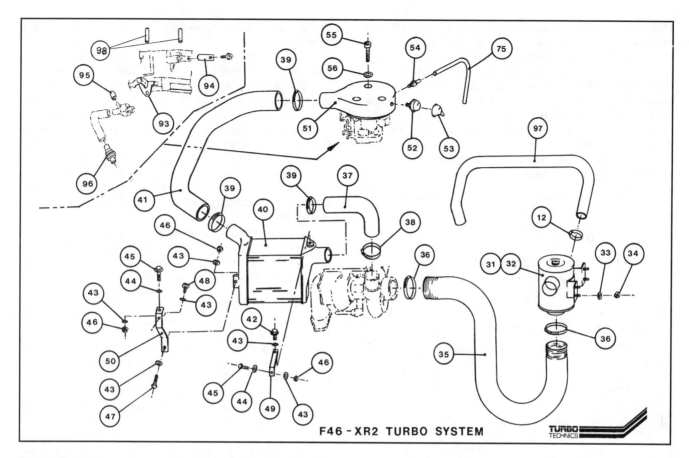

F46 ~ XR2 TURBO SYSTEM

Fiesta XR2 turbo system – induction components. [*Turbo Technics*]

the charge air cooler mounting and the horns are relocated to the side.

The T25 turbocharger is fitted with a swing-valve wastegate which is completely contained within the cast turbine housing so that no extra exhaust piping is needed for it. A cast-iron elbow is used to change from the horizontal exhaust flange on the turbocharger to the vertical direction needed for the exhaust down-pipe. The turbocharger assembly comes as standard fitted with a pneumatic servo actuator for the wastegate. This takes its pressure from a tapping on the outlet of the compressor housing.

The next stage in the conversion (see the diagram) is to assemble to the turbocharger the exhaust elbow, the water cooling pipes for the centre bearing housing, and the oil drain pipe. The turbocharger is then bolted onto the exhaust manifold at the turbine flange and the complete assembly is fixed to the engine using new high-temperature gaskets.

A tee-junction is fitted between the existing oil pressure switch and the engine, and the oil feed pipe for the turbocharger is connected to this. The pipe connecting the coolant header tank to the main radiator, and the hot pipe to the heater, are cut and tee pieces are inserted. The water cooling pipes from the turbocharger are then

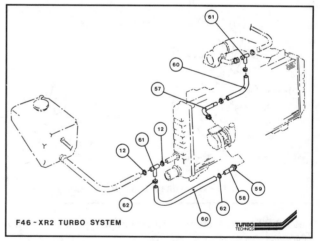

F46 - XR2 TURBO SYSTEM

Fiesta XR2 turbo system – water-cooling components. [*Turbo Technics*]

connected to these points.

The engine oil sump is removed and a hole is drilled in the side into which an elbow is brazed, providing a connection point for the turbocharger oil drain. This is arranged so that the drain discharges into the sump high above the normal working oil level to ensure that there is no obstruction to the frothy oil flow.

The feed and return pipes between fuel tank and

engine have to be completely replaced. A pipe from the tank is connected to the new electric fuel pump which is bracket-mounted onto the chassis above the steering rack. From the pump another pipe leads on to a pressure regulator fitted to the bulkhead, which in turn has a connecting pipe to the carburettor. The drain from the pressure regulator connects via a new return pipe back to the fuel tank. A pipe will be connected from the air plenum above the carburettor to the fuel pressure regulator in order to give automatic fuel pressure adjustment to match changes in boost pressure.

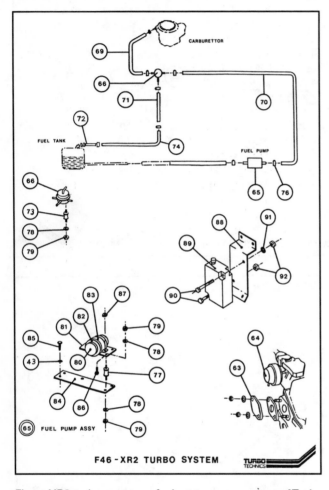

Fiesta XR2 turbo system – fuel system components. [*Turbo Technics*]

An inertia switch is mounted on the engine compartment bulkhead and is connected into the fuel pump circuit to cut off the fuel feed in the event of a crash. A special wiring harness provides all the electrical connections for the pump and crash switch, linking in to the existing vehicle electrical system.

The exhaust system is now finished off by installing the new down-pipe which connects the turbine elbow to the original exhaust pipe at the first junction point. A support is fitted, with a flexible hanger, for the new pipe. A heat shield is fitted to the exhaust manifold to protect the ignition leads from radiation from the hot exhaust.

The carburettor now has to be modified. The existing vacuum capsule is removed and the connection blanked off. The secondary throttle is modified to allow a new mechanism to be linked to the final movement of the primary throttle. Two stand-pipes are fitted to connect to the float chamber vents, and other holes in the float chamber are sealed. The float positioning is reset. The fuel entry pipe contains a flow restrictor, and this has to be opened up by drilling. All the jets are changed to new sizes. The modified carburettor is now refitted to the engine and the new air plenum chamber is assembled to it.

For the early engines (up to September 1986) the carburettor is different and has to have its top face machined, although it needs no change to the throttle mechanism. A different air plenum is used.

The charge air cooler is mounted on brackets to the side of the radiator. Rubber pipes are fitted to join the air filter to the compressor inlet, the compressor outlet to the charge air cooler, and the cooler to the plenum chamber above the carburettor. Another rubber pipe connects the crankcase breather to a secondary inlet on the air filter.

A non-return valve has to be fitted in the line from the breather oil separation pot to the inlet manifold, and a new pipe is fitted from the separation pot to the air filter.

An over-boost pressure switch is fitted to the air plenum and this is connected via a new wiring harness into the ignition circuit.

The distributor now has to be modified. The cap and rotor arm are removed, as is the electronic detector and amplifier to reveal the standard vacuum advance capsule. This is replaced by the new unit which combines vacuum advance and pressure retard. A new pipe has to be fitted to connect from the carburettor throttle body to the new vacuum/pressure capsule. The ignition timing then has to be reset to give a reference point of 12° before top dead centre when the engine is idling and the vacuum is disconnected.

The spark plugs are changed to a hotter grade and a synthetic engine oil is used to protect the turbocharger. To take account of the increased power available from the engine, harder bushes are fitted to the front suspension and steering, and the tracking is adjusted for 1 mm toe-out. The standard brakes and clutch are quite adequate to handle the increased power and no further suspension modifications are needed.

When the conversion is complete, the boost pressure control will be set to give 0.40/0.42 bar on full throttle at 3,500 engine revolutions per minute. This should also give 0.28/0.35 bar at full throttle and 2,500 rpm.

Under these conditions the XR2 engine will have a maximum power of 125 bhp at 5,500 rpm and a maximum torque of 183 Nm at 3,800 rpm. The 0-60 miles per hour dash is achieved in a quick 7.8 seconds, and a top speed of 120 mph is attainable. With the low

A turbocharged Jaguar engine installation. [*Turbo Technics*]

inertia of the T25 turbocharger there is no perceptible turbo lag on acceleration.

Because of the close co-operation between Turbo Technics and Ford, this turbocharger conversion does not affect the standard vehicle warranty. The cost of the conversion includes an extension to the standard warranty to cover the additional parts of the turbocharger system.

2.8-litre Capri

Let us now look at the changes needed for turbocharging a larger Ford engine, the classic cast-iron block 2.8-litre V-6 used in many vehicles including the Capri, XR4i, XR4x4 and earlier Granada models. The conversion considered here is the 200 bhp, fuel injected version for the Special Edition Capri. The basic engine is

unchanged and a single Garrett T3 turbocharger is mounted on the left side of the engine (right side on left-hand drive models), with an air-to-air charge air cooler added in front of the radiator.

Unless the vehicle is new, Turbo Technics will insist on carrying out their initial check-out first and will undertake any remedial work to ensure that the vehicle conforms to the standard specifications before starting the conversion.

The existing exhaust down-pipes are cut 520 mm in front of the first mufflers and are removed. The exhaust manifold on the left side is removed and replaced by a new high-nickel cast-iron one which incorporates a pulse converter arrangement. A cross-over pipe is then fitted between this manifold and the original manifold on the right-hand bank of cylinders. This cross-over pipe is made in two sections for ease of installation. The two pipes are welded together once in place.

The T3 turbocharger is mounted by its turbine flange onto the new exhaust manifold. A new two-section exhaust pipe connects the turbine outlet flange to the original piping. This new larger-diameter single down-pipe is made in two sections for ease of fitting and ends in a Y-piece which then connects to the original twin mufflers.

As with the smaller engine, an elbow is brazed into the side of the sump to accept the turbocharger oil drain connection which is made in two sections to achieve the correct angles between the turbocharger and the sump connection point. The lubricating oil feed for the turbocharger is again taken from the existing oil pres-

Capri 2.8i turbo system – exhaust components. [*Turbo Technics*]

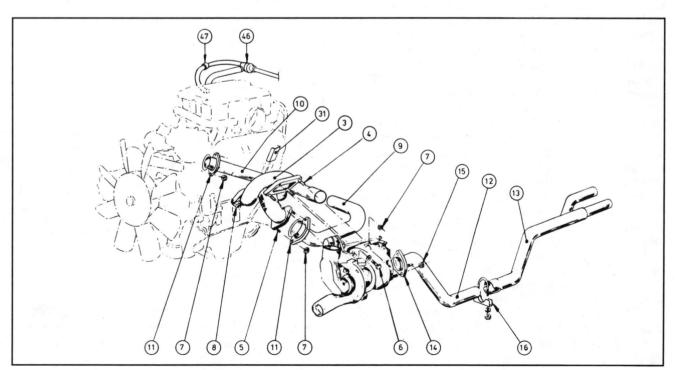

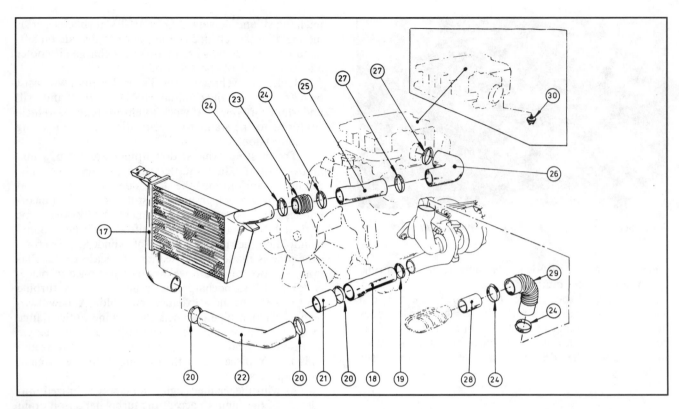

Capri 2.8i turbo system – induction components. [*Turbo Technics*]

sure switch mounting by inserting a tee-piece. A braided metal-sheathed high-pressure hose connects from here to the oil feed point on the central bearing housing of the turbocharger. The T3 relies on air and oil cooling for the bearing assembly so there are no water connections to be made on this engine.

The charge air cooler is mounted on brackets in front of the main radiator, so the connecting hoses are provided with adapters to allow them to be passed through the bulkhead. The compressor inlet is connected to the existing air filter, the compressor outlet to the cooler inlet, and the cooler outlet to the existing air plenum chamber above the centre of the engine. The plenum is drilled to accept an over-boost pressure switch which is wired to cut out the ignition if the wastegate should fail or excess boost pressure occur for any reason. The engine breather piping needs to be modified by fitting a diverter valve, one-way valve and restrictor.

The vacuum advance capsule on the distributor for ignition timing is replaced by a combined vacuum advance/boost pressure retard capsule. This unit will give a retard of 8/10° with 0.40 bar boost pressure, at all speeds. The coil and spark plug high-voltage leads are all changed to high-temperature silicone insulated ones and an additional heat shield is fitted over the centre plug on the left-hand side which is just beneath the exhaust manifold. The spark plugs are changed to wide-heat-range types with 0.75 mm gaps.

The standard fuel injection system is retained, but a profile block is fitted to the air flow metering cone. The system is balanced to give matched flows from each injector.

Capri 2.8i turbo system – induction components. [*Turbo Technics*]

Because of the use of the air-cooled turbocharger, it is crucial that only high-temperature-working synthetic or semi-synthetic lubricating oil is used. This will avoid any risk of turbocharger bearing damage due to heat

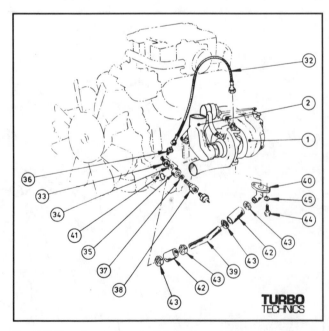

Capri 2.8i turbo system – lubrication components. [*Turbo Technics*]

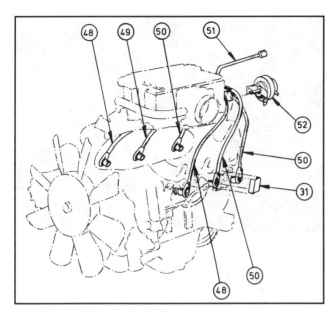

Capri 2.8i turbo system – ignition components. [*Turbo Technics*]

soak-back after engine shutdown. Turbo Technics recommend the use of Shell Gemini oil with this conversion.

The standard braking system is retained, but upgraded disk pads are fitted at the front. Harder suspension location bushes are fitted at key points.

When the conversion is complete, rolling-road testing will check that a carbon monoxide level of 1-1.5% at the warm idle speed of 900 rpm is obtained. In third gear at 3,000 rpm the boost pressure should be 0.40/0.45 bar, and at 1,750 rpm it should be 0.25 bar minimum. Under these conditions the engine will be capable of delivering a maximum power output of 200 bhp at 5,500 rpm and a maximum torque of 312 Nm at 3,750.

If the boost pressure is increased to 0.60/0.65 bar and the compression ratio is reduced to 8.9:1 to avoid detonation, the maxima can be raised to 230 bhp at 5,500 rpm and 373 Nm at 4,000 rpm. In the XR4x4 this can produce a 0-60 mph time of 6 seconds and a top speed of 140 mph.

2.9-litre Sierra XR4x4

The third engine whose after-market supercharging we are looking at is the Ford 'Cologne' 2.935-litre V-6. This engine is now used in the Sierra XR4x4 and the Granada/Scorpio cars. It is a Bosch K-Jetronic fuel injected, 60° vee engine fitted with Ford's EEC-IV electronic engine management system. It has push-rod operated overhead valves with two valves per cylinder. In standard Ford condition it delivers 150 bhp maximum at 5,700 rpm, with a maximum torque of 233 Nm at 3,000 rpm. This gives the XR4x4 a 0-60 mph time of 8.5 seconds and a top speed of 127 miles per hour.

The cylinder heads are first removed to allow the compression ratio to be reduced from the standard 9.5:1 to 8.6:1. This is done using a computer-controlled milling machine to remove metal from within the combustion chambers. New bolts will be used when the heads are refitted to the block, to ensure that there is no weak point when the engine is subjected to the increased temperatures.

New compact exhaust manifolds are used which have been designed to make the best use of the pulse energy. These are cast in a high-nickel-content iron. A Garrett T2 turbocharger is mounted by its turbine flange on to each of the new exhaust manifolds. The downpipes then connect to the existing twin pipe/muffler exhaust system so that future servicing is simplified.

The turbochargers are a Turbo Technics special version of the T2 with dynamic seals for fast response. Water cooling of the central housing is used to ensure long life for the bearings. The T2 has an integral, swinging-arm-type wastegate which is completely within the turbine housing, so that there is only one hot flange connection to make to the exhaust system.

The air supply is taken in through the standard filter and air flow metering unit and is then connected by hoses to the twin compressor inlets. The outlets from the compressors are connected by further hoses to a split-path charge air cooler which is mounted in front of the main engine cooling radiator. The cooled air returns via two more hosepipes to connect to the original plenum chamber mounted on the throttle body.

The original electronically controlled fuel injection system is retained, but two additional fuel injectors are mounted on a special adapter at the inlet to the throttle body. These injectors, under the control of the engine management system, are brought into action when on high boost.

A new digital electronic control system of Turbo Technics' own manufacture is used to re-map all the fuel and ignition characteristics, control the additional injectors and bring in the turbocharger boost pressure control. The wastegate operation is controlled by using a solenoid-operated modulating valve which is installed in the boost pressure line between the compressor outlet and the wastegate servo actuator.

Connections are made to the engine coolant system to tap off feeds for the turbocharger water cooling. Lubricating oil pressure feeds and drains back to the sump are provided for both turbochargers in a similar manner to that described for the other engines.

A special higher-capacity clutch is fitted as standard, and recommended options include uprated front brakes with ventilated disks, stiffer suspension springs and harder location bushes at the front, and stiffer springs and gas dampers at the rear, together with harder sub-frame mounting rubbers.

After the conversion is complete, Turbo Technics expect the engine to deliver a maximum power of 225 bhp at 5,500 rpm, and maximum torque of 366 Nm at 2,500 rpm. With a peak boost pressure of 0.45 bar, the 0-60 miles per hour time has come down to 6.7 seconds, and the top speed is in excess of 144 miles per hour.

A higher-rating package includes fitting forged pistons, honing the cylinder bores, enlarging the valve ports and fitting nimonic exhaust valves. The exhaust down-pipes are made in stainless steel, and the suspension and brake modifications are included as standard in the package as well as new alloy wheels and high-rated tyres. A higher-ratio transmission final drive is available as an option.

The additional power in this package is obtained by raising the maximum boost pressure to 0.75 bar and adjusting correspondingly the control values in the electronic engine management system. The changes raise the peak power from 225 bhp to 280 bhp, reducing the 0-60 mph time yet further down to 5.2 seconds.

The Minker car

The Turbo Technics upgrade package for the Sierra XR4x4 was a by-product of another development which is typical of the ultimate 'after-market' approach – the creation of a new specialist car based on an existing production model. The Turbo Technics 'Minker' starts off with a standard production line Ford four-wheel-drive Sierra which is stripped down and completely rebuilt into something totally new.

The 2.9-litre engine is modified in a manner similar to that described above but with more extensive changes. It is fitted with forged aluminium pistons with strengthened connecting rods and is 'blue-printed' and rebalanced for optimum tolerances on all components throughout. Oil is directed to the undersides of the pistons to help cooling. The cylinder heads have the combustion chambers reworked and the ports opened up, with a final compression ratio of 7.5:1. Nimonic exhaust valves are fitted feeding out to the pulse-optimised manifolds. A stainless steel exhaust piping system with straight-through mufflers is fitted.

The twin Garrett T2 turbochargers are set up to give a maximum boost pressure of 1.04 bar. As before, they are fully water-cooled. The charge air cooler is the same as that used on the XR4x4 uprate. The same Turbo Technics electronic control system is used with different settings, together with the supplementary fuel injectors. All of this gives a maximum power output of

Induction system of the Minker engine. [*Turbo Technics*]

323 bhp at 6,000 rpm and a maximum torque of 469 Nm at 2,800 rpm.

The body shell is changed to give better aerodynamics and greater down force from the rear wing and front spoiler – a total of 159 kilograms at 110 miles per hour. The shorter Sierra Sapphire-type hood has been fitted to the engine bay, with additional louvre vents to increase cooling air flow. Side skirts also help with the aerodynamics as well as giving the vehicle a very stylish look. Cast alloy 7 x 15-inch wheel rims are fitted with Goodrich 205/50VR15 low-profile high-performance tyres. The interior trim and instrumentation are all that you would expect for a car of this quality.

The suspension dampers at front and rear are changed for uprated adjustable types, and new springs are also fitted. Power is fed to the existing four-wheel transmission system via an uprated clutch and the Ford MT75 gearbox. A completely new braking system is fitted incorporating ventilated front disks.

The finished Minker has a quite phenomenal performance while still behaving very docilely when driven in town traffic. The 0-60 miles per hour time is 4.8 seconds! This beats the performance of a whole range of exotic vehicles, including the Audi Quattro 20V, Chevrolet Corvette ZR-1, Ferrari Testarossa, Lamborghini Countach 5000QV, Nissan 300ZX, and Porsche 911 Turbo 3.3, for a lower initial investment. The maximum speed is governed not to exceed 150 miles per hour.

Appendix A

Engine details

This Appendix gives detailed information, supplied by the manufacturers, for engines with forced induction systems available in series production during the years 1985 to 1991. The tables are presented in alphabetical order of manufacturer and for each there are two tables. The first lists the engine details and the second lists the vehicles normally fitted with these engines. There are numerous special versions and trial installations which are not generally included in these tables, and some manufacturers are omitted where the appropriate data could not be obtained. Units of measurement included in the tables are those used by the individual manufacturers where they deviate from the general conventions used elsewhere in the book. The letters 'na' indicates non-applicability; a blank space indicates that the data was not available from the manufacturer.

The engine data table headings are as follows:

Type   the manufacturer's type reference
Cycle   the operating cycle: D – diesel, G – spark ignition gasoline
Size   the nominal swept volume capacity; litres or cubic inches
Form   cylinder layout: I – in-line, V – vee, F – opposed flat
$\mathbf{P_{max}}$ maximum power: kW or bhp
$\mathbf{N_p}$ speed at maximum power: rpm
$\mathbf{T_{max}}$ maximum torque: Nm or lbs ft
$\mathbf{N_t}$ speed at maximum torque: rpm
CR   geometrical compression ratio
BMEP   maximum brake mean effective pressure
Sup   type of pressure charger: $S_.$ – unspecified type of mechanical supercharger, S_r – Roots, S_p –rotary piston, G – G-lader, T – turbocharger, T_2 – twin turbochargers, C – Comprex
Make   supplier of charger: A – ABB, G – Garrett, I – IHI, K – KKK, M – manufacturer's own, Mi – Mitsubishi, Mk – Mikuni
$\mathbf{P_{max}}$ maximum boost pressure: bar or psi
AC   charge air cooler: A – air/air, W – air/water
WC   turbocharger housing cooling: A – air, W – water cooled
$\mathbf{P_{cont}}$ method of pressure control: W – wastegate, V – variable geometry, A – air dump valve
Fuel   fuel delivery system: I_d– direct combustion chamber injection, I_s – swirl chamber injection, I_p – port injection, I_c – central injection, C_s – suck–through carburettor, C_b – blow-through carburettor
Cont   pressure control system: D – direct servos, E – partial electronic, M – full electronic management system
Emiss   emission control systems: C – catalytic converter, E – evaporation system, R – exhaust gas recycling, L – lean burn, O – oxygen sensor

The vehicle data table headings are as follows:

Model generally known model name
Year introductory year of model
Engine engine type reference as used in above table
Notes any additional comments

AUDI see Volkswagen Audi Group

BMW

Type	Cycle	Size litre	Form	P_{max} kW	N_p rpm	T_{max} Nm	N_t rpm	CR	Sup	Make	P_{max} bar	AC	WC	P_{cont}	Fuel	Cont	Emiss	Notes
24td	D	2.443	I6	85	4800	220	2400	22.0	T	G	0.85		W	I_d		M	n/a	electronic inj'n

Model	Year	Engine	Notes
324TD	1985	24td	electronic injection in '89
524TD	1985	24td	electronic injection in '89

Citroen

Type	Cycle	Size litre	Form	P_{max} kW	N_p rpm	T_{max} Nm	N_t rpm	CR	Sup	Make	P_{max} bar	AC	WC	P_{cont}	Fuel	Cont	Emiss	Notes
M25/666	G	2.5	I4	122	5000	294	3250	8.5	T	G	0.44	A	A	W	I_p	D		
M25/669	D	2.5	I4	88	3900	258	2000	21.0	T	G	0.8	A	A	W	I_d	D		
A8A	D	1.769	I4	65	4300	181	2100	22.0	T	K		A	A	W	I_d	D		
PHZ	D	2.088	I4	80	4300	235	2000	20.5	T						I_d	D		anti-pollution

Model	Year	Engine	Notes
BX Turbo Diesel	1988	A8A	
CX 25i Turbo 2	1986	M25/666	
CX 25 Diesel Turbo 2	1987	M25/669	saloon/limo/Safari/Familiale
XM Turbo D12	1990	PHZ	anti-pollution version

Daihatsu

Type	Cycle	Size litre	Form	P_{max} kW	N_p rpm	T_{max} Nm	N_t rpm	CR	Sup	Make	P_{max} bar	AC	WC	P_{cont}	Fuel	Cont	Emiss	Notes
	G	0.993	I3	74	6500	130	3500	7.8	T	I	0.63	A	A	W	I_p	E		

Model	Year	Engine	Notes
Charade GTti		as above	

Ferrari

Type	Cycle	Size litre	Form	P_{max} kW	N_p rpm	T_{max} Nm	N_t rpm	CR	Sup	Make	P_{max} bar	AC	WC	P_{cont}	Fuel	Cont	Emiss	Notes
F114B	G	2.855	V8	294	7000	496	3800	7.6	T_2	I	0.9		W	W	I_p	D		
F120A	G	2.936	V8	352	7000	577	4000	7.7	T_2	I	1.1		W	W	I_p	M	C O	

Model	Year	Engine	Notes
288GTO		F114B	
F40		F120A	

Ford (UK)

Type	Cycle	Size litre	Form	P_{max} kW	N_p rpm	T_{max} Nm	N_t rpm	CR	Sup	Make	P_{max} bar	AC	WC	P_{cont}	Fuel	Cont	Emiss	Notes
f1	G	1.596	I4	99	5500	183	2400	8.2	T	G		A	W	W	I_p	M		unleaded fuel
f2	G	1.993	I4	164	6250	281	3500	8.0	T	G		A	W	W	I_p	M		Cosworth design
f3	D	1.753	I4	56	4500	152	2200	22.0	T	G		A	W	W	I_s	E		
f4	D	2.498	I4	71	4150	201	2250		T						I_s			

Model	Year	Engine	Notes
Fiesta RS Turbo	1990	f1	
Escort RS Turbo		f1	
Sierra Sapphire RS Cosworth 4x4	1990	f2	
Sierra/Sierra Sapphire Turbo Diesel	1990	f4	
Granada Turbo Diesel		f5	
Scorpio Turbo Diesel		f5	

General Motors (Europe)

Type	Cycle	Size litre	Form	P_{max} kW	N_p rpm	T_{max} Nm	N_t rpm	CR	Sup	Make	P_{max} bar	AC	WC	P_{cont}	Fuel	Cont	Emiss	Notes
15DT	D	1.49	I4	49	4600	132	2600	22.0	T	I	0.68	na	W	W	I_s	D		RHB3 turbo
15DTR	D	1.49	I4	53	4600	143	2600	22.0	T	I	0.68	A	W	W	I_s	D		RHB4 turbo
23DTR	D	2.26	I4	74	4200	218	2200	23.0	T	K	0.9	A	A	W	I_s	D	R	
C36GET	G	3.615	I6	281	5200	570	4200	8.2	T_2	G	0.7	W	W	W	I_p	M	C O	Lotus engine

Model	Year	Engine	Notes
Opel Corsa	1988	15DT	vehicle passes US87 emission standards
Opel Kadett	1989	15DTR	vehicle passes US87 emission standards
Opel Omega	1989	23DTR	vehicle passes US87 emission standards
Vauxhall Cavalier	1989	23DTR	vehicle passes US87 emission standards
Opel Lotus Omega	1990	C36GET	limited edition
Vauxhall Lotus Carlton	1990	C36GET	limited edition

General Motors (USA)

Type	Cycle	Size litre	Form	P_{max} bhp	N_p rpm	T_{max} lb ft	N_t rpm	CR	Sup	Make	P_{max} psi	AC	WC	P_{cont}	Fuel	Cont	Emiss	Notes
1.0l	G	1.0	I3	70	5500	80	3500	8.3	T	I	8	A	W	W	I_p	D	C O	Suzuki built
1.5l	G	1.5	I4	110	5400				T									
1.8MFI	G	1.8	I4	150	5600	150			T									
2.0MFI	G	2.0	I4	165	5600	175	4000	8.0	T	G	9	na	W	W	I_p	M	C	
3.1MFI	G	3.128	V6	205	4800	220	3000	8.9	T	G			W	W	I_p	E	C R O	McLaren dev't
3.8SFI	G	3.8	V6	200	4000	300	2400		T			na		W	I_p	M	R O	
3.8SFIi	G	3.8	V6	245	4400	355	2800		T		13	A	W		I_p	M	R O	

Model	Year	Engine	Notes
Buick Skyhawk T-type	1985	1.8 MFI	to end of 1986
Buick Regal T-type	1985	3.8 SFI	
Buick Regal Grand National	1985	3.8 SFI	
Buick Riviera T-type	1985	3.8 SFI	
Buick Riviera Convertible	1985	3.8 SFI	
Buick Regal T-type	1986	3.8 SFIi	charge air cooled
Buick Regal Grand National	1986	3.8 SFIi	charge air cooled
Buick Skyhawk Custom	1987	2.0 MFI	
Buick Skyhawk Limited	1987	2.0 MFI	
Buick Skyhawk Sport	1987	2.0 MFI	
Buick Regal Limited	1987	3.8 SFIi	charge air cooled
Chevrolet Turbo Sprint	1988	1.0l	Suzuki manufactured engine
Chevrolet Spectrum Turbo	1988	1.5l	
Chevrolet Spectrum Turbo Coupe	1988	1.5l	
Pontiac Sunbird SE & GT	1987	2.0 MFI	turbo optional on SE
Pontiac Grand Am SE & LE	1987	2.0 MFI	turbo optional on LE
Pontiac Trans Am GTA	1988	3.8 SFIi	
Pontiac Turbo Grand Prix	1989	3.1 MFI	

Isuzu

Type	Cycle	Size litre	Form	P_{max} bhp	N_p rpm	T_{max} lb ft	N_t rpm	CR	Sup	Make	P_{max} in Hg	AC	WC	P_{cont}	Fuel	Cont	Emiss	Notes
D	2.8	I4	95.2		158.9	2100	17.5	T	I		25.98	na	A	W		D	R	

Model	Year	Engine	Notes
Trooper	1988	as above	

Lancia

Type	Cycle	Size litre	Form	P_{max} kW	N_p rpm	T_{max} Nm	N_t rpm	CR	Sup	Make	P_{max} bar	AC	WC	P_{cont}	Fuel	Cont	Emiss	Notes
HF	G	1.585	I4	95.6	5600	191	3700	8.0	T	G	1.7	A	A	W	C_b	D		
HFie	G	1.585	I4	104	5500	193	3500	8.0	T	G	1.7	A	A	W	I_p	M		
16v	G	1.995	I4	133	5500	314	2500	8.0	T	G	1.6	A	W	W	I_p	D		two stage boost
VX	G	1.995	I4	99.3	5500	206	3000	7.5	S_r		1.4	na	A	na	C_s	na		
Delta	G	1.759	I4	184	6750	291	4500	7.6	S,T	K		A	A	W	I_p	M		road version
Delta R	G	1.759	I4	294	8000	392	5000	7.0	S,T	K	2.8	A	A	W	I_p	M		rally version

Model	Year	Engine	Notes
HP Executive VX		VX	
Coupe VX		VX	
Delta S4	1985	Delta	Abarth engine design
Delta HF turbo		HF	
Delta HFie turbo		HFie	
Delta HF Martini		HFie	
Thema 2.0ie turbo		16v	
Thema 2.0ie SE turbo		16v	

Land Rover

Type	Cycle	Size (litre)	Form	P_{max} (kW)	N_p (rpm)	T_{max} (Nm)	N_t (rpm)	CR	Sup	Make	P_{max} (bar)	AC	WC	P_{cont}	Fuel	Cont	Emiss	Notes
2.5L	D	2.500	I4	89	4200	284	1950	22.5	T	K	0.85	A	A	W	I_s	D	na	
200Tdi	D	2.495	I4	83	4000	265	1800	19.5	T	G	0.85	A	A	W	I_d	D	na	

Model	Year	Engine	Notes
Range Rover Turbo D	1986	2.5L	
Land Rover Defender	1990	200Tdi	
Land Rover Discovery	1989	200Tdi	

Lotus

Type	Cycle	Size (litre)	Form	P_{max} (bhp)	N_p (rpm)	T_{max} (lb ft)	N_t (rpm)	CR	BMEP (bar)	Sup	Make	P_{max} (bar)	AC	WC	P_{cont}	Fuel	Cont	Emiss	Notes
910S	G	2.174	I4	264	6500	261	3900	8.0	20.5	T	G	0.84	W	W	W	I_p	M	C O	direct ignition

Model	Year	Engine	Notes
Esprit Turbo SE1990	1990	910S	

Maserati

Type	Cycle	Size (litre)	Form	P_{max} (bhp)	N_p (rpm)	T_{max} (kg m)	N_t (rpm)	CR	Sup	Make	P_{max} (bar)	AC	WC	P_{cont}	Fuel	Cont	Emiss	Notes
BT1	G	2.491	V6	185	5500	30.5	3000	7.7	T_2	I	0.75	A	A	W	C_b	M	na	
BT2	G	2.491	V6	192	5500	30.5	3000	7.4	T_2	I	0.75	A	W	W	C_b	M	na	
BT3	G	2.790	V6	183	5600	38	3600	7.4	T_2	I	0.75	A	W	W	I_p	M	na	no catalyst
BT3	G	2.790	V6	165	5600	38	3600	7.4	T_2	I	0.75	A	W	W	I_p	M	C O	catalyst
BT4	G	2.790	V6	250	5600	39	3600	7.4	T_2	I	0.75	A	W	W	I_p	M	na	no catalyst
BT4	G	2.790	V6	225	5600	37	3600	7.4	T_2	I	0.75	A	W	W	I_p	M	C O	catalyst

Model	Year	Engine	Notes
Biturbo	1986	BT1	
Biturbo	1988	BT2	
228	1990	BT3	catalyst optional
430	1990	BT3	catalyst optional
222 SE	1990	BT4	catalyst optional

Mazda

Type	Cycle	Size (litre)	Form	P_{max} (kW)	N_p (rpm)	T_{max} (Nm)	N_t (rpm)	CR	Sup	Make	P_{max} (bar)	AC	WC	P_{cont}	Fuel	Cont	Emiss	Notes
	D	1.998	I4	61	4000			21.1	C	A		A	na	W	I_d	E		

Model	Year	Engine	Notes
Capella	1989	as above	

Mitsubishi Motors Corporation

Type	Cycle	Size (litre)	Form	P_{max} (kW)	N_p (rpm)	T_{max} (Nm)	N_t (rpm)	CR	BMEP (kg/cm²)	Sup	Make	P_{max} (bar)	AC	WC	P_{cont}	Fuel	Cont	Emiss	Notes
3G81TI	G	0.548	I3	37	6500	66	3500	8.5	17.4	T	Mi		A	W	W	C_*	C O		
4G54TI	G	2.555	I4	129	5000	314	3000	7.0	15.7	T	Mi		A	W	W	I_c	C O E		

Type	Cycle	Size litre	Form	P_{max} bhp	N_p rpm	T_{max} Nm	N_t rpm	CR	Sup	Make	P_{max} psi	AC	WC	P_{cont}	Fuel	Cont	Emiss	Notes
4G61TI	G	1.595	I4	107	6000	206	2500	8.0	17.7	T	Mi		A	W	W	I_p		C	O
4G63TI	G	1.997	I4	151	5000	294	3000	7.8	18.9	T	Mi		A	W	W	I_p		C	O
6G71SI	G	1.998	V6	110	5500	221	3000	8.0	14.2	S*	Mk		A	na	na	I_s		C	O
4D56TI	D	2.476	I4	69	4200	226	2000	21.0	11.7	T	Mi		A	W	W	I_s		E	C
4D65T	D	1.795	I4	58	4500	162	2500	21.5	10.6	T	Mi		na	W	W	I_s		E	C
4DR6T	D	2.659	I4	69	3500	206	2000	17.5	9.9	T	Mi		na	W	W	I_d		E	

Model	Year	Engine	Notes
Galant Σ./Eterna Σ	1984	4D65T	
Chariot	1984	4D65T	
Delica	1986	4D06TI	
Jeep	1986	4DR6T	
Minicab	1987	3G81TI	
Galant	1987	4G63TI	
Debonair	1987	6G71SI	
Starion	1988	4G54TI	
Mirage	1988	4G61TI	
Lancer	1988	4G61TI	
Eterna	1988	4G63TI	
Eterna diesel	1988	4D65T	
Pajero	1988	4D56TI	
Minica	1989	3G81TI	
Eterna Sava	1989	4D65T	
Mirage	1990	4D65T	
Lancer diesel	1990	4D65T	

Nissan

Type	Cycle	Size litre	Form	P_{max} bhp	N_p rpm	T_{max} Nm	N_t rpm	CR	Sup	Make	P_{max} psi	AC	WC	P_{cont}	Fuel	Cont	Emiss	Notes
2SX	G	1.809	I4	171	6400	228	4000	8.5	T	G		A			I_p	M		direct ignition
3ZX	G	2.960	V6	280	6400	372	3600	8.5	T_2			A			I_p	M	C	var.valve time

Model	Year	Engine	Notes
200SX	1989	2SX	
300ZX	1990	3ZX	

Peugeot Talbot

Type	Cycle	Size litre	Form	P_{max} kW	N_p rpm	T_{max} Nm	N_t rpm	CR	Sup	Make	P_{max} bar	AC	WC	P_{cont}	Fuel	Cont	Emiss	Notes
XUD7T	D	1.769	I4	57.5	4300	157	2100	22	T	K					I_p			
XUD7TE	D	1.769	I4	66	4300	180	2100	22	T	K/G					I_p			
XUD11AT	D	2.088	I4	80	4300	245	2000	21.5	T	Mi	0.8				I_p			

Model	Year	Engine	Notes
205 D Turbo		XUD7T	
309 GRDT		XUD7T	
405 GRDT		XUD 7 TE	
405 GTDT		XUD 7 TE	
605 SRdt		XU D11 ATE	

Porsche

Type	Cycle	Size litre	Form	P_{max} kW	N_p rpm	T_{max} Nm	N_t rpm	CR	Sup	Make	P_{max} psi	AC	WC	P_{cont}	Fuel	Cont	Emiss	Notes
911t	G	3.299	F6	221	5500	430	4000	7.0	T	K	0.7	A		W	I_p	E		
911t90	G	3.299	F6	236	5750	450	4500	7.0	T	K	0.7	A		W	I_p	M	C	wastegate cat.
944t	G	2.479	I4	162	5800	329	3500	8.0	T	K	0.75	A		W	I_p	E		
944t89	G	2.479	I4	184	5800	350	4000	8.0	T	K	0.82	A		W	I_p	M	C	
959	G	2.85	F6	331	6500	500	5500	8.3	T_2	K	1.0	A_2	W	W	I_p	E		sequential turbo

Model	Year	Engine	Notes
911 Turbo	1983	911t	earlier version 1975
911 Turbo	1990	911t90	
944 Turbo	1985	944t	
944 Turbo	1989	944t89	
959	1986	959	Group B competition car

Renault

Type	Cycle	Size litre	Form	P_{max} kW	N_p rpm	T_{max} Nm	N_t rpm	CR	Sup	Make	P_{max} bar	AC	WC	P_{cont}	Fuel	Cont	Emiss	Notes
r1	G	1.397	I4	88.5	5750	165	3750	7.9	T	G		A	A	W	C_b	E		
J/turbo	G	1.995	I4	129	5200	270	3000	8.0	T	G	0.9	A	W	W	I_p	M		abs. press. cont
r3	G	2.458	V6	147	5750	285	2500	8.6	T	G			A		I_p	M		
r4	G	2.458	V6	136	5750	290	2200	8.0	T	G			A		I_p	M	C	

Model	Year	Engine	Notes
5 Series GT Turbo		r1	
21 Series Turbo	1988	J/turbo	
21 Series Turbo Quadra	1988	J/turbo	4-wheel drive
GTA Turbo Alpine	1986	r3	
GTA Turbo Alpine	1986	r4	emissions control model
GTA Le Mans	1990	r4	emissions control model

Rolls-Royce

Type	Cycle	Size litre	Form	P_{max} kW	N_p rpm	T_{max} Nm	N_t rpm	CR	Sup	Make	P_{max} bar	AC	WC	P_{cont}	Fuel	Cont	Emiss	Notes
	G	6.75	V8					8.0	T	G	0.5	A	A	W A	I_p	M	C O	

Model	Year	Engine	Notes
Bentley Turbo R	1985	as above	

Rover

Type	Cycle	Size litre	Form	P_{max} bhp	N_p rpm	T_{max} kg m	N_t rpm	CR	BMEP psi	Sup	Make	P_{max} psi	AC	WC	P_{cont}	Fuel	Cont	Emiss	Notes
A	G	1.275	I4	94	6130	11.8	2650	9.4	166	T	G	7	na	A	W	C_b	E	na	oil cooler
O	G	1.994	I4	152	5100	23.4	3500	8.5	210	T	G	10	A	A	W	C_b	D	na	

Model	Year	Engine	Notes
Metro	1984	A	ended in 1989
Maestro	1989	O	1989 only
Montego	1985	O	

Subaru

Type	Cycle	Size (litre)	Form	P_{max} (bhp)	N_p (rpm)	T_{max} (lb ft)	N_t (rpm)	CR	Sup	Make	P_{max} (psi)	AC	WC	P_{cont}	Fuel	Cont	Emiss	Notes
	G	1.8	F4	134	5600	144	2800	7.7	T	I	10	na	W	W	D	R		

Model	Year	Engine	Notes
L Series Turbo	1985	as above	

Toyota

Type	Cycle	Size (litre)	Form	P_{max} (bhp)	N_p (rpm)	T_{max} (lb ft)	N_t (rpm)	CR	Sup	Make	P_{max} (bar)	AC	WC	P_{cont}	Fuel	Cont	Emiss	Notes
t1	G	1.998	I4	201	6000	203	3600	8.8	T	M	0.83	A	W	W	I_p	M	C	
t2	G	2.954	I6	234	5600	258	3200	8.4	T	M	0.53	A	W	W	I_p	M	C	
t3	D	2.446	I4	88	3500	159	2400	21.0	T	M	0.81	A	W	W	I_d	M		
t4	D	4.164	I6	165	3600	266	1800	18.6	T	M	0.65	A	W	W	I_d	M		

Model	Year	Engine	Notes
Celica GT4	1990	t1	
Supra Turbo	1988	t2	
Landcruiser II	1990	t3	
Landcruiser VX	1990	t4	

Volkswagen/Audi Group

Type	Cycle	Size (litre)	Form	P_{max} (kW)	N_p (rpm)	T_{max} (Nm)	N_t (rpm)	CR	Sup	Make	P_{max} (bar)	AC	WC	P_{cont}	Fuel	Cont	Emiss	Notes
EA111	G	1.3	I4	85	6000	148	3600	8.0	G	M	0.72	A	A	A	I_p	M	na	
EA111e	G	1.3	I4	82	6000	148	3600	8.0	G	M	0.72	A	A	A	I_p	M	C O	
v1	D	1.588	I4	44	4500	110	2700	23.0	T		0.82	na	A	W	I_d	D	C	Umwelt engine
v2a	D	1.588	I4	59	4500	155	2700	23.0	T	K	0.76	A	A	W	I_d	D	na	
v2b	D	1.588	I4	59	4500	155	2700	23.0	T	K	0.85	A	A	W	I_d	D	na	
v2c	D	1.588	I4	59	4500	155	2700	23.0	T	K	0.82	A	A	W	I_d	D	na	
G60	G	1.781	I4	118	5600	225	4000	8.0	G	M	0.72	A	A	A	I_p	M	C O	
v3	D	1.986	I5	75	4500	192	2500	23.0	T		0.76	A	A	W	I_d		na	
v4	G	2.226	I5	123	5500	241	3000	8.4	T	K	0.79	A	A	W	I_p	M	C O	
v5	G	2.226	I5	161	5900	309	1950	9.3	T	K	1.12	A	A	W	I_p	M	C O	
v6	G	2.226	I5	147	5800	270	3000	8.6	T	K	0.79	A	A	W	I_p	E	na	

Model	Year	Engine	Notes
Audi 80 Turbo Diesel		v2a	
Audi Quattro	1980	v6	
Audi Quattro 20V	1989	v5	
Audi S2	1991	v5	
Audi 100 Turbo	1990	v4	
Audi 100 Turbo Quattro	1990	v4	
Audi 100 Avant Turbo Diesel		v3	

VW Polo coupe GT G40							1986		EA111		or catalyst version					
VW Golf CL Umwelt diesel							1990		v1							
VW Jetta GX Umwelt diesel							1990		v1							
VW Golf GTD diesel							1989		v2c							
VW Jetta GL turbo diesel							1989		v2c							
VW GolF GTi G60							1990		G60							
VW Passat CLTD & GLTD							1989		v2b							
VW Corrado G60							1989		G60							

Volvo

Type	Cycle	Size litre	Form	P_{max} bhp	N_p rpm	T_{max} Nm	N_t rpm	CR	Sup	Make	P_{max} kPa	AC	WC	P_{cont}	Fuel	Cont	Emiss	Notes
B18FT	G	1.721	I4	119	5400	175	3300	8.1	T	G	45	A	W	W	I_p	M	C O	
B230GT	G	2.316	I4	170	4800	265	3450	8.7	T	M_i	51	A	W	W	I_p	E	E	diagnostic
B230FT	G	2.316	I4	165	4800	264	3450	8.7	T	M_i	51		W	W	I_p	E	C O E	diagnostic
D24T	D	2.383	I6	109	4800	205	2500	23.0	T	G	85			W	I_s	D		
D24Tic	D	2.383	I6	122	4800	235	2400	23.0	T	G	85	A	W	W	I_s	D		

Model	Year	Engine	Notes
440 turbo	1986	B18FT	
460 turbo	1986	B18FT	
740 turbo	>1991	B230GT	UK market up to 1991
760 turbo	>1991	B230GT	UK market up to 1991
740	1990	B230FT	option; standard 1991
760	1990	B230FT	option; standard 1991
740 turbo diesel	1985	D24T	
760 turbo diesel	1985	D24Tic	

Appendix B

Calculation methods

The following material is based on a technical paper by P. F. Freeman and B. E. Walsham[24] and information supplied by Garrett Automotive.

A simple turbocharger matching technique is described which has been shown to give an accuracy within 10%, but this is dependent on the accuracy of a number of initial assumptions which have to be made. It is assumed that the choice of target matching point has already been decided from the factors discussed in Chapters 19 and 20. To simplify the presentation, the following symbols (in alphabetic order) are used to define the different quantities used in the calculations:

AF	Air/fuel ratio	Fraction
BSFC	Brake specific fuel consumption	μg/sec
C_{pa}	Constant pressure specific heat for air (1005)	kJ/kg
C_{pe}	Constant pressure specific heat for exhaust gas (1158)	kJ/kg
D_{as}	Standard air density at 288K and 1.013 bar	kg/m^3
DR	Density ratio of delivered air to ambient air	Fraction
E_c	Compressor isentropic efficiency	Fraction
E_{er}	Enthalpy rise across engine	kJ/sec
E_i	Charge air cooler effectiveness	Fraction
E_{ta}	Apparent turbine efficiency	Fraction
E_{th}	Engine thermal efficiency	Fraction
E_v	Engine volumetric efficiency	Fraction
LCV	Lower calorific value of fuel	MJ/kg
M_a	Air mass flow	gms/sec
M_f	Fuel mass flow	gms/sec
M_{tn}	Turbine non-dimensional mass flow	kg/sec x $\sqrt{K}$/bar/1000
N	Engine speed	revs/minute
P	Ratio of P_1/1.013 (standard ambient pressure)	Fraction
P_1	Compressor inlet pressure	bar absolute
P_2	Compressor outlet pressure	bar absolute

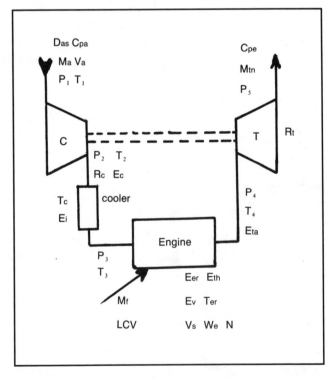

Schematic showing where the various quantities used in the calculations are measured.

Symbol	Description	Units	Symbol	Description	Units
P_3	Engine inlet pressure	bar absolute	T_2	Compressor outlet temperature	°K
P_4	Turbine inlet pressure	bar absolute	T_3	Engine inlet temperature	°K
P_5	Turbine outlet pressure	bar absolute	T_4	Turbine inlet temperature	°K
PD	Ratio of pressure drop across cooler (P_3/P_2)	Fraction	T_5	Turbine outlet temperature	°K
Q_c	Ratio of heat lost to coolant/input heat	Fraction	T_c	Charge air cooler coolant temperature	°K
R_c	Compressor pressure ratio	Fraction	T_{er}	Gas temperature rise across engine	°K
R_t	Turbine expansion ratio	Fraction	V_a	Actual volumetric air flow	m³/sec
T	Ratio of $T_1/288$ (standard ambient temperature)	Fraction	V_{ac}	Corrected volumetric air flow	m³/sec
T_1	Compressor inlet temperature	°K	V_s	Swept volume of engine	litre
			W_e	Engine power	kW

Consider the case where a turbocharger/engine match is required at a particular engine speed and power. The given information will be speed, power and swept volume. Estimates will therefore have to be made of the volumetric efficiency, the air/fuel ratio, the fuel consumption, and the fraction of heat lost to the coolant, and these are usually based on experience with similar engines. Values for T_1, P_1 and P_5 will also have to be assumed, although these are usually the ambient conditions. If a charge air cooler is to be fitted, values for E_i, T_c and PD need to be estimated.

Given these initial assumptions, first determine the fuel mass flow:

$$M_f = (W_e \times BSFC)/1000 \tag{1}$$

From this comes the necessary air mass flow and the volumetric air flow:

$$M_a = M_f \times AF \tag{2}$$
$$V_a = (M_a \times T)/(D_{as} \times P \times 1000) \tag{3}$$

The corrected volumetric air flow is then given by:

$$V_{ac} = V_a/\sqrt{T} \tag{4}$$

This calculated value of the corrected air flow, V_{ac}, allows the use of standard compressor maps, which are plotted on a basis of constant relative inlet Mach number.

The density ratio across the compressor, and charge air cooler if fitted, may now be calculated. However, it should be noted that this is based on total conditions rather than static ones. The latter would require an input of compressor geometry which is not appropriate to this level of calculation. The error introduced is very small. The density ratio is given by:

$$DR = (V_a \times 120)/(V_s \times N \times E_v) \tag{5}$$

If no charge air cooler is fitted, an iterative sequence is entered to specify the compressor operating point. The air flow is already known, so from a suitable compressor map an appropriate value of pressure ratio and efficiency may be chosen. Then the compressor outlet temperature is determined by:

$$T_2 = T_1 + (T_1/E_c)(R_c^{0.286} - 1) \tag{6}$$

where 0.286 is the value of $(\gamma-1)/\gamma$ for inlet air, and γ, the ratio of specific heats, is approximately 1.4.

A new value of the density ratio is now calculated:

$$DR_{new} = (T_1/T_2) \times R_c \tag{7}$$

This new density ratio is compared with the required value from equation (5), and new values of R_c and E_c are taken from the map until the solutions from equations (5) and (7) are similar.

If a charge air cooler is to be used, instead of equation (7) equations (8) and (9) are used:

$$T_3 = T_2 - E_i(T_2 - T_c) \tag{8}$$
$$DR_{new} = (T_1 \times R_c \times PD)/T_3 \tag{9}$$

Then the calculations are repeated as before to find the correct point on the compressor map.

The engine calculations may now be made to obtain T_4. First determine the engine thermal efficiency:

$$E_{th} = 1000/(LCV \times BSFC) \tag{10}$$

From a curve of heat loss to coolant in relation to fuel flow, or similar data, an appropriate value for Q_c can be obtained. Then:

$$E_{er} = LCV \times M_f \times (1 - E_{th} - QC) \tag{11}$$

giving a gas temperature rise across the engine of:

$$T_{er} = E_{er}/(C_{pa} \times M_f \times (1 + AF)) \tag{12}$$

whence the turbine inlet temperature is:

$$T_4 = T_2 + T_{er} \tag{13}$$

or if a charge air cooler is fitted:

$$T_4 = T_3 + T_{er} \tag{14}$$

It is now necessary to assume an apparent turbine efficiency. The adjective 'apparent' is used because this is a figure derived from a mean measured exhaust manifold pressure and also includes the turbocharger bearing losses. This figure is usually high and can be over 100% at low exhaust pulse frequencies.

The power balance between the compressor and turbine is now used to derive the turbine expansion ratio:

$$R_t = \{ 1/[1 - (AF \times T_1 \times (R_c^{0.286} - 1))/((AF + 1) \times 1.152 \times E_c \times E_{ta} \times T4)]\}^{4.03} \qquad (15)$$

where 4.03 is $\gamma/(\gamma-1)$ for exhaust gas, the ratio of specific heats, γ, being taken as 1.33, and 1.152 is the ratio of C_{pe}/C_{pa}.

The turbine parameters thus defined are now referred to a turbine swallowing capacity. This requires the correlation of turbine expansion ratio and a mass flow parameter to size the turbine. The mass flow parameter, M_{tn}, is, as with the compressor, an inlet Mach number corrected figure.

$$M_{tn} = ((M_a + M_f) \times \sqrt{T_4})/(R_t \times P_5 \times 1000) \qquad (16)$$

If a suitable turbine is not available, the calculations must be restarted with alterations to the input data until all the conditions are met, and a suitable turbocharger can be specified for the application.

Similar equations are used if the starting conditions are a fixed boost level instead of engine power.

Basic principle of A/R calculation

An A/R 'nozzle' rating is computed using the principle of continuity of flow and the requirement that the volute feeds the turbine wheel tip with a free vortex flow field. It is assumed that the flow is two dimensional and compressibility and frictional effects are ignored. The accompanying diagram depicts a typical turbine housing and defines the terms and derivation of A/R.

The free vortex law is based upon the principle of the conservation of angular momentum; in order to satisfy angular momentum, tangential velocity must vary inversely with radius. Thus, from the throat of the housing the tangential velocity component is accelerated down to the turbine wheel tip. In order to obtain optimum turbine efficiency with a 90° radial inflow turbine wheel design, it is a requirement that the tangential velocity component of the gas approaching the wheel tip have approximately the same magnitude as the wheel tip peripheral velocity. Thus, depending upon the diameter of the wheel and its design rotational speed, different magnitudes of the tangential velocity vector are required.

The following symbols are used:

Q   volumetric flow rate of exhaust gas (m³/min)
A   cross-sectional area of volute at the tongue (metre²)
V_T tangential component of velocity (metres/min)
N_w wheel speed (revs/min)
R_w radius of wheel tip
R   a radius of the scroll

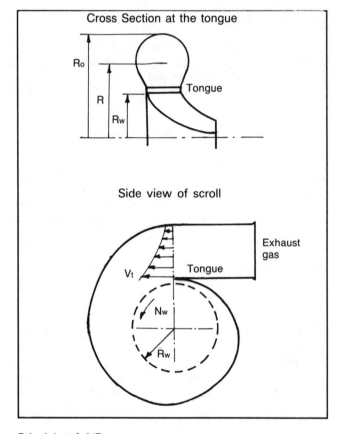

Principle of A/R measurement

Free vortex flow requires that $(V_T \times R)$ remains a constant. The continuity of the flow, with V being some function of R, requires that:

Q = A × V_T

thus:

Q = (A × constant)/R

or,

Q = A/R × K

The constant K is given by $2\pi R_w^2 N_w$ (metres/min)

If we solve for R,

Q/K = A/R

R = A/(A/R) = R_{DC}

R_{DC} is called the radius to dynamic centre. This locates that point which divides the scroll area such that half the flow passes above and half below that radius. The V_T at R_{DC} is the mean value of flow velocity.

Appendix C

Maintenance check-lists

The following notes apply to turbochargers, where the similarity between different manufacturers' designs is sufficiently close to allow general comments to be written. For mechanically driven superchargers, the variety of construction techniques means that only good engineering practice can be recommended without going into specific detail.

On-engine routine checking

WARNING: Turbochargers operate at high speed and high temperatures. Keep fingers away from openings and avoid contact with hot surfaces.

- Routinely check all air duct and gasket connections for tightness and leaks. Make any necessary repairs immediately, to prevent loss of power and engine overheating.
- Poor inlet air filtration leading to excessive dirt build-up on the compressor wheel and housing can cause loss of power and overheating. If the compressor ingests this dirt, the turbocharger and the engine could be damaged. Use a non-caustic cleaning solvent to remove dirt build-up.
- Follow the engine manufacturer's recommendations for the proper types of oil and oil filters, and observe scheduled oil change intervals to ensure the normal service life for the turbocharger bearings. A synthetic lubricating oil is commonly recommended for use in turbocharged engines.
- Avoid high speed engine operation in the first few seconds after starting, especially from cold. Allow time for oil flow to be established to the turbocharger bearings before spinning it up to high speed.
- Make sure that the exhaust manifold to engine connection is secure and that the gasket does not leak.
- Ensure that the turbine mounting onto the exhaust manifold is secure and that there are no signs of leaks. Heat discoloration and/or exhaust deposits may indicate an exhaust gas leak.
- Check the turbine outlet to exhaust system flange joint for tightness and signs of leakage.
- If an integral wastegate is fitted, check that its operating linkage is free to move.
- Check for any oil leaks from the centre housing and end housings. Leakage indicates a possible engine or turbocharger problem.
- Check the oil feed line for tightness and any sign of leakage.
- When running, note any unusual noise or vibration:
  - Noise level cycling can indicate a blocked air cleaner, a restriction in the air cleaner to compressor duct, or a heavy dirt build-up in the compressor housing or on the compressor wheel.
  - High-pitched noise can indicate air leakage between air cleaner and engine, or an exhaust gas leak between engine exhaust manifold and turbocharger inlet.
- Watch for any oil smoke at hot idle, indicating worn bearings/failed seals.

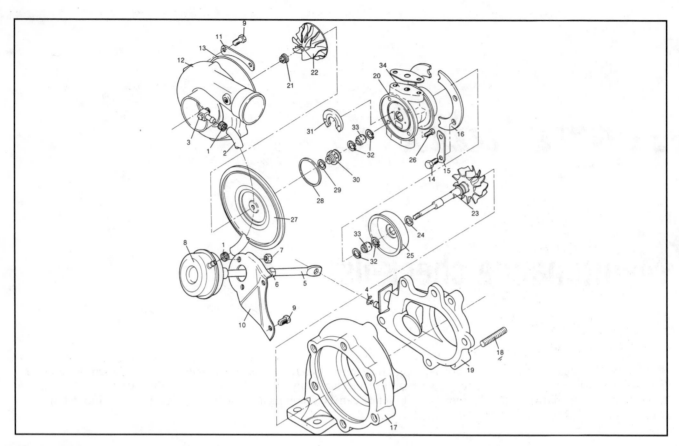

Exploded diagram of the T3 turbocharger. [*Garrett*]

Disassembly maintenance

- Remove the air inlet and exhaust ducting. Turn the rotating assembly by hand via the compressor inlet or turbine exhaust ports and feel for dragging or binding. Push assembly sideways while turning, to check for wheel rub. If the wheels rub, replace the turbocharger.
- Remove the oil drain line and check for any build-up of sludge or coke in the drain or the centre housing port.
- After the complete turbocharger is removed from the engine, thoroughly re-examine for leaks, freedom of rotor movement and wastegate movement.
- Before disassembly:
  - clean the exterior of the turbocharger with a non-caustic solvent;
  - remove cooling water fittings as necessary, identifying and marking the inlet and outlet ports.
- Dismantle the wastegate assembly (if fitted) as follows:
  - remove hose clamps and hose from wastegate actuator inlet and compressor housing;
  - remove retaining clip securing actuator rod to crank assembly pin;
  - carefully lift the rod off the lever;
  - remove the bolts securing the actuator to the compressor housing.
- Remove the exhaust elbow/wastegate assembly from the turbine housing if this is separate.
- Scribe marks on the compressor and turbine housings to ensure that they and their clamps can be re-assembled in the same position later.
- Remove the compressor and turbine housings from the central housing assembly. It may be necessary to rotate the housings to get access to all the fixing bolts. Discard the gaskets and replace with new at re-assembly.
- Following disassembly, inspect the major components for damage and make sure that there are no missing parts. If there is any damage a replacement unit will normally be needed. DO NOT dismantle the central housing assembly.
- Before cleaning, inspect all parts for surface discoloration, rubbing or impact damage that might not be evident after cleaning.
- Carefully check the turbine housing for any signs of scaling or cracking.

- Clean all parts in a non-caustic cleaning solution. Use a soft-bristle brush, a plastic scraper, and dry compressed air to remove residue:
    - do not use abrasive cleaning methods which might damage machined surfaces;
    - do not immerse the complete central housing assembly in solvent;
    - do not blow under the compressor wheel with compressed air;
    - do not permit the wheel/shaft assembly to spin when blowing off solvent and residue.
- Check the exhaust assembly for any damage to the wastegate:
    - scoring, wear, cracking or erosion of the by-pass valve face or seat;
    - misalignment of the by-pass valve and its port;
    - any wear in the operating linkage which could cause maloperation;
    - nicks, dents or warping of the mating surface that could prevent proper sealing with the turbine housing.

A compressor impeller which has suffered damage by rubbing against the housing after excessive thrust bearing wear. [*Garrett*]

- Inspect the bearing clearances. Measuring these usually requires special tools only available at the turbocharger service agent but a manual check can give some idea of the likely condition. Radial clearance is likely to be in the 0.05-0.15 mm range, and axial clearance in the 0.02-0.08 mm range. The manufacturer's maintenance leaflets will give the correct values.
- If there is any damage to the compressor or turbine wheel, or there is any doubt about the condition of the bearings, the complete central unit should be replaced. It is not a 'do-it-yourself' service job to change any part of this assembly; a specialist workshop is needed with the appropriate high speed balancing equipment, jigs and tools, as well the spare parts.

Re-assembly

- New gaskets should always be used. Some manufacturers recommend replacing the fixing bolts and wastegate hose as well.
- If either the turbine housing or a separate exhaust elbow with the wastegate is replaced, both must be changed. If the wastegate actuator does not have an adjustable rod end, it should be changed for one that does.
- If new housing components are used, transfer the alignment marks from the old ones to the new.
- The bolts holding the compressor and turbine housings to the central unit should be tightened to the torque recommended by the manufacturer.
- Whenever a turbocharger is installed, or re-installed, pre-oil the bearings before mounting it on the engine:
    - plug the oil drain hole and fill the central housing with clean engine oil;
    CAUTION: with water-cooled models, be sure to fill the oil passages, and not the cooling passages, with the oil.
    - turn the compressor/turbine wheel assembly by hand through several revolutions to thoroughly coat all the bearing surfaces with oil; drain the excess oil before mounting the turbocharger on the engine.

Appendix D

Conversion factors

The measurement units used in this book are based on the international standard 'Systeme International d'Unites' system; usually abbreviated to SI Units.

In this system the basic units of mass, length and time are the kilogram, the metre and the second. All the other units are derived from these:

```
1 metre (m)       = 1,000 millimetres (mm)
1 centimetre (cm) = 10 millimetres
1 kilometre (km)  = 1,000 metres
1 kilogram (kg)   = 1,000 grams (gms)
1 litre (l)       = 1,000 cubic centimetres
1 Newton (N)      = 1 kilogram x 1 metre per second squared (m/s²)
```

Note that the kilogram is a unit of mass. The Newton is the force which, acting on a mass of one kilogram, gives to that mass an acceleration of one metre per second per second. In the old Imperial system, the pound (lb) was the unit which was used to describe both mass and force. Today, pound (lb) and pound force (lbf) are used to distinguish between mass and force.

The acceleration (g) due to the force of gravity is 9.81 metres per second per second. Therefore a one kilogram mass weighs 9.81 Newtons.

Torque is given by force multiplied by the radius of action. The SI unit of torque is the Newton metre (Nm).

Heat is internal energy and is capable of doing work. Heat flows from a hot to a cold surface. The basic SI unit of temperature is the degree Kelvin; the more convenient scale is Celsius, which has the same size unit as the Kelvin but a different zero point.

Kelvin ($°K$) = Celsius ($°C$) + 273.15

Energy cannot be created or destroyed – it can only be converted from one form to another. Work is defined as force multiplied by distance moved, and the basic SI unit is the Joule.

1 Joule (J) = 1 Newton x 1 metre

Power is the rate of doing work, and the basic SI unit is the Watt.

1 Watt (W) = 1 Joule per second

Pressure is measured as force per unit area. The basic SI unit is the Pascal, although the bar is the more commonly used unit. The bar approximates to the average atmospheric pressure.

```
1 Pascal (P) = 1 Newton per square metre    (N/m²)
1 bar        = 100,000 Pascal
```

The following conversions between the SI units and the British Imperial system are likely to be useful in automotive applications:

1 inch	= 25.4 millimetres	1 Btu	= 1.055 kJ
1 millimetre	= 0.03937 inch	1 Chu	= 1.9 kJ
0.001 inch	= 0.025 millimetre	1 horsepower	= 746 Watts
1 foot	= 304.8 millimetres	horsepower (hp) =[torque (lb-ft) x speed (rpm)]/5250	
1 mile	= 1.6 kilometres	1 lb/in² (psi)	= 0.07 bar
1 cubic inch	= 16.4 cubic centimetres	1 inch Mercury	= 34 millibar
1 litre	= 61.02 cubic inches	1° Fahrenheit	= (°C x 1.8) + 32
1 gallon	= 4.536 litre	Rankine (°R)	= °F + 459.67
1 pound mass	= 0.454 kilogram	1 foot/second	= 0.3 metre/second
1 pound force	= 4.45 Newtons	1 mile/hour	= 1.6 kilometres/hour
1 lb-ft torque	= 1.36 Nm	1 mile/gallon	= 0.34 km/litre or 290 litres/100 km
1 ft lb work	= 1.4 Joule		

Specific heat is the heat input per degree rise in temperature. For a gas there are two different values:

c_p – specific heat at constant pressure
c_v – specific heat at constant volume

The ratio of the two specific heats is used in the various gas equations and is indicated by the Greek letter gamma (γ).

$\gamma = c_p/c_v = 1.667$ for a perfect gas; 1.4 for air

Useful gas characteristic values:

	R (kJ/kg-K)	γ (at 15°C)	c_p (kJ/kg-K)	c_v (kJ/kg-K)
Air	0.2870	1.402	0.992	0.714
Oxygen	0.2598	1.40	1.013	0.6495
Nitrogen	0.2967	1.40	0.984	0.7237
CO	0.2968	1.401	1.013	0.740
CO_2	0.1890	1.306	0.842	0.618

The perfect gas equation:

$$pv = RT$$

where p = pressure (N/m²);
v = specific volume (m³/kg);
R = gas constant (J/kg-K);
T = absolute temperature (°K).

A perfect gas is approximated by air at normal low pressures.

Constant volume process:	$V_2/V_1 = 1.0$	$p_2/p_1 = T_2/T_1$
Constant pressure process:	$p_2/p_1 = 1.0$	$V_2/V_1 = T_2/T_1$
Isothermal process:	$T_2/T_1 = 1.0$	$V_2/V_1 = p_1/p_2$
Adiabatic process:	$pv^\gamma =$ constant	$p_2/p_1 = (V_1/V_2)^\gamma$
	$T_2/T_1 = (V_1/V_2)^{\gamma-1}$	$T_2/T_1 = (p_2/p_1)^{(\gamma-1)/\gamma}$

The kinetic energy of a gas is given by:

$\frac{1}{2}mv^2$ (Nm)

A very rough rule of thumb is that an engine will require 6.5 lbs of air per horsepower hour.

Glossary

The following is a list of words which have been used in this book and which may not be generally familiar. Each word or phrase is accompanied by a brief explanation.

Actuator: A device used by an electronic control system to convert an electrical signal into the adjustment of some engine or vehicle control. For example: fuel injection valves, throttle movement, turbine nozzle vane movement.

Adiabatic: A process which changes the pressure or volume of a gas without the addition or loss of any heat.

Adiabatic efficiency: The ratio of the theoretical temperature rise in a compressor to the actual temperature rise.

Air standard efficiency: The theoretical overall thermal efficiency of an engine cycle based on the known highest and lowest temperatures in the cycle and assuming air as the working fluid.

Analogue: A quantity, usually electrical, which varies smoothly to represent some physical change. For example: the current through a variable resistor.

A/R: The ratio of turbine inlet throat area to the radius of the dynamic centre. It is a convenient measure of the 'swallowing' capacity of a vaneless turbine (see Appendix B).

Bar: A basic unit of gas pressure. It approximates to the normal atmospheric barometric pressure (see Appendix D).

BHP: See Brake horsepower

Blow down energy: The energy in exhaust gases which is released by the opening of an exhaust valve, as a result of the instantaneous difference between the cylinder pressure and the exhaust system back pressure.

Blow-through: A carburettor installation which follows a supercharging compressor.

BMEP: See Brake mean effective pressure.

Boost pressure: The additional pressure generated by a supercharger above the normal atmospheric pressure.

Brake horsepower: The actual available power at the output shaft of an engine after allowing for mechanical losses, and the power needs of auxiliaries and supercharger. It is the power which would be measured by a brake on the output shaft (see Dynamometer).

Brake mean effective pressure: The mean effective cylinder pressure calculated back from brake horsepower (see Mean Effective Pressure).

BSFC: See Specific fuel consumption.

Catalytic converter: A device placed in the exhaust system which uses catalytic chemical reactions to convert carbon monoxide, hydrocarbons and nitric oxides into non-carcinogenic compounds (see Chapter 7).

Centrifugal compressor: A compressor which uses the kinetic energy of a fast moving gas to obtain an increase in pressure.

Charge air cooler: A heat exchanger which reduces the temperature of the engine inlet air before it enters the cylinders. It is usually used to lower the temperature after a supercharging compressor.

Closed loop control: A control system which measures the resulting output after actions have been taken and adjusts the control rules and actions to achieve the result required.

Compound engine: An internal combustion engine which uses an exhaust gas turbine to provide additional engine power by some form of coupling to the output shaft.

Compressor: A device which takes a gas at one pressure, and applies mechanical work in some manner in order to deliver the gas at a new higher pressure. Compressors used for supercharging are either positive displacement or kinetic energy types.

Critical speed: A speed at which the vibration of a rotating component coincides with the natural frequency of vibration of the structure of the component. At this speed the vibrations will be amplified and can build up to damaging levels. Any object will have numerous critical speeds which are multiples of each other. Usually only the first and perhaps the second critical speeds are important.

Diagram efficiency: The difference between the theoretical power of a particular engine and the measured power obtained from the values of pressure and volume on an indicator diagram.

Diffuser: A shaped gas passage which efficiently slows down the speed of the gas and increases its pressure.

Digital: Values of measured quantities which are stored as numbers. Electronic computers usually use digital data rather than analogue data.

DIN: Reference to a standard method of measurement or system of units as defined by the German standards institution.

Dynamic pressure: The component of the total pressure of a gas which results from the kinetic energy of movement of the gas.

Dynamometer: A test machine for determining engine power and related characteristics. An engine can be mounted on the dynamometer and run under controlled conditions. A load is placed on the output shaft, usually by hydraulic or electrical means. Early dynamometers used a water-cooled friction brake, and as a result the word 'brake' is still used to identify dynamometer measured values.

Effective compression ratio: The equivalent geometric compression ratio for an engine which would be required to give the same resulting final compression pressure as that obtained after supercharging.

EGR: See Exhaust gas recirculation.

Engine management system: An electronic control system, usually using digital computers, which measures and controls all the related parameters of engine operation as one integrated process.

Exhaust gas recirculation: A method of reducing nitric oxide production by feeding a proportion of the exhaust gas back into the inlet of an engine.

Gamma: The Greek symbol γ which is used to represent the ratio of constant pressure to constant volume specific heat values for a gas.

Gas constant: The numeric constant, R, which is used in the basic gas law equation, $PV = RT$. Its value depends upon the actual measuring units for P, V and T.

Gas turbine: A rotating paddle-wheel-type of device which obtains mechanical work from a high-temperature gas. The term may also be applied to a complete system which incorporates an air compressor, combustion chamber, turbine and power take-off.

Geometrical compression ratio: The ratio of the total volume of an engine cylinder (swept volume plus clearance volume) to the clearance volume. It is determined by the physical dimensions of the engine and will differ from the effective compression ratio in a supercharged engine.

Heat exchanger: A device where two fluids are brought into close proximity, but kept separate, allowing heat to transfer from one fluid to the other. The gas or liquid which flows through will be exposed to large-area fins in order to maximise the heat transfer. In a regenerative heat exchanger, there will only be one set of passages and the fluids will flow through this passage alternately. Heat is transferred from one fluid to the relatively massive walls of the exchanger during one passage and then back from the walls to the other fluid in the second pass.

IHP: See Indicated horsepower.

Indicated horsepower: The power output which is available from an engine before taking into account friction and other losses. It is determined from the area of the pressure/volume 'indicator' diagram.

Indicator diagram: A graph of the variation of cylinder pressure related to cylinder volume obtained by measurements on an engine.

Isothermal: A gas process which changes pressure and/or volume without changing temperature.

Kinetic energy: The energy stored in a moving object as a result of its speed of movement.

Lambda: The Greek letter λ which denotes the ratio of actual air/fuel ratio to the stoichiometric, correct combustion value.

Lambda probe: An oxygen sensor which is placed in the exhaust system to determine the lambda value.

Mach number: The ratio of the speed of a fluid to the speed of sound at that point.

Mean effective pressure: The pressure which, if it applied throughout the power stroke of an engine, would produce the same output power as the actual measured variable values. If it is determined by reference to dynamometer output measurements it will be the 'brake mean effective pressure' (BMEP).

Methanol: Methyl alcohol, CH_3OH, is sometimes used as a racing fuel. It has less than half the energy per volume of gasoline but its cooling properties make it attractive for use in very highly rated engines. It can be used in conjunction with water for injection cooling (see Chapter 14).

Milliseconds: Thousandths of a second.

Moment of inertia: The resistance of a rotating object to any change of the speed of rotation.

Natural aspiration: An engine which relies upon the movement of the piston in the cylinder to draw in a fresh charge, without any forced assistance from a supercharger.

Nitrous oxide: A liquified gas, N_2O, used to provide extra oxygen and cooling for peak power output from racing engines.

Nozzle: A shaped gas passage which efficiently accelerates the gas flow, with an accompanying drop in pressure.

Particulate trap: A device which is fitted to some diesel engines to catch the fine particles of soot which can be released into the exhaust. At regular intervals the trap has to be subject to a high-temperature cycle which burns the trapped carbon and hydrocarbon particles.

Pressure wave: An abrupt change of the pressure of a gas, for example by the opening of a valve, can generate a pressure wave which moves away from the source at the speed of sound.

Pulse converter: A shaped junction in a gas passage which causes pressure waves and pulses to be passed through with little attenuation and little transfer to the other arm of the junction.

Radius of gyration: The radius of a very thin ring of the same mass as a rotating object and which would have the same moment of inertia.

Resonance tuning: Gas pressure waves in a tube can build up their amplitude if their frequency of occurrence is related to the length of the tube. This characteristic is used to increase the effective pressure and flow of the gas.

SAE: The Society of Automotive Engineers in the USA, which defines many standards used in the automotive industry, including reference data points for testing engines.

Sensor: A device which measures some relevant quantity on an engine and converts it into a signal, usually electrical, to a control system. For example: coolant temperature, boost pressure, throttle valve position.

Software: The programs of instructions stored in a digital computer which determine how it will function – Everything which is not hardware!

Specific fuel consumption: The weight of fuel required to produce a unit of power from an engine for a unit of time. If it is calculated from the brake horsepower it will be referred to as the 'brake specific fuel consumption' (BSFC).

Specific heat: The heat input per degree rise in temperature. It is a general property which has a different value for every material. For gases, there are two different values depending on the measurement being taken at constant pressure or constant volume.

Static pressure: The portion of the total pressure of a gas which is not dependant on the kinetic energy of flow. For a stationary gas, the static pressure is equal to the total pressure.

Stoichiometric: The ideal air/fuel ratio for perfect combustion. For gasoline it is approximately 14:1.

Suck-through: An installation where the carburettor is before the supercharger.

Supercharger: A device which increases the inlet pressure to an engine above atmospheric and increases the mass of air drawn in on each stroke. Can use resonance tuning or pressure waves, but is usually based on some form of compressor.

Torque: The twisting strength available at the output shaft of an engine. It is not directly related to the output power.

Torque back-up: The extent to which engine torque increases as the engine speed drops. Very desirable to give good ability to cope with hill climbing.

Total pressure: The sum of the static and dynamic pressure components within a gas.

Turbine: A paddle-wheel-like device which can draw energy from a fluid flow and convert it into the rotary motion of a shaft to deliver mechanical work.

Turbocharger: The combination of a gas turbine and a centrifugal compressor into one unit. It uses the exhaust gas energy of an engine to provide induction supercharging.

Vane: One of a series of blades fitted into a turbo-compressor or gas turbine to form a diffuser or nozzle system.

Variable geometry turbine: A turbine which can have adjustments made to nozzle vanes in order to change its effective A/R ratio.

Volumetric efficiency: For a naturally aspirated engine, the ratio between the actual volume of air drawn in during one induction stroke and the geometric swept volume. It reflects the pressure losses in inlet filters, ducts and valves.

Wastegate: A high-temperature valve fitted at the inlet to an exhaust gas turbine which can release exhaust gases into a by-pass pipe in order to control the energy delivered to the turbine.

References

1   Prof A. Rateau: *"The use of the turbo-compressor for attaining the greatest speeds in aviation"*. Proceedings of the Institution of Mechanical Engineers, 1922.

2   Symposium of papers on supercharging. Proceedings of the Institution of Mechanical Engineers, Vol 129, 1935.

3   A. Meyer: *"The combustion gas turbine"*. Proceedings of the Institution of Mechanical Engineers, Vol 141, 1939.

4   S. A. Moss: *"Gas turbines and turbosuperchargers"*. Transactions of the American Society of Mechanical Engineers, July 1944.

5   E. T. Vincent: *"Supercharging the internal combustion engine"*. McGraw-Hill, 1948.

6   H. R. Ricardo: *"Supercharging of internal combustion engines"*. Proceedings of the Institution of Mechanical Engineers, Vol 162, 1950.

7   E. Chatterton: *"Compound diesel engines for aircraft"*. Journal Royal Aeronautical Society, Vol 58, 1954.

8   Symposium on superchargers and supercharging. Proceedings of the Institution of Mechanical Engineers, Automobile Division, 1956-7.

9   R. Miller & H. U. Lieberkerr: *"The Miller supercharging system for diesel and gas engines"*. Proceedings CIMAC, 1957.

10 G. A. Ball, A. J. Bell & L. B. Mann: *"The development of the Chrysler automotive centrifugal compressor"*. SAE Technical Progress Series, Vol 3, 1961.

11 J. H. Lewis, G. Burrel & F. W. Ball: *"The Oldsmobile F-85 Jetfire Turbo Rocket Engine"*. Society of Automotive Engineers, June 1962.

12 F. Wankel: *"Rotary piston machines – A classification of design principles for pumps, engines and compressors"*. Iliffe, 1965.

13 W. Klaurig & K. Will: *"Automatic operation of highly rated, spark ignition, turbocharged gas engines with special regard to their torque characteristics"*. Proceedings CIMAC, 1968.

14 F. J. Wallace & W. A. Linning: *"Basic Engineering Thermodynamics"*. Pitman, 1970; ISBN 0 273 31476 9.

15 J. M. Clarke, D. F. Walker & P. H. Hamilton: *"A new class of rotary piston machines suitable for compressors, etc"*. Proceedings of the Institution of Mechanical Engineers, Vol 186, 1972.

16 K. G. Parker: *"Turbocharging production cars"*. Journal of Automobile Engineering, Vol 4, Dec 1973.

17 E. R. R. Fuchs and others: *"Turbocharging the 3-litre V6 Ford Essex engine"*. Proceedings of the Institution of Mechanical Engineers, Vol 188, 1974.

18 I. W. Goodlet: *"Turbocharging of small engines"*. Proceedings of the Institution of Mechanical Engineers, Vol 188, 1974.

19 J. Melchior & T. Andre-Talamon: *"Hyperbar system of high supercharging"*. Society of Automotive Engineers, SAE 740723, September 1974.

20 K. Zinner: *"Supercharging of internal combustion engines"*. Springer Verlag, 1974: ISBN 0 387 08544 0.

21 D. H. Gollings: *"Development of a new generation of simplified turbocharger systems"*. Society of Automotive Engineers, SAE 771013, 1977.

"International Conference on Turbocharging & Turbochargers". Institution of Mechanical Engineers Conference Publication 1978-2, April 1978: ISBN 085298 395 6.

22   C49/78 Dr M. S. Janota: Opening address.

23   C58/78 J. Goddard, B. C. Jasper & D. C. McWhannell: *"A turbocharged spark ignition engine with thermal reactor, performance and emission characteristics"*.

24   C59/78 P F. Freeman & B. E. Walsham: *"A guide to some analytical turbocharger matching techniques"*.

25 H. Mezger: *"Turbocharging engines for racing and passenger cars"*. Society of Automotive Engineers, SAE 780718, August 1978.

26 Hugh McInnes: *"Turbochargers"*. H P Books, Tucson, Arizona, USA, 1978: ISBN 0 912656 49 2.

27 T. F. Wallace: *"Buick's turbocharged V-6 powertrain for 1978"*. Society of Automotive Engineers, SAE 780413, 1978.

28 Conference papers Feb/March 1979: *"Turbochargers and Turbocharged Engines"*. Society of Automotive Engineers Inc. SP-442.

29 A. Baker: *"The Comprex supercharger"*. The Automotive Engineer, Vol 4, No 4, Aug/Sept 1979.

30 H. H. Dertian, G. W. Holiday & G. W. Sandburn: *"Turbocharging Ford's 2.3 litre spark ignition engine"*. Society of Automotive Engineers, SAE 790312, 1979.

31 *"The passenger car power plant of the future"*. Conference Proceedings of the Institution of Mechanical Engineers, 1979/13.

32 W. Dommes & A. Werner: *"The turbocharged engine of the Audi Quattro"*. Automobiltechnische Zeitschrift, Vol 82, No 7-8, Jul-Aug 1980.

33 T. A. Kollbrunner: *"Comprex supercharging for passenger diesel car engines"*. Society of Automotive Engineers, SAE 800884, August 1980.

34 D. Scott: *"Fixed-head car diesels for volume production (three turbocharged overhead-camshaft diesels from BMW-Steyr Motoren GmbH)"*. Automotive Engineering, Vol 88, No 12, Dec 1980.

35 R. F. Ansdale: *"A reconnaissance of supercharging technology 1902-1980"*. Society of Automotive Engineers, SAE 810003, February 1981.

36 M. C. Brands, J. R. Werner, J. L. Hoehne & S. Kramer: *"Vehicle testing of the Cummins turbocompound diesel engine"*. Society of Automotive Engineers Inc. SAE 810073, 1981.

37 G. M. Schruf & A. Mayer: *"Fuel economy for diesel cars by supercharging"*. Society of Automotive Engineers, SAE 810343, February 1981.

38 Society of Automotive Engineers Progress in Technology Series 1981: *"Turbocharged diesel and spark ignition engines"*. Society of Automotive Engineers Inc. SAE/PT-81/23: ISBN 0 89883 111 3.

39 A. Allard: *"Turbocharging and supercharging"*. Patrick Stephens Ltd, 1982: ISBN 0 85059 494 4.

"International Conference on Turbocharging & Turbochargers 1982": Institution of Mechanical Engineers Conference Publication 1982-3, April 1982: ISBN 085298 491 X.

40   C33/82 T. Okazaki, K. Uchiyama, K. Yamada & H. Tsubouchi: *"Development of high speed small turbochargers for passenger cars"*.

41   C49/82 J. S. Clark & B. D. Owen: *"Turbocharging the 1.3 litre British Leyland Metro car"*.

42 N. Watson & M. S. Janota: *"Turbocharging the internal combustion engine"*. Macmillan, 1982: ISBN 0 333 24290 4.

43 G. Gyarmathy: *"How does the Comprex pressure-wave supercharger work?"* Society of Automotive Engineers, SAE 830234, March 1983.

44 M. Kurasawa, K. Miyashita, T. Kobayashi, M. Saito, K. Shibui & J. Yasanobe: *"RBH3 turbocharger for small passenger cars"*. IHI Eng. Rev., Vol 16, No 1, 1983.

45 J. Mason, P. Chapman, J. Meyer, A. Parois & M. Smith: *"Design and performance of the T2 turbocharger"*. American Society of Mechanical Engineers, October 1983 Tokyo International Gas Turbine Congress.

"Seminar on Supercharging and Turbocharging of Petrol Engines". Institution of Mechanical Engineers, 17 Oct 1983.

46   M. T. Overington: *"Positive displacement superchargers"*.

47   McCutcheon, Byrne, Styhr: *"Development of ceramic turbine wheel for passenger car turbocharger"*.

48 N. Watson: *"Dynamic turbocharged diesel engine simulator for electronic control system development"*. J. Dyn. Syst. Meas. Control, Vol 106, No 1, 1984.

49 R. C. Benn & J. R. Mihalisin: *"Turbo 25; a low cost turbocharger alloy development"*. ASM '85 Materials Week, 14-17 Oct 1985, American Society of Metals.

50 D. E. Winterbourne, J. R. Nichols & G. I. Alexander; *"Efficiency of the manifolds of a turbocharged engine"*. Proceedings of the Institution of Mechanical Engineers, pt D, Vol 199, No D2, 1985.

51   M. Bantle & H. Bott: *"Der Porsche Typ 959 – Gruppe B – ein besonderes Automobil"*. Automobiltechnische Zeitung (ATZ), No 5, 1986.

"International Conference on Turbocharging & Turbochargers". Institution of Mechanical Engineers Conference Publication 1986-4: ISBN 085298 5908 3

52   C115/86 H. Egli: *"Evolution & outlook of turbochargers for vehicle engines"*.

53   C106/86 M. F. Lasker: *"Experience with ceramic rotor turbochargers"*.

54   C112/86 H-J. Esch & P. Zickwolf: *"Comparison of different exhaust gas turbocharging procedures on Porsche engines"*.

55   C118/86 H. G. Rosenkranz, H. C. Watson, W. Bryce & A. Lewis: *"Driveability, fuel consumption and emissions of a 1. 3 litre turbocharged spark ignition engine developed as replacement for a 2. 0 litre naturally aspirated engine"*.

56   C107/86 Y. Sumi & K. Yamane: *"Recent developments of high-response turbochargers for passenger cars"*.

57   C109/86 E. Jenny, P. Moser & J. Hansel: *"Progress with variable geometry and Comprex"*.

58   C124/86 F. W. Spinnler & F. A. Jaussi: *"The fully self-regulated pressure wave super-charger Comprex for passenger car diesel engines"*.

59   R. R. Lundstrom & J. M. Gall: *"A comparison of transient vehicle performance using a fixed geometry, wastegate turbocharger and a variable geometry turbocharger"*. Society of Automotive Engineers, SAE 860104, February 1986.

60   K. Miyashita, T. Kitazawa, A. Ohkita & N. Ikeya: *"Development of high efficiency ball-bearing turbocharger"*. IHI Eng. Rev., Vol 19, No 4, 1986.

61   K. Akiyama, N. Ikeya, K. Miyashita & N. Misaki: *"Acceleration response of turbocharged passenger cars"*. IHI Eng. Rev., Vol 20, No 1, 1987 (Ishikawajima-Harima Heavy Industries Co)

62   E. Jenny & M. Naguib: *"Development of the Comprex pressure wave supercharger: in the tradition of thermal turbomachinery"*. Brown Boveri Review, August 1987, Vol. 74.

63   A. Hishikawa, Y. Okazaki & P. Busch: *"Developments of variable area radial turbines for small turbochargers"*. Society of Automotive Engineers, SAE Technical Paper 880120, March 1988.

64   A. Mayer: *"Comprex supercharging eliminates trade-off of performance, fuel economy and emissions"*. Society of Automotive Engineers, SAE 881152, August 1988.

65   J. P. Norbye: *"Automotive fuel injection systems"*. Foulis, 1988: ISBN 0 85429 755 3.

66   M. Hitomi, Y. Yuzuriha & K. Tanaka: *"The characteristics of pressure wave supercharged small diesel engine"*. Society of Automotive Engineers, SAE 890454, February 1989.

67   G. Zehnder, A. Mayer & L. Matthews: *"The free running Comprex"*. Society of Automotive Engineers, SAE 890452, March 1989.

"4th International Conference on Turbocharging & Turbochargers", May 1990. Institution of Mechanical Engineers Conference Publication 1990-6: ISBN 085298 719 6.

68   C405/013 G. Cser: *"Double resonance system – a new way to improve the low-speed operation of supercharged engines"*.

69   C405/032 A. Mayer, I. E. L. Nasher & J. Perewusnyk: *"Comprex with gas pocket control"*.

70   C405/036 B. E. Walsham: *"Alternative turbocharger systems for the automotive diesel engine"*.

71   C405/037 J. Hall & F. J. Wallace: *"Optimal control of an integrated engine transmission with controllable pressure charging"*.

72   C405/049 J. E. T. Blake: *"The application of ball bearings to automotive turbochargers"*.

73   C405/054 M. W. G. Brown & A. B. Horner: *"Effects of controlled turbine bypass on a commercial turbocharged engine"*.

74   C405/057 H. Richter & N. Hemmerlein: *"Experiences with supercharging the Porsche 944 engine"*.

Useful addresses

The following is a list of (mainly UK) addresses and telephone numbers of companies which manufacture products relevant to the supercharging of automotive engines:

ABB Turbo Systems, CH-5401 Baden, Switzerland – larger turbochargers and Comprex.

Robert Bosch Ltd (0895 838383), PO Box 98, Broadwater Park, North Orbital Road, Denham, Uxbridge, Middlesex UB9 5HJ – fuel injection systems; lambda probes.

Brodie Brittain Racing (0280 702389), Oxford Road, Brackley, Northamptonshire NN13 5DY – after-market turbocharging; engine management systems.

Cosworth Engineering Ltd (0604 752444), St James Mill Road, Northampton NN5 5JJ – advanced engine developments.

Covrad Heat Transfer Ltd (0203 675544), Sir Henry Parkes Road, Canley, Coventry, West Midlands CV5 6BN – charge air coolers.

Detection Techniques (0280 816781), Buckingham Industrial Park, Buckingham MK18 1XJ – engine management system specialists.

DPR Forced Induction Systems Ltd (0935 32177), Watercombe Lane, Lynx Trading Estate, Yeovil, Somerset BA20 2 hp – Sprintex superchargers.

Eaton Limited (081-572-7313), Eaton House, Staines Road, Hounslow, Middlesex TW4 5DX – Eaton Roots superchargers.

ERP Limited (0273-309928), 41 Wanderdown Road, Ovingdon, Brighton, East Sussex BN2 7BT – after-market engine management systems.

Fleming Thermodynamics Limited (041 952 0933), 16/17 Fleming Court, Clydebank Business Park, Clydebank, Glasgow G81 2DR – designers of the Sprintex supercharger.

Garrett Automotive Limited (0695 22391), Potter Place, West Pimbo, Skelmersdale, Lancashire WN8 9PH – automotive turbochargers.

Garrett Turbo Service (061 485 6244), Stanley Green Estate, Cheadle Hulme, Cheadle, Cheshire SK8 6QS – turbocharger after-market support.

Holset Engineering Co. Ltd., Huddersfield Works, Turnbridge, Huddersfield, West Yorkshire HD1 6RD – truck diesel turbochargers.

Ishikawajima-Harima Heavy Ind. Co. Ltd, 2-16 Toyosu, 3-chome, Koto-ku, Tokyo, 135 Japan – automotive turbochargers.

Aktiengesellschaft Kuhnle, Kopp & Kausch, D6170, Frankenthal/Pfalz, West Germany – automotive turbochargers.

Llanelli Radiators (0554 758101), Llanelli, Dyfed SA14 8HU – charge air coolers.

ND Marston Limited (0274 582266), Marston House, Otley Road, Shipley, West Yorkshire BD17 7JR – charge air coolers.

Power Engineering (0895 55699), Unit 8, Union Buildings, Wallingford Road, Uxbridge, Middlesex UB8 2SR – after-market turbocharging installations; G-lader developments.

Sabre Engines Ltd (0202 893720), Ferndown Industrial Estate, 22 Cobham Road, Wimborne, Dorset BH21 7PW – turbocharged marine engines.

Setrab (UK) Limited (0933-222747), Bradfield Close, Finedon Road Industrial Estate, Wellingborough, Northamptonshire NN8 4RQ – oil coolers.

Superchargers UK (0264-59798), 4 Prince Close, Walworth Industrial Estate, Andover, Hampshire SP10 5LL – Eaton supercharger distributors.

Torque Developments Limited (081-591-0442), Unit 6, Riverside Industrial Estate, Thames Road, Barking, Essex – after-market supercharging; rolling road.

Turbo Technics (0604 764005), 17 Gallowhill Road, Brackmills, Northampton NN4 0EE – after-market turbocharging specialists; engine management systems.

Weber Concessionaires Ltd (0932 788805), Dolphin Road, Sunbury-on-Thames, Middlesex TW16 7HE – carburettor specialists.

Index